Oracle Visual Builder Cloud Service Revealed

Rapid Application Development for Web and Mobile

Sten Vesterli

Apress®

Oracle Visual Builder Cloud Service Revealed: Rapid Application Development for Web and Mobile

Sten Vesterli
Vaerloese, Denmark

ISBN-13 (pbk): 978-1-4842-4928-4
https://doi.org/10.1007/978-1-4842-4929-1

ISBN-13 (electronic): 978-1-4842-4929-1

Managing Director, Apress Media LLC: Welmoed Spahr
Acquisitions Editor: Jonathan Gennick
Development Editor: Laura Berendson
Coordinating Editor: Jill Balzano

Cover image designed by Freepik (www.freepik.com)

Distributed to the book trade worldwide by Springer Science+Business Media New York, 233 Spring Street, 6th Floor, New York, NY 10013. Phone 1-800-SPRINGER, fax (201) 348-4505, e-mail orders-ny@springer-sbm.com, or visit www.springeronline.com. Apress Media, LLC is a California LLC and the sole member (owner) is Springer Science + Business Media Finance Inc (SSBM Finance Inc). SSBM Finance Inc is a **Delaware** corporation.

For information on translations, please e-mail rights@apress.com, or visit http://www.apress.com/rights-permissions.

Apress titles may be purchased in bulk for academic, corporate, or promotional use. eBook versions and licenses are also available for most titles. For more information, reference our Print and eBook Bulk Sales web page at http://www.apress.com/bulk-sales.

Any source code or other supplementary material referenced by the author in this book is available to readers on GitHub via the book's product page, located at www.apress.com/9781484249284. For more detailed information, please visit http://www.apress.com/source-code.

Printed on acid-free paper

*For my wife Lotte
and our children Michael and Maria
and others like them
who work to make the world a better place
through word, code, and deed.*

Table of Contents

About the Author

Sten Vesterli is one of the world's leading experts on Oracle technology and has worked almost every development tool produced by Oracle in the last several decades, including ADF, APEX, JET, VBCS, Forms, Reports, Designer, Oracle Portal, Oracle WebDB, Oracle BPEL, Oracle Collaboration Suite, and even Oracle Power Objects.

He is a frequent speaker at Oracle conferences around the world and has given hundreds of presentations at Oracle OpenWorld and at ODTUG KScope, IOUG Collaborate, UKOUG, DOAG, and many other user group conferences. His presentations are highly rated by the participants, and he has received the ODTUG best speaker award twice.

Known for his ability to explain technology clearly, Sten writes the popular *Oracle Watch* newsletter and articles for *Oracle Profit*, *Oracle Scene*, and other publications. He has previously written five books on Oracle technologies and is excited to present this first book on Oracle Visual Builder Cloud Service.

Sten was a member of Oracle's elite Oracle ACE Director program for a decade until his penchant for telling the unvarnished truth got him excommunicated. An independent consultant based in Denmark, Sten works with customers worldwide, helping them get the most from their investment in Oracle software.

He holds a private pilot license for single-engine aircraft, and his personal projects have included an Ironman and an ultramarathon in Denmark, climbing Mont Blanc in France, a 2-week hike in Greenland, skydiving in Denmark, a 3-week trek around Annapurna in Nepal, paragliding in the Alps, rock climbing in Sweden, glacier walking in Norway, and scuba diving in Thailand.

You can find Sten online at `www.vesterli.com`, on LinkedIn, and on twitter @stenvesterli.

About the Technical Reviewers

Oracle Groundbreaker Ambassador/Oracle ACE Director **Andrejus Baranovskis** is a technical expert (full stack developer) in and founder of Red Samurai Consulting, based in Lithuania. His technical expertise is based on 15 years of continuous work developing enterprise IT systems across the globe (the USA, Canada, Germany, the UK, Denmark, Portugal, South Africa, Hong Kong, etc.). He is primarily focused on Oracle products – Oracle Fusion Middleware, Development Tools, and Oracle Cloud. He is involved in legacy systems modernization to Oracle JET (JavaScript) and Oracle ADF (Java). His typical tasks include technical architecture implementation, development framework setup, team training, and performance tuning for Oracle ADF and Oracle JET. He is the founder of the Katana ML product (`http://katanaml.io/`); this product helps to apply Machine Learning in the enterprise domain by extracting rules and patterns from data and converting these rules into Machine Learning models. Andrejus is a prolific technical blogger; he shares his knowledge on his blog (`www.andrejusb.blogspot.com`) and sample code on GitHub (`https://github.com/abaranovskis-redsamurai`). He is a writer for the online publication *Towards Data Science* (`https://towardsdatascience.com/@andrejusb`).

Solutions Architect with over 15 years of experience with a focus on Oracle and Java EE technologies, working as Team Leader, Senior Developer positions, **Florin Marcus** provides specializes in performance tuning and development best practices of large enterprise systems. He is often invited as a speaker on various Oracle conferences.

Acknowledgments

From Oracle, I want to thank Brian Fry, Duncan Mills, Jules Lane, Shay Shmeltzer, and Steve Morton for making Visual Builder Cloud Service demo environments available, for their blog posts detailing important points, and for answering my questions.

From Apress, I thank Jonathan Gennick for believing in a Visual Builder Cloud Service book and Jill Balzano for shepherding the project to completion.

I also want to thank my technical reviewers, Andrejus Baranovskis and Florin Marcus, for their comments and suggestions.

Finally, I want to express my love and gratitude for my wonderful wife, who has been unfailingly supportive when I mark yet another batch of weekends "book chapter deadline" in our calendar.

Introduction

This book introduces you to Oracle Visual Builder Cloud Service (VBCS), which allows you to build and deploy an attractive, user-friendly web or mobile application in one day or less.

In today's fast-paced world, the ability to rapidly deliver running code is the most crucial and sought-after skill a developer can have. Oracle has brought together their enterprise experience, advanced usability, and cloud engineering to produce this innovative platform giving developers unprecedented productivity.

With the visual and browser-based approach of VBCS, developers of all expertise levels can quickly solve simple business problems. For more sophisticated applications, experienced developers can dive into the code and add Groovy and JavaScript business logic. Most VBCS applications run in the Oracle Cloud to get the full benefit of the VBCS tool, but it is possible to build VBCS web applications and deploy them to other clouds or on-premise.

To get started with this book, you need to sign up for an Oracle Cloud account at `https://cloud.oracle.com`. Oracle offers free trials with several hundred dollars' worth of cloud credits. Unfortunately, the free trial is limited to 30 days, so you should make sure you will have enough time available to evaluate the product when you start the trial.

Chapter 1 introduces you to the tool and shows how to build a simple application. Chapter 2 explains how to create business objects to store your data inside Visual Builder Cloud Service, and Chapter 3 shows how to create service connections to data sources outside VBCS.

Chapter 4 describes the features for building great-looking and user-friendly applications, including the powerful visualization components. Chapter 5 discusses how to handle data in your application, and Chapters 6 and 7 explain how to add custom business logic to the business layer and the user interface layer of your VBCS application. Chapter 8 shows the exciting Visual Builder Add-in for Excel, which allows an end user to work with VBCS data directly from an Excel spreadsheet. Chapter 9 shows how to use VBCS to build mobile applications for Android and iOS and as progressive web applications.

Chapter 10 explains the security features in VBCS, and Chapter 11 describes how to manage whole VBCS applications. Chapter 12 provides a detailed look at how to use VBCS in an enterprise setting, including how to integrate with Oracle Developer Cloud Service and use Git version control, how to automate building VBCS applications, and how to deploy them outside VBCS. Finally, Chapter 13 explains how to integrate VBCS with Oracle Process Cloud Service.

I'm happy you have picked up this book and believe Visual Builder Cloud Service will be a great addition to your skillset.

CHAPTER 1

Building Your First Web Application

The purpose of Oracle Visual Builder Cloud Service (VBCS) is to allow you to build applications quickly – not quickly as "in a few weeks," but quickly as "in a few hours."

In this chapter, we will do just that.

Visual Builder Cloud Service Architecture

As the name implies, Visual Builder Cloud Service is cloud-based. Your application is developed in the Oracle Cloud, and the default runtime environment is the cloud. Your data can be stored anywhere, as long as you can access them via a REST web service.

A VBCS application normally consists of a web user interface and/or a mobile user interface connected to VBCS business objects and/or service connections as shown in Figure 1-1.

© Sten Vesterli 2019
S. Vesterli, *Oracle Visual Builder Cloud Service Revealed*, https://doi.org/10.1007/978-1-4842-4929-1_1

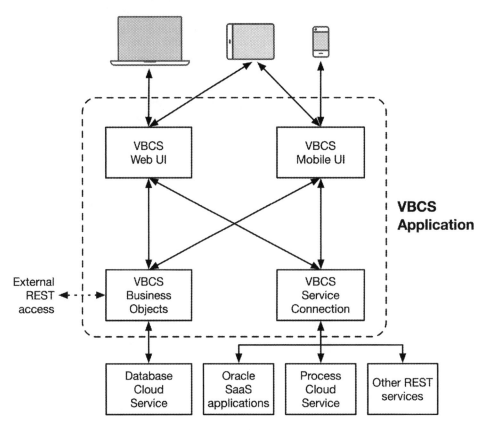

Figure 1-1. *Visual Builder Cloud Service architecture*

The Front End

The front end of a VBCS web application is JavaScript and HTML, using open source Oracle JET JavaScript components. The declarative approach and the wizards in VBCS make it very fast to build basic applications, saving time for even experienced developers. If necessary, these applications can then be extended and improved with hand-crafted JavaScript and HTML.

Tip   It is even possible to move the JavaScript and HTML out of VBCS and host it on your own server. You lose a few services that the VBCS runtime environment normally provides you with, like integration with Identity Cloud Service and use of the VBCS proxy for external REST calls. We'll discuss this in a later chapter.

The mobile applications you build with VBCS are real on-device iOS and Android mobile apps that use Apache Cordova for access to device features. The VBCS development tool makes it easy to access features like camera and location, and you can add Cordova plug-ins for additional functionality.

The Back End

The VBCS business objects and service connections provide a uniform interface for your web application and/or mobile application to connect to.

In the simple case, you just define your own *VBCS Business Objects*. VBCS will automatically store them in the Database Cloud Service associated with your Visual Builder Cloud Service instance without you having to worry about creating tables and indexes or defining storage parameters. The tables in the database will be presented to your VBCS application as REST services.

Tip   You can even expose your VBCS business objects as REST services to external applications. We'll return to that in Chapter 2.

You can also use *VBCS Service Connections* to connect to Oracle Software-as-a-Service (SaaS) applications, Oracle Process Cloud Service (PCS) instances, or any standard REST services.

VBCS is a great tool for building small additional applications on top of Oracle SaaS applications like Finance Cloud, HCM Cloud, or CRM Cloud. These applications offer a number of REST APIs you can invoke, and VBCS offers a catalog to make it really easy to use them.

To connect to PCS, you access the process data PCS makes available through REST interfaces that VBCS understands how to connect to.

Finally, you can access data using standard REST calls, no matter where in the world your data is located. This enables you to call third-party services if necessary and even allows you to use data stored on-premise in your own data center if you expose them to properly authenticated and authorized external users.

The Use Case

In this chapter, we create a simple web application for an "incoming" travel agency to handle tasks. The company might need to provide transfer busses from the airport to a hotel, restaurant meals, sightseeing tours, or other services for visitors arriving in the company's home city or country.

To manage passengers, vehicles, and services, we will create a list of tasks with a start and end time and place, a description, number of passengers, and a service to be provided. Since many of the services will be provided by subcontractors, we also need the ability to select a subcontractor from a list, and for many services it is also relevant to select equipment like a vehicle of a certain capacity.

Creating a VBCS Instance

When you have signed up for Visual Builder Cloud Service, you receive an email with the URL of your cloud dashboard. If you don't have that information available, you can start at *https://cloud.oracle.com* and click *Sign In*. The Oracle Cloud sign in page appears as shown in Figure 1-2.

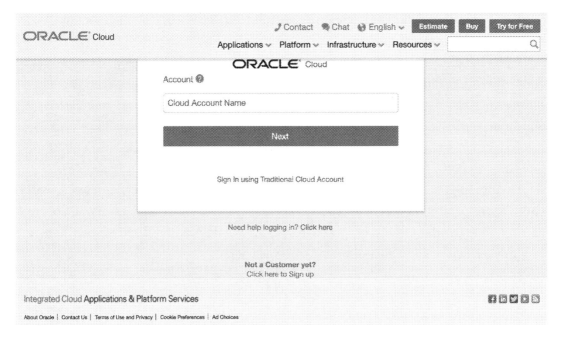

Figure 1-2. *The Oracle Cloud sign in page*

Provide your cloud account name and click *Next*. After you have logged in with your Oracle Cloud Account, your *Oracle Cloud My Services Dashboard* appears as shown in Figure 1-3.

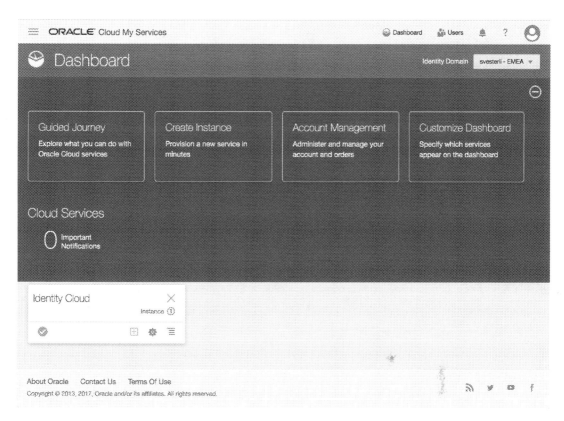

Figure 1-3. *Oracle Cloud My Services Dashboard, initial*

This dashboard shows your existing cloud service instances, and you can create new ones. When the first user logs on to your cloud account for the very first time, the dashboard will probably only show an Identity Cloud instance. If you have already used other Oracle Cloud Services before, these will also be shown.

Tip   You can configure which services are shown by clicking *Customize Dashboard.*

In order to get started with Visual Builder Cloud Service, you need to create an *instance* of VBCS. If somebody has already created one, it will show up on the dashboard and you can use that. If not, you will have to create one.

There are two ways to set up a VBCS instance:

- Using a Quick Start

- Using an Oracle Cloud stack template

The *Quick Start* instance uses default settings and needs nothing more from you than an instance name. This is the option to choose for a developer who wants to get started quickly with VBCS and see what it can do for the organization.

For a production instance, you probably want your cloud administrator to make an explicit decision on the various parameters you can set for a VBCS instance. The cloud administrator should use an *Oracle Cloud stack template.* Oracle provides default templates which will configure all the necessary services (Visual Builder, Database Cloud, Storage Cloud), and the cloud administrator can download and edit these templates to produce an environment that is appropriate for the organization and the intended use.

Refer to Chapter 3 of the *Administering Oracle Autonomous Visual Builder Cloud Service* manual for a more detailed description of how to set up a VBCS instance.

Caution   The Quick Start instance does not include database backup.

Creating a Quick Start Instance

To create a Quick Start instance, you start from the dashboard by clicking *Create Instance.* Select *All Services* and then scroll down to find the Visual Builder service as shown in Figure 1-4.

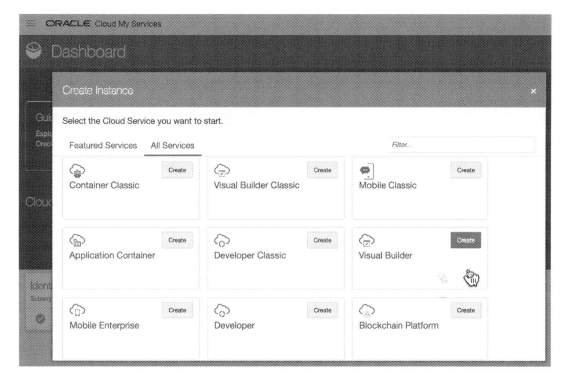

Figure 1-4. *Creating a Visual Builder instance*

Caution   Choose *Visual Builder*, not *Visual Builder Classic*. The "Classic" instances are only for organizations that have applications built with an earlier version of VBCS.

The default *Create Instance* window only allows you to define the name of your VBCS instance. At the bottom of the window, it tells you what it will create for you. This includes two nodes of Visual Builder Cloud Service, Oracle managed, and a database.

You can click the *Custom* button at the top right of the *Create Instance* window to change a few settings like the data center region your instance will be based in. Choosing *Custom* also gives you the option to download the provisioning instructions sent to the provisioning REST service as shown in Figure 1-5.

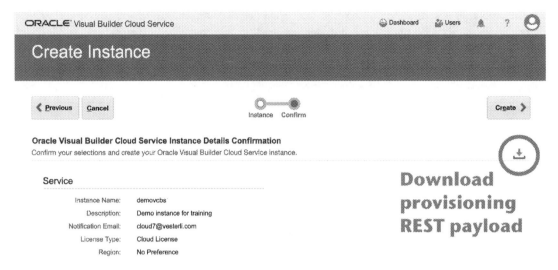

Figure 1-5. *Downloading the provisioning REST payload*

The payload you download will look something like this:

```
{"serviceVersion":"1.0","managedSystemType":"oracle","edition":"SUITE",
"enableNotification":"true","serviceName":"stenvbcs","serviceLevel":"
PAAS","subscriptionId":"1234567","notificationEmail":"sten@vesterli.
com","isBYOL":"false"}
```

This can be useful if you want to automate the creation of VBCS instances using Oracle Cloud provisioning REST services.

Note that a Quick Start instance does not include database backup. If you want database backup (e.g., if you are creating a production instance), you should use a stack template.

When you click *Create*, the instance creation starts. The Oracle Visual Builder Cloud Service console window appears, showing your new instance with status *Creating service* ... It used to take several hours for your instance to be created, but recently I have experienced create times of less than 15 minutes. However, I have also experienced instances that weren't created after 6 hours and have had to contact Oracle Support to find out what went wrong. Your mileage will vary.

Once your instance is created, it will appear in the dashboard together with the newly created database instance as shown in Figure 1-6.

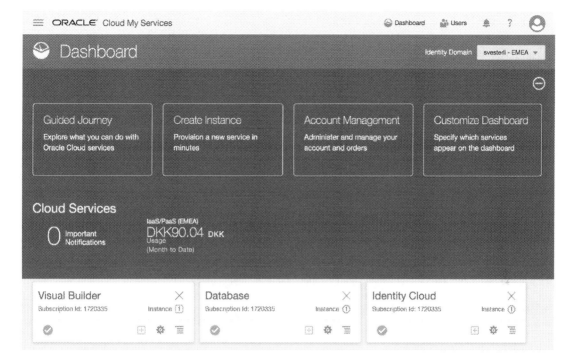

Figure 1-6. *The cloud dashboard with Visual Builder and Database instances*

Creating a Stack Template Instance

To create a VBCS instance using a cloud stack template, you use the navigation menu at the top left corner of the dashboard window. Expand the *Services* node, scroll to the very bottom (past *Visual Builder* and *Visual Builder Classic*), and choose *Cloud Stack*.

In the *Oracle Cloud Stack* window, choose the *Templates* tab. You will see a lot of predefined stacks of cloud services – search for "visual" to find a *Visual Builder Cloud Service* stack. At the time of writing, there were two:

- Oracle Visual Builder Cloud Service (Oracle-VISUALBUILDERAUTO-OM-Template), which creates an autonomous (Oracle-managed) instance

- Oracle-VisualBuilder-CM-Template, which creates a customer-managed instance

9

The Oracle-managed instance can't be changed, and you can't stop it. The customer-managed template can be changed to match your needs, and if your cloud service is billed by usage ("Pay-as-you-go"), you can stop your VBCS instance to save money when you don't need it. If you click the customer-managed template, you can see which services it will create, as shown in Figure 1-7.

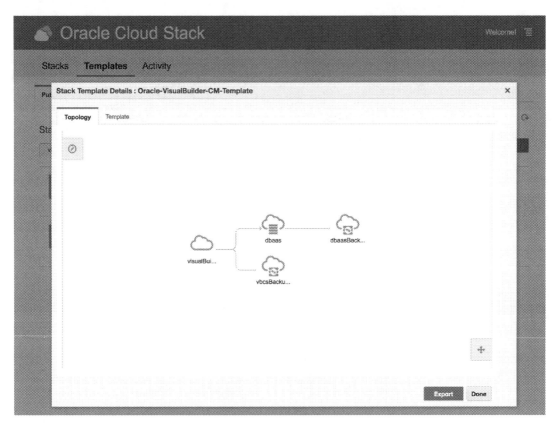

Figure 1-7. *Topology of a cloud stack template*

You can click the *Template* tab to see the actual commands the template contains. It will look something like this:

```
---
  template:
    templateName: Oracle-VisualBuilder-CM-Template
    templateVersion: 1.0.74-1901300359
    templateCategory: RESTRICTED
```

templateDescription: Includes everything needed to use Oracle Visual Builder Cloud Service Classic to rapidly develop and host web and mobile applications for the enterprise. Customer manages the environment.

```
#----------------------------------------
# PARAMETERS
#----------------------------------------
parameters:
  #---------------------------------------
  # Configuration
  #---------------------------------------
  serviceName:
    label: Service Name
    description: "Unique service name for this instance."
    type: String
    mandatory: true
    maxLength: 48
  sshPublicKey:
    label: SSH Public Key
    description: SSH public key
    type: ssh
    mandatory: trueQ/div>
    sensitive: true
  vbcsNumberNodes:
    label: Initial Number of Nodes
    description: Number of Nodes (OCPUs) allocated for the service. If no
    downtime during patching is desired, you must specify 2 or more nodes.
    type: Number
    mandatory: false
    default: 1
    sensitive: false
    minValue: 1
  #---------------------------------------
  # SERVICE
  #---------------------------------------
```

...

You can click *Export* to download the template YAML file, edit it to match your needs, and then *Import* it back into the Oracle Cloud Stack window.

It is a task for your cloud administrator to define the right topology, number of nodes, backup policy, and so on.

To start creating an instance from a stack template, you click the little cloud icon with a plus sign. This will call up the *Instance Details* screen where you define the service name, provide an SSH key, set database password, and more. When you have provided all the necessary information, click *Next*, verify everything on the confirmation page, and click *Create*.

Building the Application

As discussed in the section on Visual Builder Cloud Service architecture, a VBCS application uses business objects that need a data source in the form of REST web services. If you already have REST web services to create, retrieve, update, and delete data, you're ready to jump straight to building the user interface. In this section, we will build a simple application from scratch, that is, we will build both business objects for the data and a user interface for the user to work with.

Getting to the Home Page

To create a VBCS application, you start from the Visual Builder Cloud Service home page. You can have several VBCS instances in your cloud account, and each of these will have its own home page and its own applications.

To get to the home page from the console, you can click the navigation icon in the bottom right corner of the *Visual Builder* tile on the dashboard and then click *Open Service Console*. This will bring up the *Visual Builder Console* shown in Figure 1-8.

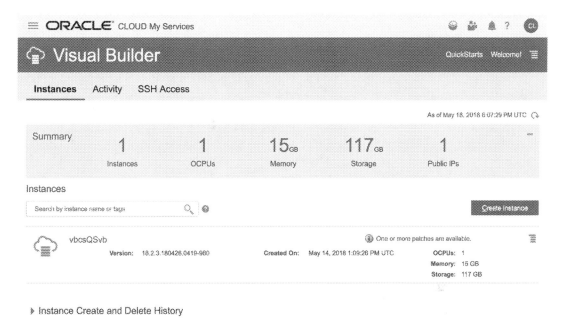

Figure 1-8. *The Visual Builder Console*

From here, you click the navigation icon to the right of a VBCS instance and choose *Open Visual Builder Cloud Service Home Page.* In the preceding figure, there is only one instance and one navigation icon, but you could have several.

Note   Each instance requires its own resources. Thus, there is an additional cost if you are running more instances.

The Visual Builder home page appears. At the time of writing, the home page had two different views. It starts in the newer *Visual Applications* view, which at the time of writing looked as shown in Figure 1-9.

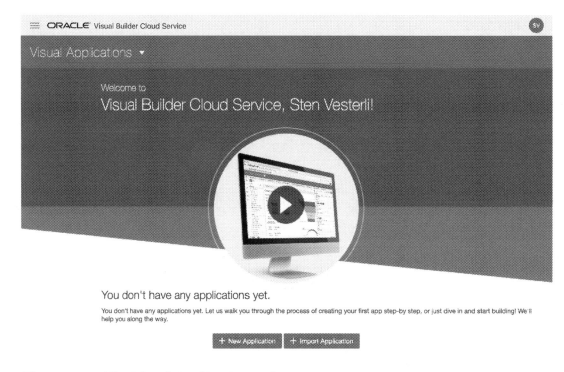

Figure 1-9. *The Visual Applications tab*

This is where you should be building your applications.

It is possible to click the little triangle next to the *Visual Applications* heading to change to the *Classic Applications* view. As shown in Figure 1-10, this looks almost identical.

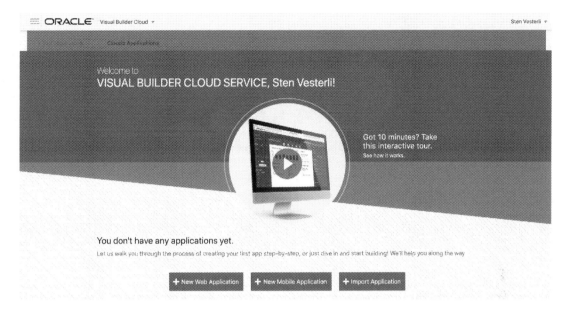

Figure 1-10. *The Classic Applications view*

Caution   You should not build new "Classic" applications. This view is retained for backward compatibility with earlier VBCS versions, and any application you build from the *Classic Applications* view will be of the older type without access to the latest features.

Creating the Application

To create an application, make sure you are on the *Visual Applications* home page (see Figure 1-9) and click *New Application*. You will be prompted to provide

- Application name (which will be shown in all the screens to manage the application).

- Application ID (which becomes part of the URL to your application).

- Optionally, a description. Make it a habit to provide a description – once you start working with VBCS in earnest, you are likely to be building a lot of applications.

You can also choose a template. The default *Empty Application* template creates a simple application without any extra features.

When you are done with this dialog, the Visual Builder main user interface appears as shown in Figure 1-11. If you are not using Google Chrome, you will probably see a warning saying "Some features may not function correctly in this browser." In my experience, VBCS works fine in Firefox, but you should probably take Oracle's advice and develop using Google Chrome.

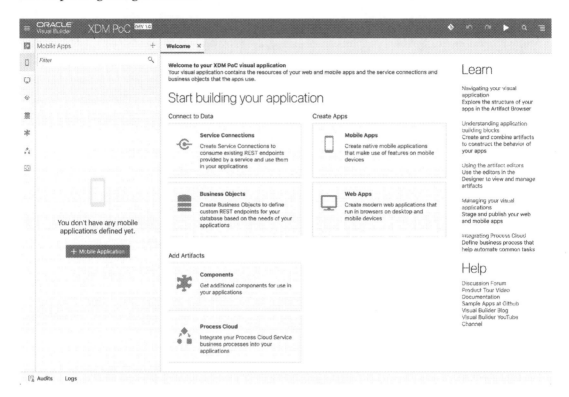

Figure 1-11. *The Visual Builder main user interface*

Most of the window is taken up by the VBCS main work area. In the preceding figure, it displays the *Welcome* tab, but you can have many tabs open in the work area to work with business objects, flows, and pages. To the left of the main work area is the navigator, which will show the elements of your application. Finally, to the far left along the edge of the screen, you see seven icons corresponding to the main areas of Visual Builder Cloud Service:

- Mobile Applications

- Web Applications

- Service Connections

- Business Objects

- Components

- Processes

- Source View

In this chapter, we will be building a simple web application, so we will only be using the *Business Objects* and *Web Applications* areas.

Creating the Business Object

Our use case is only concerned with one business object: Tasks. To create a business object for our tasks, you select the *Business Objects* area to the left and then click the plus sign next to the *Business Objects* heading. The *New Business Object* dialog appears as shown in Figure 1-12.

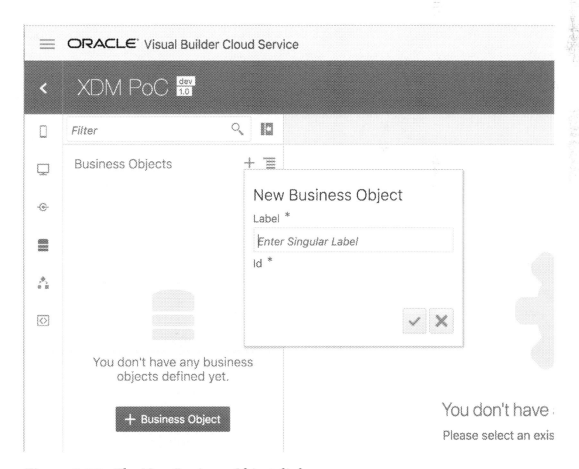

Figure 1-12. *The New Business Object dialog*

Once you provide a label and click the *Create* (checkmark) icon, your new business object is opened in a separate tab in the work area. We'll discuss all the options here in later chapters, but in this chapter, we focus on quickly creating a simple VBCS application. To add custom fields to your newly created business object, choose the *Fields* tab. You will see that VBCS has already created an ID field and some fields for recording the history of an object. These are standard in all VBCS business objects.

Use the *New Field* button to create some additional fields as shown in Figure 1-13.

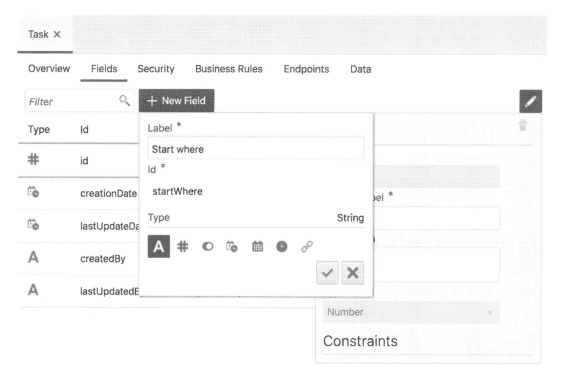

Figure 1-13. *Creating fields in business objects*

If you want to follow along with the example in this chapter, create the following fields:

- Date (type Date)

- Start where (type String)

- Start when (type Time)

- Description (type String)

- End where (type String)

- End when (type Time)
- Pax (type Number)

The word **Pax** is widely used in the travel industry as shorthand for *Passenger*.

When you have created all the fields, you can click them to modify their properties. Make *Date, Start where, Start when,* and *Description* required. Your business object should look as shown in Figure 1-14.

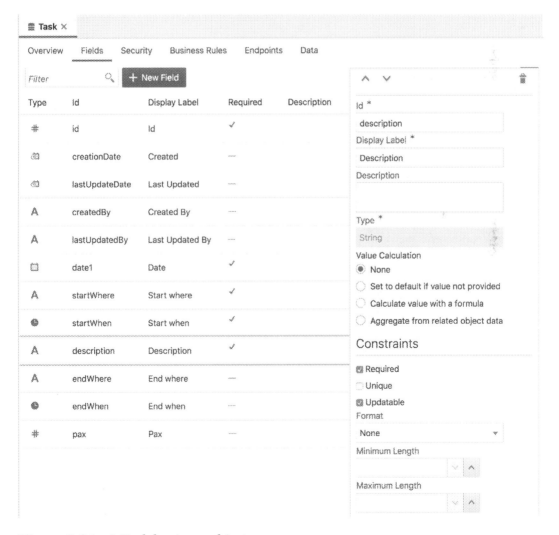

Figure 1-14. *A Task business object*

Once you have your business object with the necessary fields, go to the *Data* tab, click *Add Row*, and create a few rows of test data.

Note   We will get back to how to import data from Excel or CSV files in a later chapter. You can even create complete business objects from your data files, but we're keeping it simple in this chapter.

That's all you need to do to create a business object you can use in your application.

If you are interested, you can go to the *Endpoints* tab and see the REST web service endpoints that VBCS has automatically created for you. You can even publish these services for other applications to use. We'll get back to that in a later chapter.

Creating the Web Page

The next step is to create the web page where the user can interact with task data. This happens in the *Web Applications* area that you select by clicking the corresponding icon in the menu bar along the left edge of your VBCS window. It's the one that looks like a computer screen.

The navigator will now be empty, because you have not created any web applications inside this VBCS application. Click the plus sign next to the *Web Apps* heading to create a web application and provide an ID. The navigation panel fills in with a tree view of your web application, and start page (called main-start) opens in a new tab in the work area as shown in Figure 1-15.

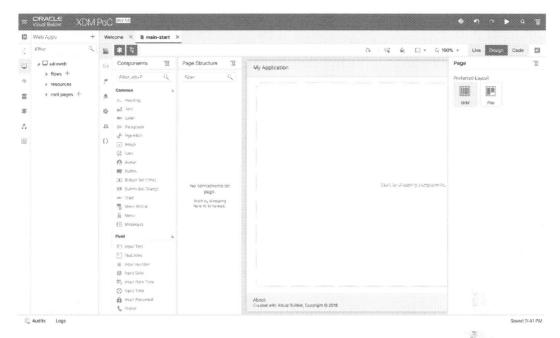

Figure 1-15. *A new web application*

Note the icons in the toolbar just below the `main-start` tab heading:

- On the left, the one that looks like a puzzle piece shows and hides the *component palette* (it is shown in the preceding figure).

- Also on the left, the one that looks like a folder tree shows and hides the *page structure* (it is hidden in the preceding figure).

- On the right, the box with the arrow expands and collapses the property inspector pane (it is expanded in the preceding figure).

Note   Confusingly, there are two "puzzle piece" icons: one at the far left (which switches to the main components tab) and one in the icon bar at the top of the work area (which toggles the component palette on that tab on and off).

To place your task business object on the page, scroll down in the component palette until you get to the *Collection* heading and drop a Table component onto your page as shown in Figure 1-16.

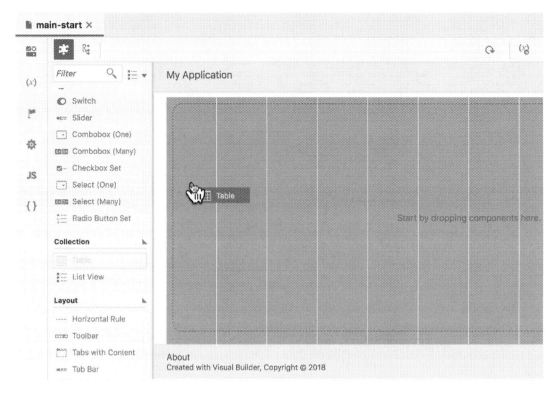

Figure 1-16. *Dropping a Table component onto a page*

Your page will show a table with some sample data as shown in Figure 1-17.

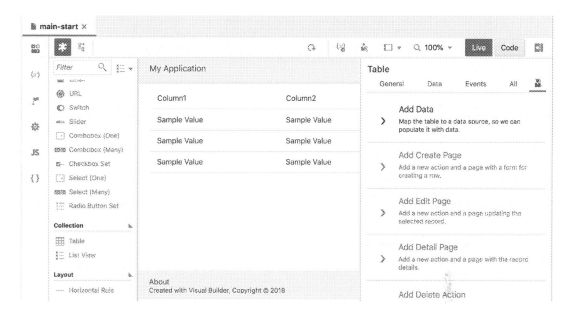

Figure 1-17. *A page with a Table component*

To connect your table to the business object, you need to expand the Property Inspector if it is not already shown. When the Table component is selected, the Property Inspector shows a number of tabs relevant for that component. The right-hand tab (with the university student icon) shows the Quick Starts, and one of these is *Add Data*. This wizard will prompt you for all the necessary information to connect your table with a data source.

In the first step, you choose an endpoint. In this case, we only have one business object under the Business Objects heading as shown in Figure 1-18.

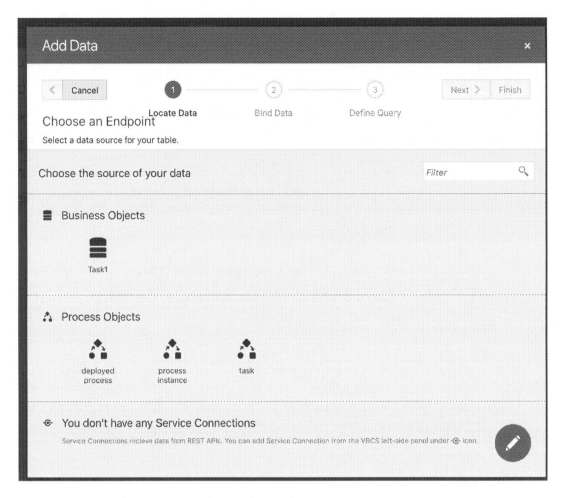

Figure 1-18. *Selecting an endpoint for tasks*

When you have selected a business object and have clicked *Next*, then second step of
the *Add Data* wizard, add the columns you want to display. Select them in the order you
want them displayed on your screen. You don't have to select all columns.

In the last step of the wizard, you have an option to provide query parameters. We'll
skip that for this example and click *Finish*.

You should now see the data from your task business object on your screen. You
can click the *Run* icon (the triangle) in the top right corner of your screen to run your
application in a new tab and see the application as the end user will. It might look
something like Figure 1-19.

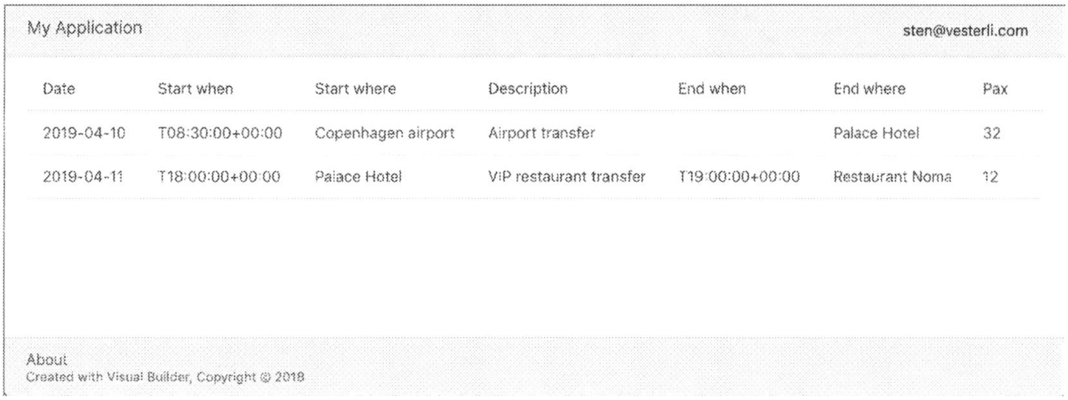

Date	Start when	Start where	Description	End when	End where	Pax
2019-04-10	T08:30:00+00:00	Copenhagen airport	Airport transfer		Palace Hotel	32
2019-04-11	T18:00:00+00:00	Palace Hotel	VIP restaurant transfer	T19:00:00+00:00	Restaurant Noma	12

My Application — sten@vesterli.com

About
Created with Visual Builder, Copyright © 2018

Figure 1-19. *A running VBCS application*

Note   We'll see how to fix the default time representation in a later chapter.

Staging and Deploying the Application

Once you have built the application, the next steps are to test it and then release it into production. Visual Builder Cloud Service supports these lifecycle events really well.

Releasing to Test

When you as a developer are satisfied with the application, you can *stage* it. This means that a copy of your application is created and placed into another environment that is part of your VBCS instance. Your testers can access a stable version of the application in this environment, even as you might continue development on the dynamic development version.

You can stage your application by clicking the application menu icon at the *right* end of the top bar in the VBCS window. There is a similar-looking icon at the left end of the top bar, but that one takes you to the VBCS home page. This will give you a number of application options as shown in Figure 1-20.

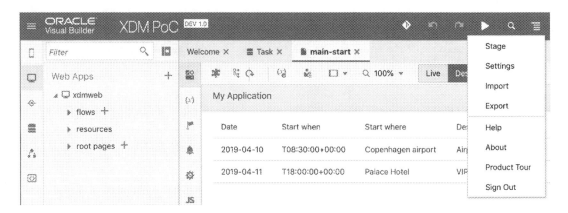

Figure 1-20. *Application management options*

To release your application to test, choose *Stage* from this menu. You will be given the option to either stage the application with a clean database where your testers will have to create their own data or ask VBCS to copy the data in your development database to the staging environment.

When you click the *Stage* button, VBCS creates the test version of your application (and data if you chose that). This might take a little while. When the staging process completes, you will see your application now has status *Stage* and still version 1.0.

Fixing Bugs

If your testers come up with anything that is not the way it is supposed to be, you need to change the application.

Tip   Testers get really annoyed if you change the application while they are testing it. Create a new version for your bug fixes.

To create a new version for your fixes, select *New Version* from the application menu. VBCS will suggest a version for you. If you are fixing bugs in version 1.0, in accordance with *Semantic Versioning* (see `https://semver.org`), your bug fix version should be 1.0.1. When you click *Create*, you get a new version of the application that has status *Development*. You can edit this new version to fix whatever problem your testers have discovered, and then stage the fixed version.

Releasing to Production

When your application has passed testing, it is time to put it into production. To do so, you choose *Publish* from the application menu. Again, you are given the option to either publish the application with a clean database or include data from the staged application your testers worked on. It is recommended to publish the application with a clean database.

When you click the *Publish* button, VBCS creates the production version of your application from the staged version. When the publishing process completes, you will see your application with status *Live* and the same version number your testers approved. Your application is now ready to be used by your users!

Conclusion

In this chapter you saw how easy it is to create a small application, complete with data source and user interface. Did you record how long it took you? Once you get familiar with Visual Builder Cloud Service, you will be able to run through the process from inception to your first staged JavaScript and HTML web application ready for testing in less than an hour, including screens for creating and editing objects.

In the next chapter, we'll discuss in more detail how to work with business objects.

CHAPTER 2

Building Business Objects

As you saw in the architectural overview in the previous chapter, your Visual Builder Cloud Service application uses REST web services to connect the web or mobile application with data. You can either use existing REST services or create VBCS business objects. If you create VBCS business objects, VBCS automatically creates REST web services in a form that is easy to use from the VBCS page designer.

This chapter is about building VBCS business objects; using existing services will be covered in the next chapter.

Creating Business Objects

You create VBCS business objects when you want to use new data – data that is not stored in any existing system. If the data is already stored somewhere, you should find a way to make that data available through a REST service and create a service connection as described in Chapter 3.

If you decide you need a VBCS business object, you can create it from the business objects tab inside the application. To open this tab, click the *Business Objects* icon as shown in Figure 2-1.

© Sten Vesterli 2019
S. Vesterli, *Oracle Visual Builder Cloud Service Revealed*, https://doi.org/10.1007/978-1-4842-4929-1_2

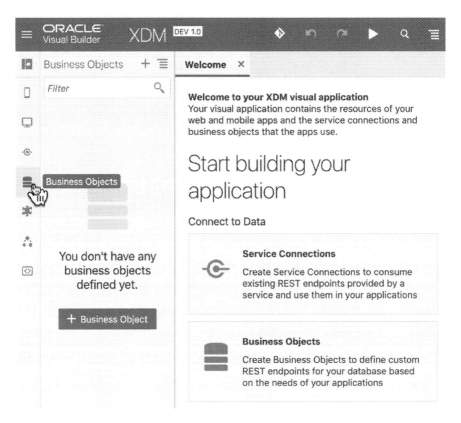

Figure 2-1. *The Business Objects icon*

Creating from Navigator

When you are on the *Business Objects* tab, the navigator shows your existing business objects. You can click an existing business object to open it in a new tab, and you can click the plus sign to create new business objects. A dialog will ask you for the name (in singular form) as shown in Figure 2-2.

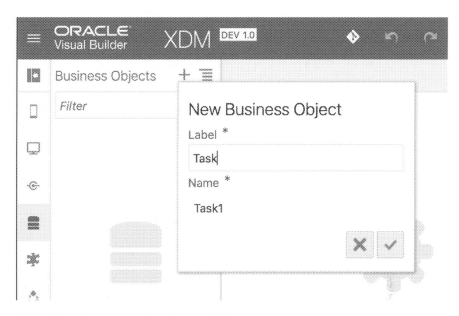

Figure 2-2. *Creating a new business object*

The system automatically creates an object ID for you. You can click the ID and change it if you want.

Note   You can use any business object name, but some names cannot be used as IDs. For example, Task is a reserved word, so my *Task* business object automatically gets the ID Task1.

When you click the checkmark icon, your business object is created and shown in the work area of the VBCS window as shown in Figure 2-3.

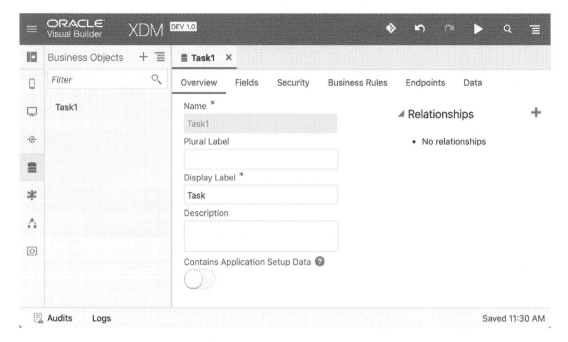

Figure 2-3. *A business object in the work area*

The initial view shows the *Overview* sub-tab of the business object, but there are also sub-tabs for *Fields, Security, Business Rules, Endpoints,* and *Data.* We will cover some of these in this chapter, and others in subsequent chapters.

Creating from Business Object Diagrammer

In addition to the normal view of business objects, VBCS also has a visual way of representing business objects and their relations: the *Business Object Diagrammer.* To start the diagrammer, you use the business objects menu (the icon next to the plus sign for creating business objects) as shown in Figure 2-4.

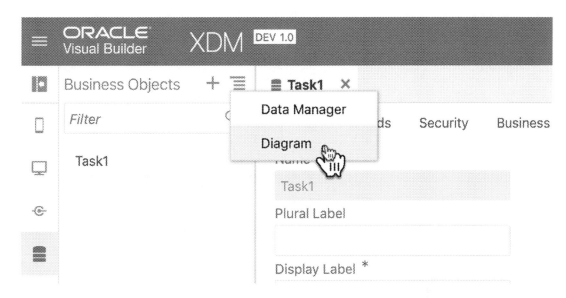

Figure 2-4. *Starting the business object diagrammer*

A diagram of all existing business objects is shown. You can click the triangle next to the title of each business object to toggle between compact and expanded view, and you can right-click anywhere on the diagram to bring up a menu of various diagramming options as shown in Figure 2-5.

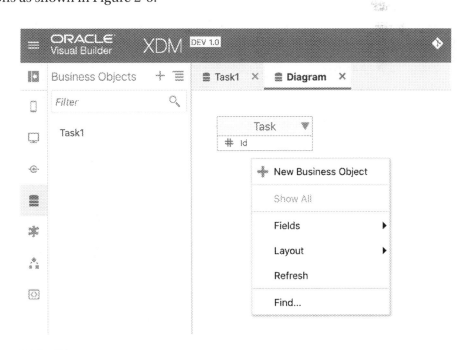

Figure 2-5. *Diagrammer context menu*

There is no way to move the business objects around if you don't like the layout VBCS presents to you. Your only options are the *Horizontal* and *Vertical* options on the *Layout* submenu.

Tip   You can right-click any business object in the navigator and choose *Find in Diagram* to open the diagram with that object highlighted.

Creating Relationships

Only the simplest applications contain only one table. In most real-life applications, you have multiple tables connected by relations. Visual Builder Cloud Service allows you to define the relations between business objects to make it easier to build master/detail pages and pages with drop-down lists for selecting reference values.

Creating from Business Object

You can create relationships from the *Overview* sub-tab in the business object by clicking the plus sign next to the *Relationships* heading in the right-hand column. This opens the *Create Relationship* window. Creating a relationship is a two-step process:

1. First you create the business object you want to create a relationship to.

2. Then you specify the relationship details.

The relationship details view allows you to define the *cardinality* of the relationship (one-to-many, many-to-one, many-to-many) as shown in Figure 2-6.

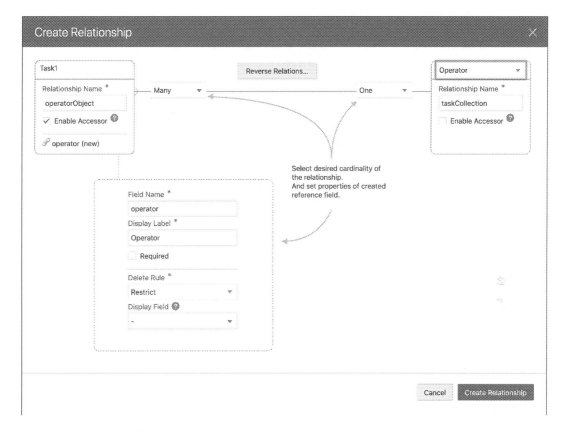

Figure 2-6. *Defining the cardinality of a relationship*

There are a number of options:

- **Many-to-one** (as shown in the preceding figure). This is normally used to create lookup relationships – in this case, each task can select one operator, and one operator can handle many tasks.

- **One-to-many**. This is used to define parent-child relationships, for example, that one person handles multiple tasks.

- **Many-to-many**. This is used for more complex relationships between two business objects. If you select this, VBCS will automatically create a new business object for you to contain all the mappings of business objects to each other.

- **One-to-one**. This is rarely used but might be useful when you have business objects with sub-types. For example, both persons and companies might have an address, so you could create an address business object that has a one-to-one relationship to both persons and companies.

Note that the relationship also defines a *Delete Rule*. This indicates what happens when you attempt to delete a record that has a relationship to other records. The options are

- **Restrict**. This means that you cannot delete a record if any other record has a relationship to it. For the preceding task/operator relationship, this would mean that you would not be able to delete an operator if any task is assigned to him.

- **Cascade**. This means that if you delete a record, all related records will be deleted. For the task/operator relationship, this would mean that if you delete an operator, all his tasks would also be deleted.

- **Set To Null**. This means that if you delete a record, the reference in the related records will be set to null. For the task/operator relationship, this would mean that if you delete an operator, the tasks would remain, but the operator field would be blank.

The checkboxes to *Enable Accessor* indicate whether you want to allow your business logic code and the REST services to access the business object at the other end of the relation. In the version of VBCS current at the time of writing, this feature is not described in the documentation. Search for blog posts to find examples of how to use this feature.

Creating from Business Object Diagrammer

You can also create and edit relationships in the business object diagrammer. To do so, you right-click a business object (the header, not any of the fields) and choose *New Relationship*. A dotted red line appears as shown in Figure 2-7.

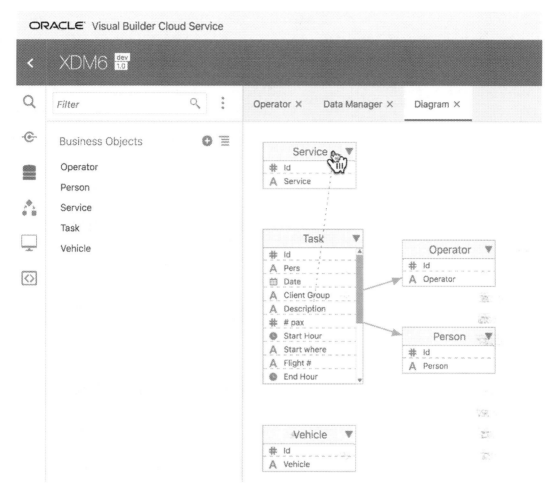

Figure 2-7. *Creating relationships from the business object diagrammer*

Click another business object to bring up the relationship details dialog, where you can define cardinality and delete rules just like when creating a relationship from the business object view.

Business Object Fields

To work with the fields in a business object, you normally use the *Fields* tab in the normal view of the business object in the main work area. The *Fields* tab is shown in Figure 2-8.

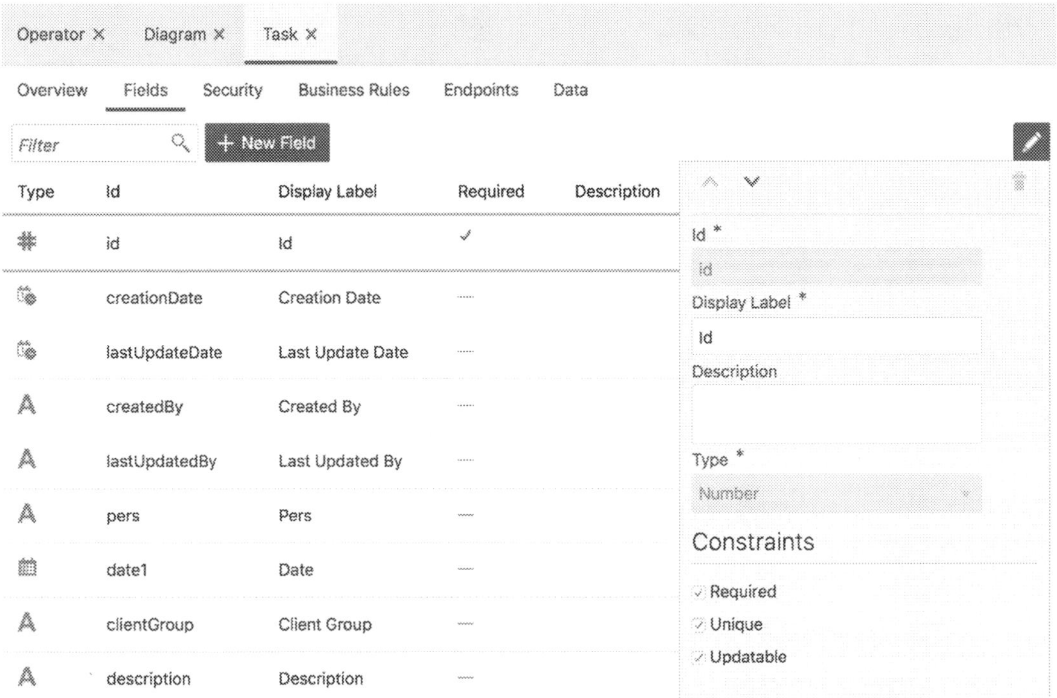

Figure 2-8. *The Fields tab of a business object*

From this tab, you can click a field to change its properties (required, unique, updatable, etc.). Note the little pencil icon in the far-right side of the filter line. You click this to display or hide the property window for the currently selected field.

Tip   Some attributes of business object fields can also be changed from the business object diagrammer.

Every business object contains five standard fields that you cannot remove (id, creationDate, lastUpdateDate, createdBy, and lastUpdatedBy). These are automatically managed by VBCS.

To add your own fields, you click the *New Field* button and provide a label and select a type. VBCS will automatically suggest an Id for the field, removing any spaces. If the label is a reserved word or has already been used in another field, VBCS will add a number to make the field Id unique.

Data Types

The version of Visual Builder Cloud Service current at the time of writing (19.1.3) has 11 data types:

- String

- Number

- Boolean

- DateTime

- Date

- Time

- Reference

- Email

- Percentage

- Phone

- Uri

The *DateTime* contains both a date and a time element (like you might be used to from an Oracle database DATE type).

The *Reference* data type is used to define lookup values. When you choose this type, you are prompted to point to a reference business object and select which field from that business object should be displayed onscreen. For example, the *Task* business object might have a reference to the *Operator* business object indicating the operator responsible for the task as shown in Figure 2-9.

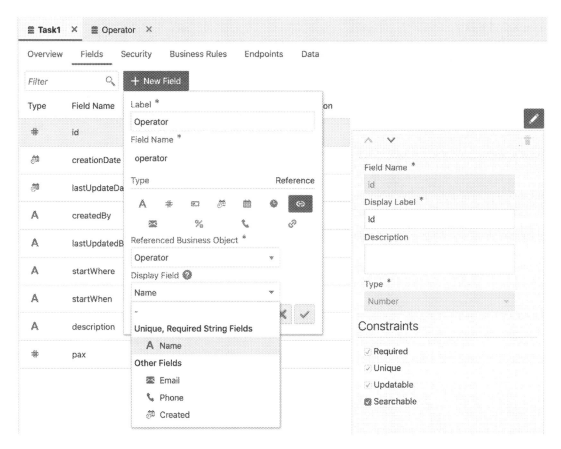

Figure 2-9. *Defining a reference type*

Note that the display field is only used to represent the data in the user interface. To make sure the end user of the application can distinguish between the display values, VBCS recommends using a field that is both *Unique* and *Required*. These fields are listed at the top of the select list for *Display Field*.

In the underlying database, VBCS uses the Id value from the reference object. If, for example, the user selects operator "CPH Limo" for a task, VBCS will store the Id value from the Operator business object (e.g., 146). This allows you to freely change the names of lookup values later without breaking the relationship.

The *Email* type comes with basic validation that the value is a plausible email address.

The *Percentage* and *Phone* types seem to be handled like any other number, that is, you cannot enter a string value in these types of fields.

The *Uri* field type is a text field. It shows a prompt "Enter a valid URL," but the default validator is a regular expression .* (which matches anything). The default rendering of a Uri field is as a hyperlink, but the link address is the VBCS application itself, not the actual Uri. Maybe a future VBCS version will make this field type more useful.

Note   The default rendering of some of the specialized types (email, phone, Uri) has the *Virtual Keyboard* property set. In mobile applications, this means the application will show the specialized keyboard of that type.

Value Calculation

In the field properties, under the *Value Calculation* header, you can define default values or calculate field values based on a formula or from data in a related business object.

Default Value Calculation

Choose *Set to default if value not provided* to define the default value that will be placed in the field if the user does not provide a value. Notice the drop-down box next to the field that appears if you choose this, illustrated in Figure 2-10.

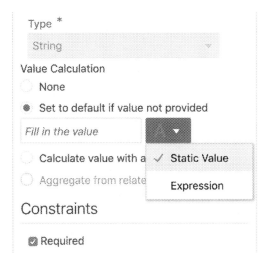

Figure 2-10. *Selecting default value type*

You can choose *Static Value* and provide a default value. The value selector depends on the data type of the field. Note that the default value is only added just before the business object instance is created. This means that your users won't see the default value in the user interface. Also, if the field is marked as *Required*, the user must provide a value in the user interface. The *Required* setting indicates that the user must actively provide a value and cannot depend on the default.

The other option is *Expression*. If you choose this, the *Expression Builder* appears as shown in Figure 2-11.

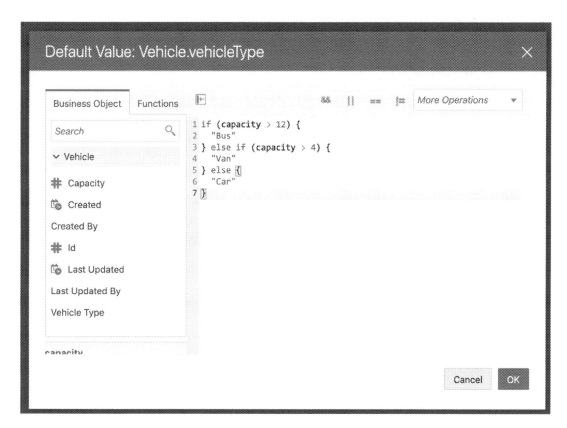

Figure 2-11. *An expression as default value*

You can use the various fields from the *Business Object* tab and a number of built-in functions from the *Functions* tab to construct an expression. This expression will be evaluated just before the business object instance is stored in the database. The syntax for an `if` statement can be found in the *More Operations* drop-down.

Formula Calculation

If you choose *Calculate value with a formula*, a field appears with a button to open the expression builder. The difference between this option and using an expression as default value is that a calculated value is always calculated – the end user will not be allowed to enter a value in a field that has a formula calculation.

Aggregation

If your business object has a parent/child relationship to another, you can also choose that the field value should be calculated based on related objects.

For example, in the travel agency example used in this book, there is a Group business object with a one-to-many relationship to a Task business object, indicating that one group can have many tasks. Tasks have a Pax (no. of persons) field, so it is possible to create an aggregation field on Groups showing the total number of persons for all tasks.

When you create a field, set *Value Calculation* to *Aggregate from related object data*, and click *Edit Aggregation*, the *Edit Aggregation* dialog appears as shown in Figure 2-12.

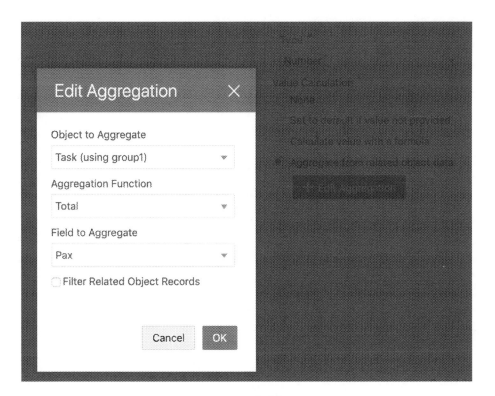

Figure 2-12. *Creating a new aggregation field*

In the *Object to Aggregate* drop-down, you can only choose objects with the right type of relationship. The possible aggregation functions are

- Average

- Count (how many related objects)

- Maximum

- Minimum

- Total (sum of the selected field)

Importing Business Objects

If you already have your data structure defined in a spreadsheet, you can create business objects from a spreadsheet data file. This method allows you to create one or more business objects in one operation and to populate them with data at the same time. To do this, you use the *Data Manager*, which is accessed from the business objects menu like the diagrammer.

The *Data Manager* has six functions as shown in Figure 2-13, and the *Import Business Objects* function is the one that is used to import data and create matching business objects.

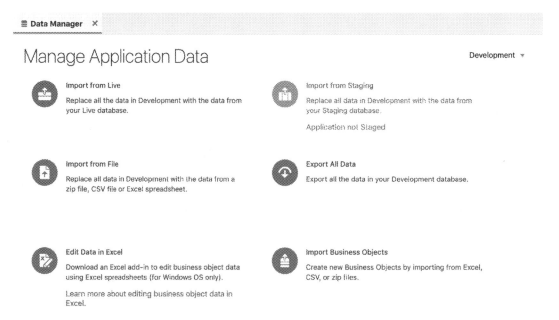

Figure 2-13. The Data Manager

When you click *Import Business Objects*, the *Import New Business Objects* wizard starts.

Note   This option is only available when you have the development environment selected in the drop-down at the top right.

You can import business objects from both comma-separated values (`.csv`) files and Microsoft Excel (`.xls/.xlsx`) files.

- If you import a `.csv` file, a business object is created with the same name as the file.

- If you import an `.xls/.xlsx` file, one business object is created for each sheet in the worksheet file with the same name as the individual worksheet.

- You can upload a ZIP file containing multiple `.csv` and/or `.xls/.xlsx` files. In this case, all files are processed as if they were uploaded individually.

In both cases, the first row must contain column headers which are used to create fields in the business objects. The import wizard does its best to determine the data type from the values in your file or spreadsheet, but you should verify and if necessary change the data type.

Tip   Format your date fields in ISO format (YYYY-MM-DD) before uploading to ensure that VBCS recognizes them as dates.

Uploading the File

Drop your file onto the *Import New Business Objects* window. The file is uploaded, and you will be shown the business objects and the number of records VBCS has found. You are likely to see some warnings this first time you import. Sometimes, the warning message is clear enough, but in other cases the easiest way to find out what is wrong is to complete the import and examine the business object created. If necessary, you can then delete the business object, change your file, and upload again.

> **Note**   The warning `Record has different number of cells than the header` is very common and occurs whenever the last cell in a row is empty.

Defining Business Objects

In the second step of the import wizard, VBCS shows you the business objects it has found in your file or files as shown in Figure 2-14.

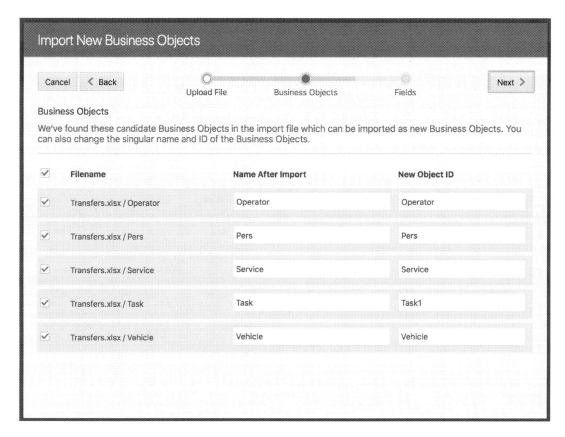

Figure 2-14. *Names for imported business objects*

On this screen, you can view and if necessary change the names and IDs of the business objects to be created. Note that if the name is a reserved word or already used, VBCS creates the object ID by appending a number to the name.

Defining Fields

In the third and final step of the wizard, you are presented with the fields the VBCS import wizard has found in your data as shown in Figure 2-15.

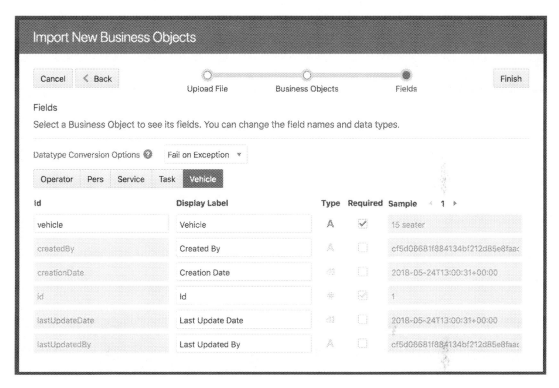

Figure 2-15. *Fields to be imported*

Note that if you are importing an Excel file or a ZIP file with multiple CSV files, there will be a series of buttons to work with each business object (`Operator`, `Pers`, `Service`, `Task`, and `Vehicle` in the preceding illustration).

Select each business object in turn. For each individual attribute

- Review and change the label as necessary.

- Change the data type if VBCS has not automatically selected the right one.

- Decide if the attribute will be mandatory (required).

Note   If you are importing multiple related business objects, see the section on importing related business objects later in this chapter.

This step of the wizard also contains the *Datatype Conversion Options* drop-down. There are three options if data cannot be converted:

- *Fail on Exception* means the whole import fails if there are any errors.

- *Skip Row Import* means any misformatted rows will not be imported, but the rest will be.

- *Set Null Value* means that any misformatted fields will be set to null, but all rows will be imported.

Performing the Import

When you have chosen the conversion option and reviewed all fields, click Finish to start the actual import and creation process. A dialog confirms your import is successful as shown in Figure 2-16.

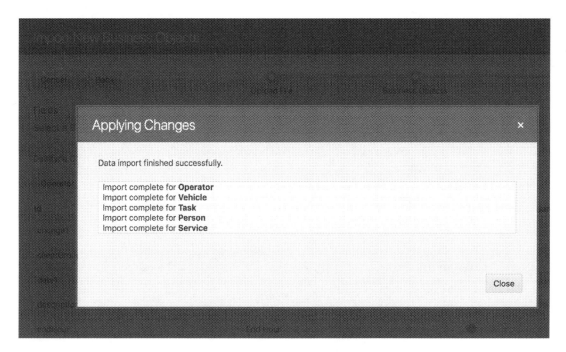

Figure 2-16. *Successful import*

Importing Related Business Objects

If you are importing multiple business objects, and the data in your CSV or Excel file already defines the relationship, you can establish this relationship during the import. There are two situations:

- You have numeric ID values.

- You have alphanumeric ID values.

Importing Numeric ID Values

In the simple case, your data contains a numeric relationship. For example, in the Excel workbook shown in Figure 2-17, there is a Person business object that contains a numeric key that indicates gender. The Gender business object converts the gender code into a user-facing text.

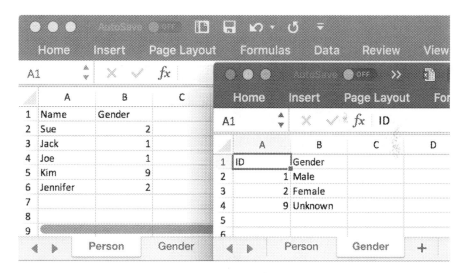

Figure 2-17. *Example of business objects with numerical relationship*

When importing business objects with this kind of relationship, you simply need to change the *Type* in the master business object to *Reference*. As shown in Figure 2-18, a dialog automatically appears when you choose *Reference*, allowing you to choose the business object that contains the reference values.

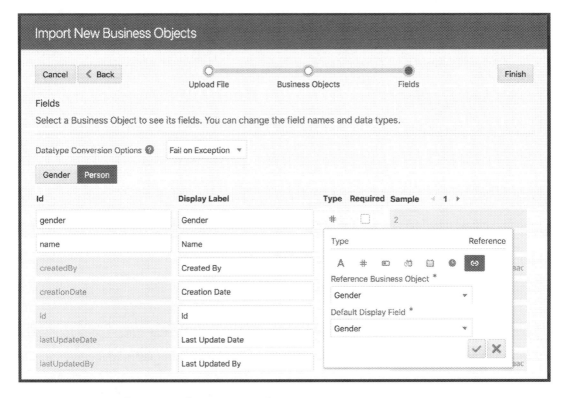

Figure 2-18. *Selecting Reference type during import*

This establishes the Gender field in the master business object as a reference value. When you later build the user interface based on Person, VBCS will automatically suggest a selection component like a drop-down list showing the values in the Gender reference business object.

Importing Alphanumeric ID Values

If your business objects are related through alphanumeric ID values, VBCS cannot automatically connect them. If you just choose *Reference*, you will get an error during the import.

However, if your data is in an Excel workbook, you can preprocess your data with an Excel VLOOKUP function. The data set in Figure 2-19 originally just contained a Pers column with initials (LF, PF, etc.), and the Pers sheet only contained the initials and names.

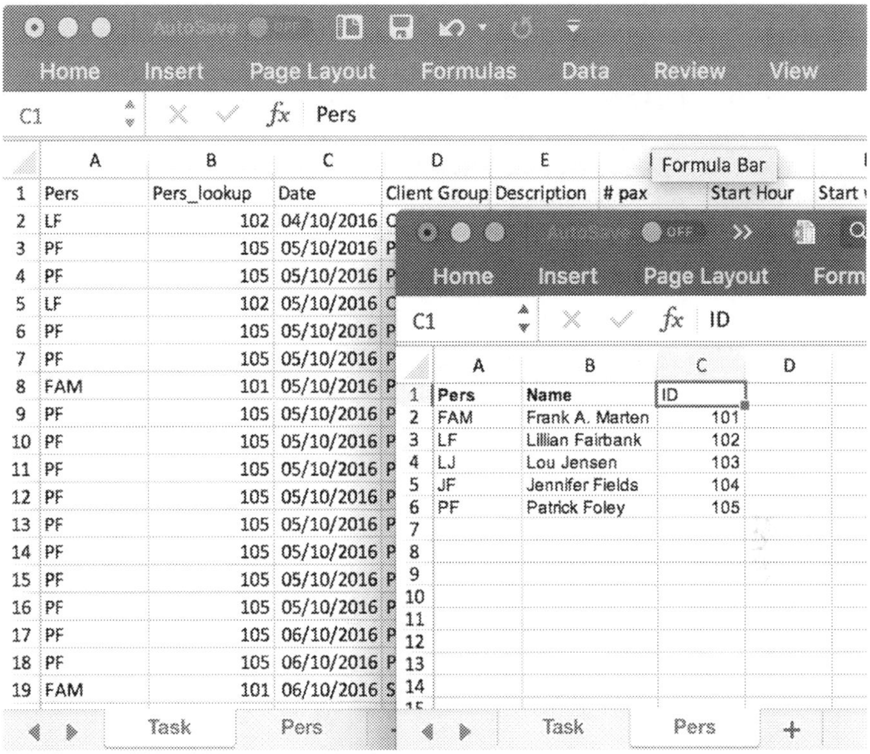

Figure 2-19. *Data with alphanumeric keys*

To help VBCS import this data, two additions were made in the Excel workbook:

- In the Pers sheet, a numeric ID column was added.

- In the Task sheet, a numeric Pers_lookup column was added. The formula for this (taken from the B2 cell) is =VLOOKUP(A2;Pers!A$2:C$6;3;FALSE). This Excel formula means "look up the content of cell A2 in the table from A2 to C6 in sheet Pers and return the content of the third column." The last parameter (FALSE) indicates that an exact match is required.

When you import these expanded business objects, you can turn the Pers_lookup columns into a *Reference* type without error. After the import, you can actually delete the field created from the original Pers column because it won't be needed in the application.

Conclusion

In this chapter, you've learned how to create your own business objects stored inside Visual Builder Cloud Service, both by explicitly defining them and by importing spreadsheet data files. You have also seen how to include calculated fields and business logic.

In the next chapter, you will see how to work with existing web services in VBCS.

CHAPTER 3

Working with Service Connections

As you know now, Visual Builder Cloud Service applications use REST web services for their data. In the last chapter, you saw how you could create VBCS business objects that are automatically exposed as REST web services. In this chapter, we will discuss how to work with existing REST web services created outside VBCS.

It is possible to use service connections that require authentication. VBCS has many authentication options including Oracle Cloud identity, various OAuth authentications, and more. Security for service connections is covered in Chapter 10.

About Service Connections

To work with service connections in an application, you select the *Service Connections* icon in the vertical tab bar along the left edge of the VBCS window. If you have the *Welcome* tab for the application open, you can also click the large Service Connections box to activate this tab. It looks as shown in Figure 3-1.

© Sten Vesterli 2019
S. Vesterli, *Oracle Visual Builder Cloud Service Revealed*, https://doi.org/10.1007/978-1-4842-4929-1_3

Figure 3-1. *Service Connections tab with no service connections defined*

To create a new service connection, you can click the big + *Service Connection* button (only shown when you have no service connections yet) or the + sign next to the *Services* heading. The *Create Service Connection* dialog appears as shown in Figure 3-2.

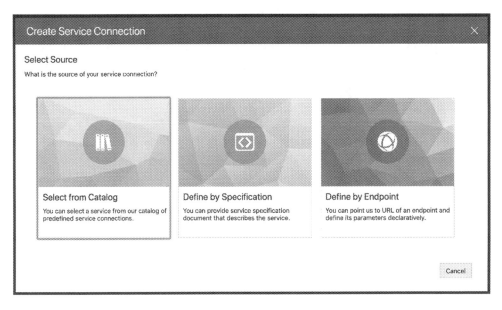

Figure 3-2. *The Create Service Connection dialog*

From here, you can create services of the three types supported by VBCS:

- Catalog services

- Specification services

- Endpoint services

The remaining sections in this chapter describe these options in more detail.

Creating from a Service Specification

If you have a service specification for your service, you should always use that as the basis for your service connection. The specification contains more information that the REST call itself, and VBCS can make use of this additional information. VBCS currently supports two types of service specifications:

- Swagger

- Oracle ADF Describe

To create a service connection from a service specification, you click *Define by Specification* when creating the connection. The Service Specification dialog appears as shown in Figure 3-3.

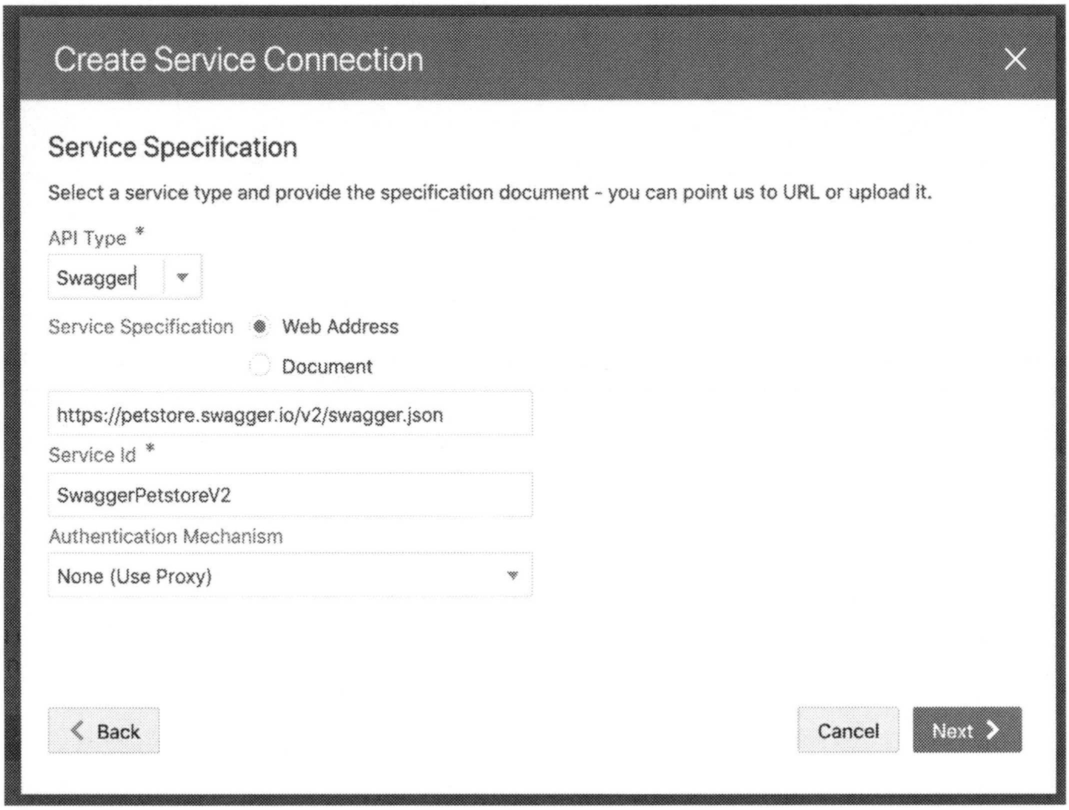

Figure 3-3. *Creating a service connection from a Swagger file*

In this dialog, you can choose either *Swagger* or *ADF Describe* as API type and provide either a URL to the specification or upload a specification document. We will describe the authentication mechanisms in Chapter 10.

Caution   It is possible to write a name containing spaces in the *Service Id* field and create the service. However, you won't be able to use it because VBCS will give you an error about the name. Write something without spaces or special characters.

You will typically be defining your service by referring to a running instance and choosing *Web Address*, but it is also possible to select *Document* and upload a specification JSON file.

Swagger

Swagger is a set of tooling for developing, documenting, and working with REST APIs. The specification is still known as a *Swagger* API in Visual Builder Cloud Service, even though the API specification is today called the *OpenAPI Specification*.

When the service you want to connect to offers an OpenAPI specification, you can use that to provide VBCS with the information it needs to work with the service.

An OpenAPI specification is a JSON file. Here you find parts of an OpenAPI specification:

```
{
  "swagger": "2.0",
  "info": {
    "description": "This is a sample server Petstore server",
    "version": "1.0.0",
    "title": "Swagger Petstore",
...
  },
  "host": "petstore.swagger.io",
  "basePath": "/v2",
  "tags": [
    {
      "name": "pet",
      "description": "Everything about your Pets",
      "externalDocs": {
        "description": "Find out more",
        "url": "http://swagger.io"
      }
    },
...
  ],
  "schemes": [
    "https",
    "http"
  ],
```

```
"paths": {
  "/pet": {
    "post": {
      "tags": [
        "pet"
      ],
      "summary": "Add a new pet to the store",
      "description": "",
      "operationId": "addPet",
      "consumes": [
        "application/json",
        "application/xml"
      ],
      "produces": [
        "application/xml",
        "application/json"
      ],
      "parameters": [
        {
          "in": "body",
          "name": "body",
          "description": "Pet object that needs to be added to the store",
          "required": true,
          "schema": {
            "$ref": "#/definitions/Pet"
          }
        }
      ],
      "responses": {
        "405": {
          "description": "Invalid input"
        }
      },
      "security": [
```

```
        {
          "petstore_auth": [
            "write:pets",
            "read:pets"
          ]
        }
      ]
    },
...
}
```

The Swagger tooling can present an OpenAPI specification in a human-readable form as shown in Figure 3-4.

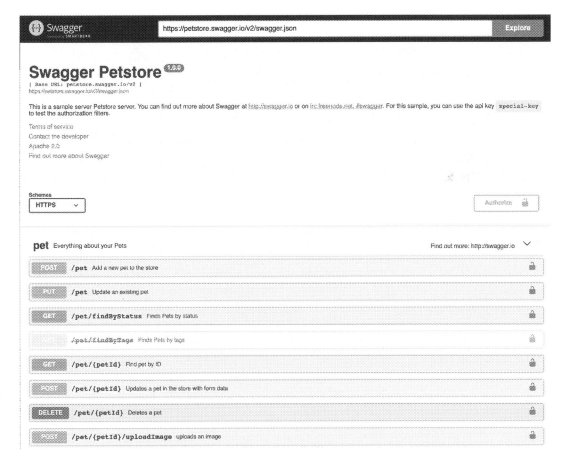

Figure 3-4. *Swagger displaying information about a REST API*

If you set API Type to Swagger, provide the URL to an OpenAPI .json file, and click *Next*, VBCS connects to the service and shows a list of available endpoints as shown in Figure 3-5.

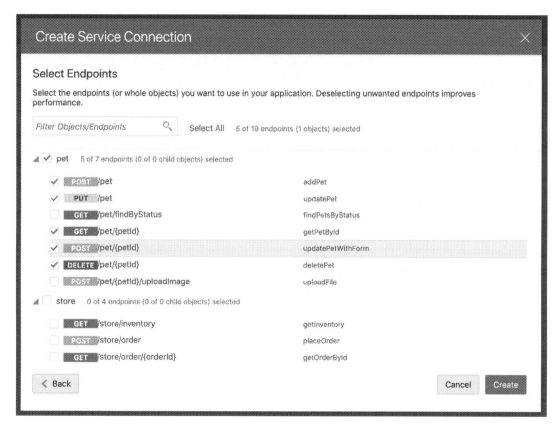

Figure 3-5. *Selecting endpoints from an OpenAPI specification*

Select only the endpoints that make sense for your application and click *Create*. VBCS creates your service connection and opens it in the main work area. You might get many different endpoint options depending on what the developer has written in the OpenAPI specification file.

ADF Describe

If your VBCS application needs to access data stored in an Oracle Application Development Framework (ADF) application, you can get all the necessary metadata from the ADF application. If the ADF developer makes the ADF Application Module available as a REST web service, the VBCS developer merely needs to point to the describe endpoint for the service.

For example, an ADF developer might have built an application that maintains employee data and published it as a REST service with URL `https://<server>:<port>/AdfEmployees/rest/v0/Employees`.

Calling this URL from a browser will deliver the employee data from the ADF application. But adding `/describe` to the URL will provide all the metadata VBCS needs. When you set *API Type* to *ADF Describe* and use a describe URL like `https://<server>:<port>/AdfEmployees/rest/v0/Employees/describe`, you will be presented with a list of endpoints as shown in Figure 3-6.

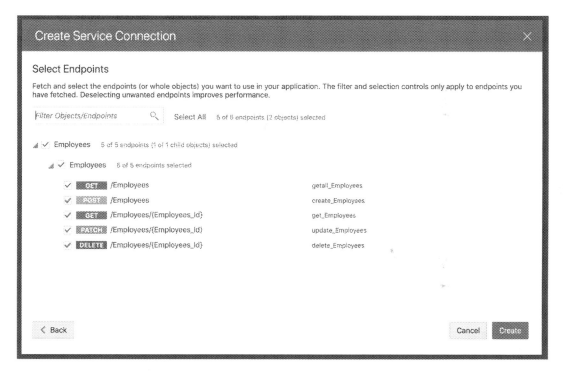

Figure 3-6. *Selecting endpoints from an ADF application*

ADF always provides two `GET` operations (for all records and for one record), a `POST` to create, a `PATCH` to update, and a `DELETE` to delete. Not surprisingly, these are the same endpoints that a VBCS business object REST service offers.

Creating from an Endpoint

If you don't have a service specification for your REST web service, you can still use it for your VBCS application. You will just have to provide some more information yourself.

To create a service connection directly from a REST endpoint, click *Define by Endpoint*. The first *Create Service Connection* dialog for an endpoint REST web service looks as shown in Figure 3-7.

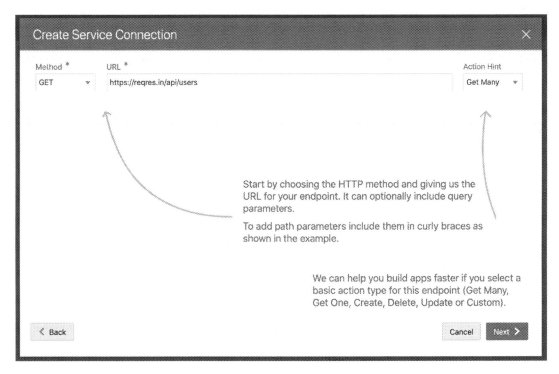

Figure 3-7. Creating a service connection for a REST endpoint

Note that when you create a service connection for a REST endpoint, you provide a URL and provide an *Action Hint* telling VBCS what that endpoint does. You usually start by defining an endpoint that retrieves multiple records because that is what VBCS needs to render a table or list of records. Choose a GET method, provide the URL to that service, and set the action hint to *Retrieve Many*.

When you click *Next*, the second *Create Service Connection* dialog appears. This has five tabs:

- The *Service* tab allows you to give your service a name.

- The *Authentication* tab allows you to specify if your service requires authentication, and if so, how to authenticate. Refer to Chapter 10 for more information about authentication.

- The *Request* tab is where you can define any parameters your service takes. You can add them as HTTP header parameters or as parameters passed as part of the URL. If you have static settings that must always be passed, you can specify them here. And if there are parameters you want to be able to set when using the service, you need to define them here.

- The *Response* tab must contain a valid response from your service. The content of the *Example* field on this tab is what VBCS uses to determine which fields your service offers.

- The *Test* tab is probably the most important because this is where you actually call your service to verify the parameters, get a response, and copy that response to the *Response* tab. Figure 3-8 shows the *Test* tab.

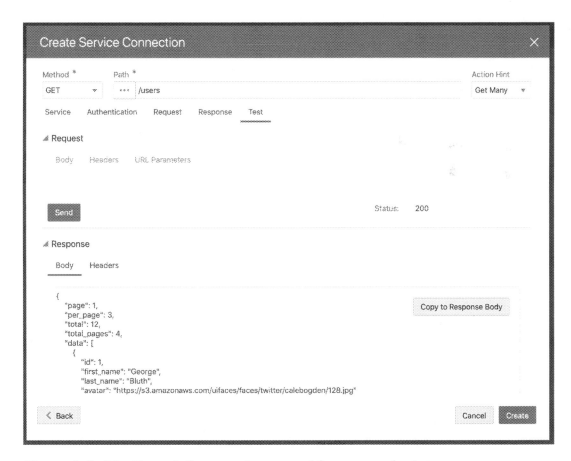

Figure 3-8. *The Test tab for a service created from an endpoint*

To test your service call, you click *Send* on this tab. The data returned from the service is placed in the *Body* field under the *Response* heading. If the data is what you expected, you can click *Copy to Response Body* to copy this sample response to the *Response* tab and then click *Create*.

Your service is then opened in a new tab and looks like any other service connection. However, the *Endpoints* tab contains only the one endpoint you just defined as shown in Figure 3-9.

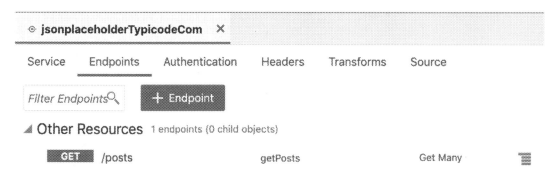

Figure 3-9. *A newly created service with just one endpoint*

If you only want to display records, it is enough to define one *Get Many* endpoint and you are done. If you also want to create, edit, or delete records, you need to click + *Endpoint* to add additional endpoints for these operations. For full Create/Retrieve/Update/Delete functionality in VBCS, you need the five standard endpoints that VBCS business objects (and ADF REST services) create. These were listed earlier in this chapter in Figure 3-6.

If something goes wrong, you will not see the various service tabs, but instead an error message as shown in Figure 3-10.

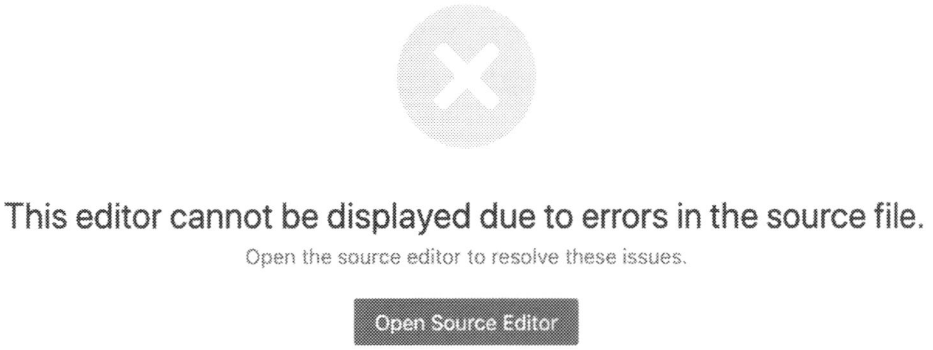

This editor cannot be displayed due to errors in the source file.

Open the source editor to resolve these issues.

Open Source Editor

Figure 3-10. *Error message for a service created from an endpoint*

You can click the *Open Source Editor* button to see the JSON file that defines your connection.

The most common error is that VBCS couldn't figure out the structure of the data your service returns. Your source file must contain a `definitions` section – if that is missing, VBCS doesn't understand the data elements returned by your service and can't map them to fields in the UI.

Using Service Connections

When you use the *Add Data* quick start to connect a collection component to a service, you will see that services defined from, for example, ADF Describe (with all the standard endpoints) are shown as an object to be selected, while services defined from individual endpoints have these listed. See Figure 3-11.

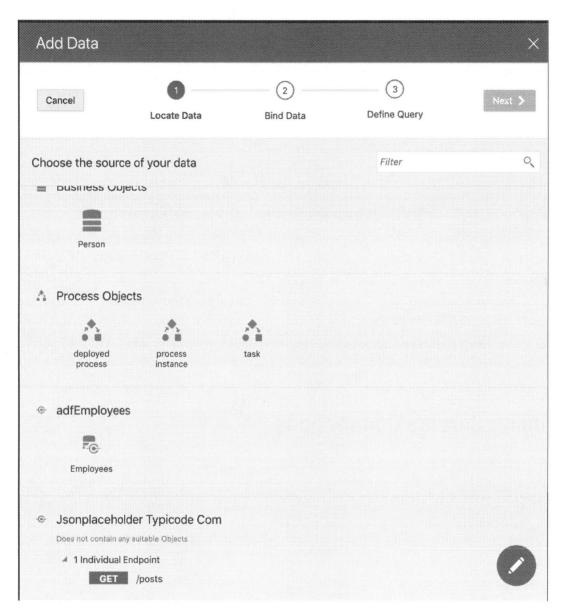

Figure 3-11. *Using the Add Data wizard on service connections*

In this figure, the adfEmployees connection is of type *ADF Describe* and is shown similarly to business objects. The individual endpoint from the Jsonplaceholder service is listed separately.

The quick starts have different requirements and can only run successfully if a service of the right type is available.

- *Add Data* requires a GET service of *Get Many* type.

- *Add Create Page* requires a POST service of *Create* type.

- *Add Edit Page* requires a GET service of *Get One* type and a PATCH service of *Update* type.

- *Add Detail Page* requires a GET service of *Get One* type.

- *Add Delete Action* requires a DELETE service of *Delete* type.

Pagination, Filtering, and Sorting

The REST services that Visual Builder Cloud Service builds for you when you define business objects contain functionality for filtering, sorting, and pagination. When VBCS builds both the services and the user interface, the UI knows what parameters it can send to the service. For example, if you build an application using pagination, the front-end components will use parameters limit and offset to define which records are required. To retrieve, for example, records 30 through 40, the query would contain offset=30&limit=10.

When you are connecting to external services, you cannot be sure that they understand the same syntax and parameters. The VBCS UI will send the same type of request, but you might have to write conversion code that converts the VBCS request into something the external service can understand.

You do this on the *Transforms* tab after creating a service connection. First, you check the checkbox *Enable filtering, sorting and pagination transforms*. A code field appears as shown in Figure 3-12.

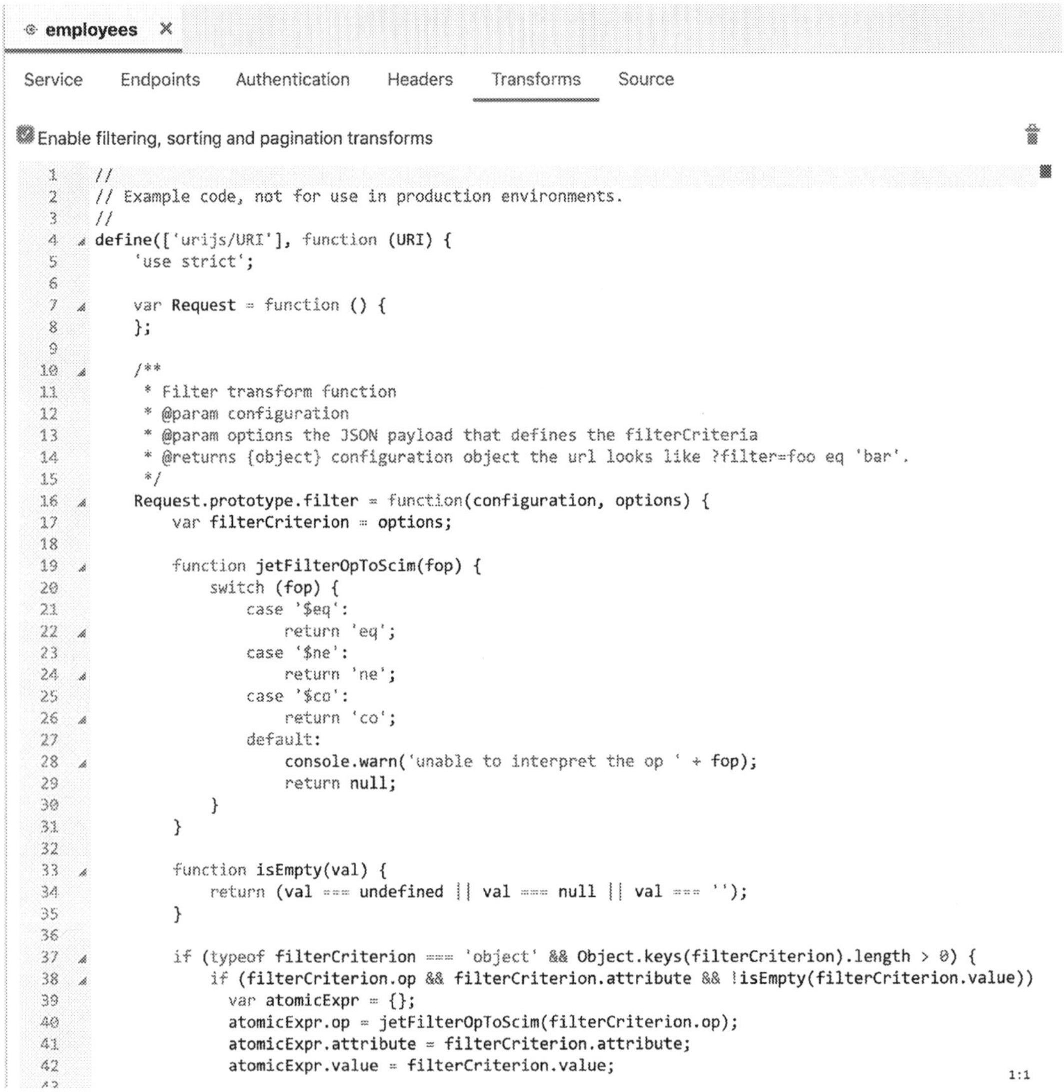

Figure 3-12. *Filtering, sorting, and pagination transforms*

VBCS helpfully provides some sample code, even though it does come with the admonition "Example code, not for use in production environments."

The filter, sort, and paginate functions all take two parameters configuration and options and return a configuration object. If you look at the sample code, you can see how it sets the url attribute of the configuration object it returns.

For example, if your service uses parameters called start and batchsize to control pagination, your paginate function could look like this:

```
/**
 * Pagination function appends batchsize and start parameters to the url
 * @param configuration
 * @param options the JSON payload that defines the pagination criteria
 * @returns {object} configuration object.
 */
Request.prototype.paginate = function(configuration, options) {
  var newUrl = configuration.url;
  newUrl = URI(newUrl).addSearch(
      {batchsize: options.size, start: options.offset}).toString();
  configuration.url = newUrl;
  return configuration;
};
```

Note that you only need to write your own transform functions if you want to use default VBCS UI component functionality that depends on these parameters (e.g., for pagination).

If you want, for example, to limit the results returned by the service connection based on user input, you can just map a variable to your query URL in the page. Step 3 in the *Add Data* quick start is *Define Query*, where you can map variable values to the URL parameters you have defined for the service.

Using the Service Catalog

If you are using any of the Oracle Software-as-a-Service products like HCM Cloud, CRM Cloud, or similar, or you are using Integration Cloud Service, you can build Visual Builder Cloud Service applications on top of the services provided by these products.

In order to work with services from the catalog, someone must tell VBCS the URL where it can find the catalog services. This can be done for all VBCS application in a VBCS instance by your instance administrator or on an application-by-application basis by the developer.

Setting Up the Service Catalog for the Instance

To set up the service catalog for all applications, your instance administrator must choose *Settings* from the VBCS main menu accessible from the menu icon next to the Oracle Visual Builder logo at the top left of the screen. See Figure 3-13.

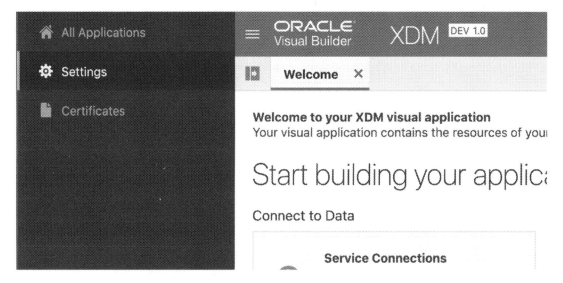

Figure 3-13. *Accessing VBCS instance settings*

Note   If you do not see this menu item, you do not have administrator rights on your instance. You must contact your administrator or set up the service catalog on an application-by-application basis instead.

The *Tenant Settings* window has a field where you write the *Fusion Applications Base URL*. This will typically be something like https://<servername> /helpPortalApi/ otherResources/latest/interfaceCatalogs.

Setting Up the Service Catalog for the Application

If you are not an administrator, you can still set up the service catalog for the specific application you are developing. To do this, you choose *Settings* from the application menu in the top right corner of your VBCS browser window. Then select the *Services* tab as shown in Figure 3-14.

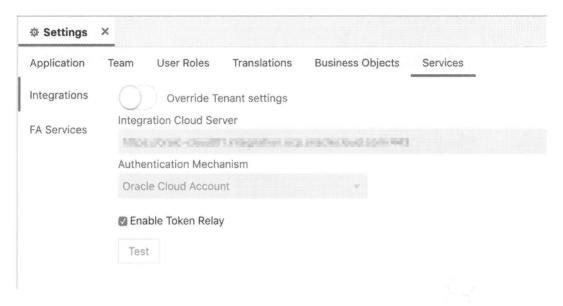

Figure 3-14. *Application service settings*

On the *Integrations* tab, you can provide the URL of your integration cloud server in order to access services from Integration Cloud Service, specify how to authenticate to that server, and test your connection.

On the *FA Services* tab, you can provide the URL of your Fusion Applications catalog, specify how to authenticate to Fusion Applications, and test your connection.

Note   If your instance administrator has set up a specific integration or FA services URL, you can override this for a specific application by moving the *Override Tenant Settings* toggle.

Working with the Service Catalog

To build applications on top of either Integration Cloud Service or one of the Fusion Applications, you choose *Select from Catalog*. You will be presented with a choice of services as shown in Figure 3-15.

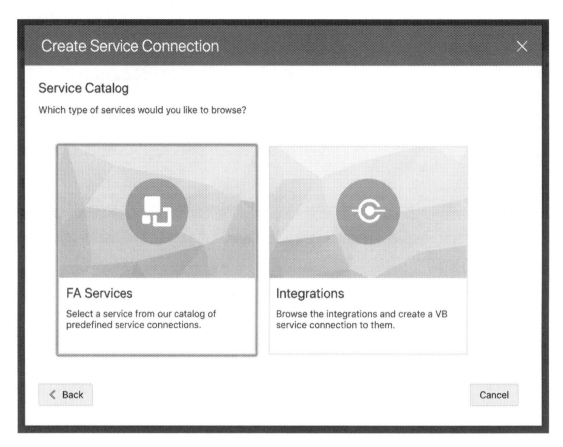

Figure 3-15. *The Service Catalog*

Clicking the *FA Services* tile takes you to a catalog of available Fusion Applications (Oracle SaaS) services. If your organization has purchased, for example, Oracle HCM Cloud, and your cloud administrator has performed the necessary incantations over your environment, you will see a list of services from HCM Cloud.

They are documented in detail in the documentation for the Oracle SaaS solution you have. For example, Figure 3-16 shows part of the REST service catalog for Oracle HCM Cloud.

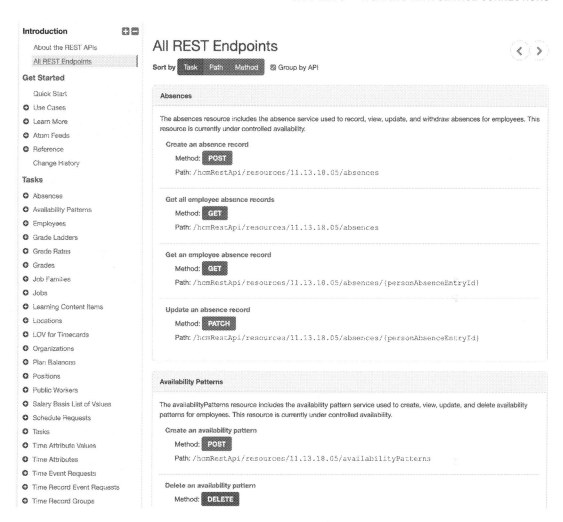

Figure 3-16. *REST services available for HCM Cloud*

If your VBCS instance is connected to Oracle Integration Cloud Service (ICS), you will also have an *Integrations* tile. Clicking this tile opens the *Create Service Connection* dialog, where you can select endpoints from all the integrations in ICS you have access to.

Note   If you get an error message or don't see the services you expect, either your user does not have access or the SaaS or integration service instance is not correctly connected to your VBCS instance. Use the *Test* button on the *Services* tab of the application settings to verify the connection.

Conclusion

In this chapter, you have learned how to connect to external services that already exist outside of Visual Builder Cloud Service. Some services are pre-integrated and can just be selected from a catalog, while others might be defined by OpenAPI (Swagger) definitions or ADF Describe. You have also seen that you can use any REST service as long as you carefully define the endpoints manually.

In the next chapter, you will learn more about building web applications based on business objects or service connections.

CHAPTER 4

Building Web Applications

In the last two chapters, you saw how to create business objects to store your data and how to connect to existing services for data. In this chapter, we will be building web applications that use this data and present it to a user in a web browser. You will see how to manage your pages and use the components in the VBCS component palette, including visualizations.

Visual Builder Cloud Service makes it easy to create responsive web applications that scale to fit the available screen area, so VBCS web applications can also be used on mobile devices of varying screen sizes. However, if you want to build a specialized mobile application, VBCS can also help you build that. We will discuss mobile applications in the next chapter.

Creating a Web Application

To get started building a web application, you select the *Web Applications* icon in the left-hand menu and then click the plus sign next to the *Web Apps* heading. You will be prompted to provide an ID for your application, and your application is ready.

Note VBCS uses the word *Application* in two meanings. On a high level, there are complete VBCS applications, but inside these, you also find something called applications. A VBCS application can contain business objects, service connections, and multiple web and/or mobile applications.

A VBCS web application consists of several parts. They are all shown in the Web Apps navigator as shown in Figure 4-1.

© Sten Vesterli 2019
S. Vesterli, *Oracle Visual Builder Cloud Service Revealed*, https://doi.org/10.1007/978-1-4842-4929-1_4

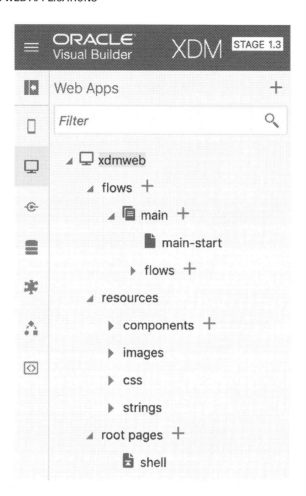

Figure 4-1. *Contents of a VBCS web application*

You will spend most of your time working with the flows in the application and the pages in these flows. In the preceding illustration, there is a main flow containing a main-start page. At runtime, your different flows are presented inside the root page (by default called shell).

In this chapter, we will first discuss how to build pages using the VBCS components and then how to work with flows.

Working with Pages

To work with a page, you open it by double-clicking it in the *Web Apps* navigator or in the visual representation of the flow that it is a part of. This opens the page in a dedicated page tab in the VBCS main work area.

Along the left edge of the page tab, you find icons for the six different views of a page:

- Designer

- Variables

- Actions

- Settings

- Functions

- Code

The Page Designer

The *Page Designer* view contains a page canvas and three additional areas you can toggle on and off as shown in Figure 4-2.

Figure 4-2. *The contents of the Page Designer view*

The leftmost icon (that looks like a puzzle piece) toggles the *component palette* on and off. To build up your page, you drag components onto the canvas from this palette.

Note   There are two "puzzle piece" icons in VBCS. The one inside a specific page tab toggles the component palette. The one at the far left of the VBCS window changes to the component view where you can manage custom components.

The next icon (that looks like a navigation tree) toggles the *Page Structure* panel on and off. For simple pages, you simply work and select items on the canvas, but for more complex pages, the page structure panel gives you an overview and allows you to easily select the component you want to work with.

The rightmost icon (with an arrow, at the other end of the top bar) expands and collapses the *Property Inspector*. The property inspector allows you to make changes to the properties of the currently selected component, so it will change as you select different components.

Page Canvas

The page canvas shows the content of your page. There are two types of layouts in VBCS: *Grid layouts* and *Flex layouts*. When the entire page is selected, the property palette allows you to choose between these two layout types.

The grid layout contains 12 predefined columns to make it easy to lay out and align components. When using the grid layout, everything is placed in one of these 12 columns and stays there.

The flex layout allows you to add components in rows of any size. You can define if you want the row to wrap if the screen is not wide enough for all items, and flex rows have many properties for alignment, justification, and item size.

Tip   The flex layout is more powerful, but also more complicated to use. Start with a grid layout and see if it meets your needs. If not, you can always drag your components onto a flex layout later.

Collection Components

You need to connect your web application components to the underlying REST services, and the VBCS collection components (*Table* and *List View*) make this easy. Table components are good for showing large amounts of tabular data in many columns and work well on large screens. List View components show fewer data elements (normally no more than four), so they are better when you don't need to show a lot of information, for example, on the smaller screens on mobile devices.

When you have placed a collection component on the page, the property palette contains a *Quick Start* icon to the right (the "graduate" icon). When you select this, you see some quick start wizards as shown in Figure 4-3.

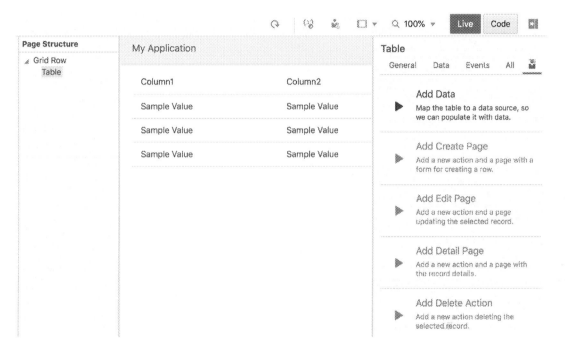

Figure 4-3. *The property palette for a collection component*

The most important of these is the *Add Data* wizard, which will create a connection from your collection component to a data source. The other wizards allow you to easily create additional pages for creating, editing, displaying, and deleting data.

Adding a Data Source for a Table

When you click *Add Data*, you will be taken through a three-step wizard where you can select the data for your collection component.

In the first step, shown in Figure 4-4, you select the endpoint that will provide your data. This screen lists your business objects, process objects (from Process Cloud Service), and any service connections you have defined.

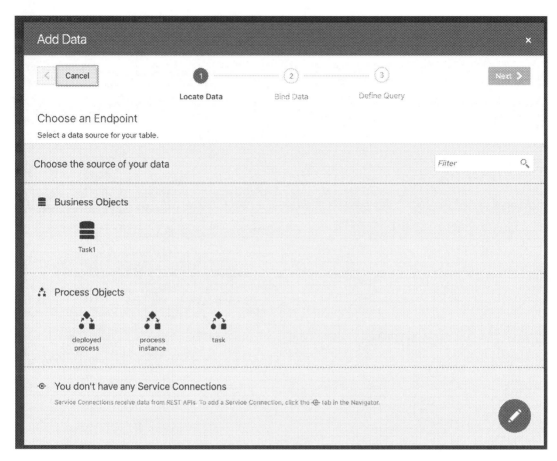

Figure 4-4. *Choosing an endpoint for a collection component*

If you want to see the specific REST endpoints, you can click the pencil icon in the bottom right corner of this dialog to see the technical details (GET, POST, etc.).

In the second step of the wizard, you select the columns you want to use in your table. They are listed in alphabetical order but added to the data source in the order you click them. You can either click them in the order you want or reorder them afterward by dragging the handle next to each data element.

Tip   Add all the elements from the service that might be relevant, even if you don't have any use for them now. VBCS creates a data source mapping for you at this time, and it is hard and error-prone to add additional data elements later.

The final step of the wizard allows you to define query parameters. This is useful if your endpoint offers a way to limit the result set, or if you want to limit the number of records returned.

When you finish the wizard, your collection component on the page canvas will show real data returned by the REST web service.

Adding a Data Source for a List View

The process when adding a data source for a List View component contains an extra step between selecting the endpoint and choosing the fields, as shown in Figure 4-5.

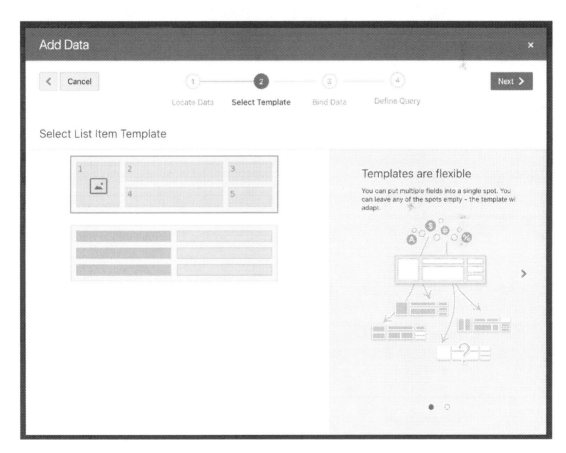

Figure 4-5. *Choosing a template for a List View component*

At the time of writing, VBCS offered two templates as previously shown:

- The top-most template is intended to show an image or icon and up to four fields in a two by two grid.

- The lower template will simply display all the items as you drop into it as a vertical list.

After you have selected a template, you map your data fields to the individual locations in the template as shown in Figure 4-6.

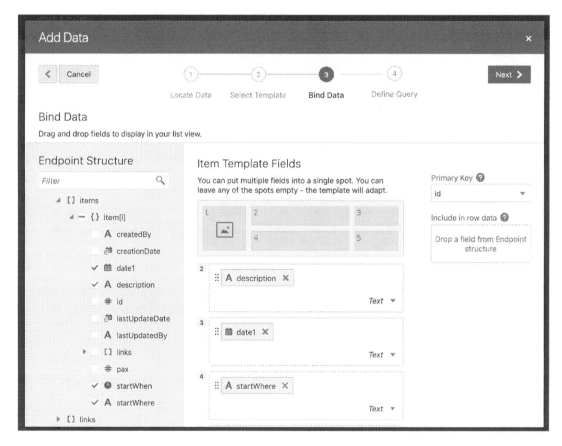

Figure 4-6. *Using a List View template*

Note that it is possible to drop multiple items into one slot and let VBCS do its best to arrange them. You can of course also leave slots empty. If you change your mind, you can reorder the elements in the page designer.

Creating Standard Pages

When you have created an overview page with a collection component, you can use the Quick Starts to add pages for creating new records, editing existing records, showing detailed information, and deleting records.

Adding a Create Page

When you click *Create Page*, you will be taken through a simple two-step wizard. In the first step, you select the data source for your create operation (business object, process object, or service connection).

In the *Page Detail* step, you select the fields you want to allow the user to provide values for.

You also need to provide the label on the button to start the page, the title of the create page, and the internal name of the create page. The first two are displayed to the user, while the last is only shown to the developer.

Tip   In some cases, the default texts suggested by VBCS will have a number appended to it (e.g., `Task1`) – remember to remove this at least from the user-facing texts. The number can get added to your service if your business component name is a reserved word, or if you have deleted and re-created the business object in the same application.

You can select the individual fields in the order you want them to appear on your create page. If you select fields in the wrong order or change your mind, you can drag the fields into a different arrangement on the create page itself.

If you want to add all fields, you can just check the topmost checkbox (next to {} `request`). This selects every field in the underlying service. You should deselect the fields that VBCS handles (Created By, Created, Id, Last Updated, Last Updated By).

Note   Using this approach adds all fields in alphabetical order to your create page. You will have to manually reorder the fields on the page.

The Result of Adding the Create Page

When you click *Finish*, you will see a new button added above your collection to open the new page. In the navigator, you will also see a new page, and if you open the main flow, you will see that your application now has two pages and flow between them as shown in Figure 4-7.

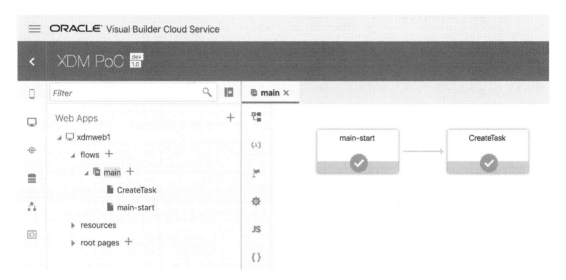

Figure 4-7. *The main flow with a create page*

Testing Your Create Flow

You can test your create flow either from within the development environment or by running the application.

To test it from within the development environment, click the *Live* button near the top right corner of the VBCS window. This sets your application to *Live* mode (indicated by a green border around the page in the page designer). In this mode, clicking the button actually executes the action corresponding to the button. In this case, the button will navigate to the create page. When you are not in *Live* mode, clicking the button simply selects it so you can edit its properties.

To test your application as it will look to the end user, you click the *Run* icon (a white triangle) above the *Live* button. This will run your application in a new browser tab.

Adding an Edit Page

To add a page where the user can edit existing data, you use the *Add Edit Page* quick start.

Tip   If the quick start icon doesn't show in the property palette, you do not have the collection component (table or list view) selected. Select it from the Page Structure panel or on the page canvas. You can only select items on the page canvas when you are in *Design* mode.

This process has three steps. In the first step, you select the read endpoint (business object, process object, or service connection). In the second step, you select the endpoint for updating the record with the new values provided by the user. When you are working with business objects, you simply select the same business object twice, and VBCS will automatically select the right REST endpoints for you.

In the *Page Detail* step, you select the fields you want the user to be able to update. Similar to the create page, you can either click individual fields one at a time in the order you want them on the edit page or check the `{} request` checkbox at the top to add all fields in alphabetical order.

Tip   Make sure the fields are in the same order on the create and update pages. VBCS does not enforce this, but your users will expect it.

You must also provide a label for the button that activates the edit page as well as the title and internal name of the edit page.

When you click *Finish*, you will see another button above your collection to open the edit page. Your application now has three pages when you look at the `main` flow, as shown in Figure 4-8.

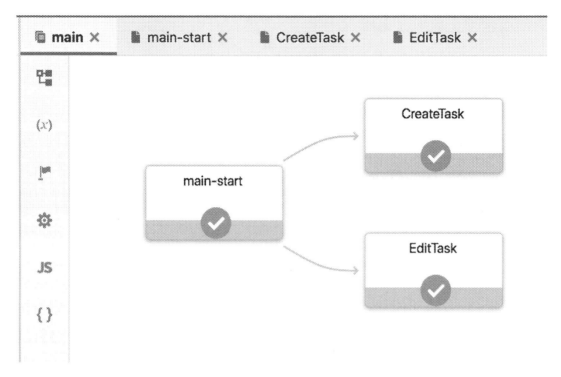

Figure 4-8. *The main flow with create and edit pages*

You can test the edit page in *Live* mode or by running the application. The *Edit* button will only be active when a record is selected in the table.

Adding a Detail Page

If your record has too many attributes to show in your collection component (table or list view), you need to provide a way for the user to see all attributes for a selected record. To create such a detail page, you use the *Add Detail Page* quick start.

This process has just two steps. In the first step, you select the endpoint for reading one record. You can just select a business object and let VBCS work out which REST endpoint to call, or you can choose a process object or a service connection. If you want to specify the REST service directly, you can also click the pencil icon in the bottom right corner of the screen to get access to the detailed REST endpoint selection.

In the second step, you select all the fields you want to show to the user. As for the other quick starts, you can either click individual fields one at a time in the order you want them on the edit page or check the {} request checkbox at the top to add all fields in alphabetical order. Select the relevant fields and show them in the same order as on the create and update pages.

You must also provide a label for the button that activates the detail page as well as the title and internal name of that page.

When you click *Finish*, you will see yet another button above your collection to open the detail page. Your application now has four pages shown in the main flow, and you can test it in Live mode or by running the application.

Adding a Delete Action

If you want to allow your users to delete records, you can use the *Add Delete Action* quick start.

In this process, you simply select the endpoint for deleting a record. Normally, you would just select a business object, choose a process object or service connection, and let VBCS figure out which REST method to call, but again, you can click the pencil icon in the bottom right corner to control the details yourself. When you click *Finish*, a delete button and corresponding action are added to your collection page. There is no extra page involved in deleting a record.

You are not prompted for the label that goes on the delete button – if you want to change it, select the button in *Edit* mode and change the *Text* property in the property palette.

Layout Components

The component palette contains a Layout heading with a lot of components. For the VBCS version current at the time of writing (19.1.3), there are 21 layout components – there might be more by the time you read this book. When you select one of them, a question mark appears to the right of the component. If you hover the mouse over the question mark, you get a very brief explanation of the component as shown in Figure 4-9.

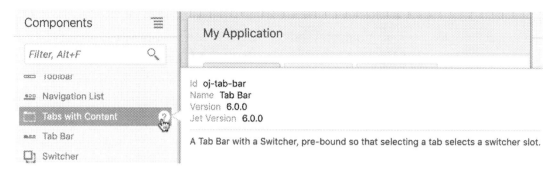

Figure 4-9. *Getting help on layout components*

If the information you get from this popup is not sufficient, you can use the *Id* property to look up the component in the Oracle JET documentation.

Behind the scenes, a Visual Builder Cloud Service application is using Oracle JET components to work its magic, and when you add layout components, you are actually dropping Oracle JET components onto the page.

For example, if you want to know more about the *Collapsible* component, pointing to the question mark tells you this is an instance of an Oracle JET `oj-collapsible` component. To learn more about this, you can go to oraclejet.org. This is the Oracle JET home page, and it looks something like Figure 4-10.

Figure 4-10. *The Oracle JET home page*

From this page, click one of the *Cookbook* links to go to the Oracle JET cookbook with recipes for all components. Naturally, you find the layout components under the *Layout & Nav* heading, where you can learn everything about the *Collapsible* component as shown in Figure 4-11.

Figure 4-11. *Oracle JET documentation of the Collapsible component*

In the Oracle JET documentation, you can see the exact HTML to use to achieve different effects – for the *Collapsible* component, everything is handled by the `<oj-collapsible>` tag. If you want a specific effect or feature you find in the Oracle JET documentation, but VBCS doesn't provide you with a way to achieve this, you can click the *Code* button in the top right corner of a page tab in VBCS to see the actual HTML code behind your page as shown in Figure 4-12.

```
 1  <div class="oj-flex">
 2      <oj-collapsible id="oj-collapsible-543729800-1">
 3          <oj-toolbar id="oj-toolbar-for-oj-list-view-543729800-1" chroming="full
 4              <oj-button id="oj-button-543729800-1" on-click="[[$page.listeners.c
 5              <oj-button disabled="[[ $page.variables.oj_list_view_543729800_1Sel
 6              <oj-button disabled="[[ $page.variables.oj_list_view_543729800_1Sel
 7              <oj-button disabled="[[ $page.variables.oj_list_view_543729800_1Sel
 8          </oj-toolbar>
 9      </oj-collapsible>
10  </div>
11  <div class="oj-flex">
12      <oj-list-view id="oj-list-view-543729800-1" class="oj-flex-item oj-sm-12 oj
13          <template slot="itemTemplate">
14              <oj-vb-list-item title1="[[$current.data.description]]" title2="[[$
15          </template>
16      </oj-list-view>
17  </div>
18
```

Figure 4-12. *The code behind a VBCS page*

In the preceding example, I have dropped a *Collapsible* component on a page and see the corresponding `<oj-collapsible>` tag in the code view.

Static Components

Under the *Common* heading in the component palette, you find some standard components you can use in your application. The *Heading, Text, Label, Paragraph, Hyperlink, Image,* and *Avatar* components are static components you can use to add additional information to your VBCS pages.

The *Image* and *Avatar* components require the URL to the image, so it has to exist on a web server somewhere. If you want to use an image that you have on your local hard disk, you first need to make it part of the VBCS application. To do this, open the node in the application navigator and right-click the *images* node. This will bring up a context menu with an *Import* item as shown in Figure 4-13.

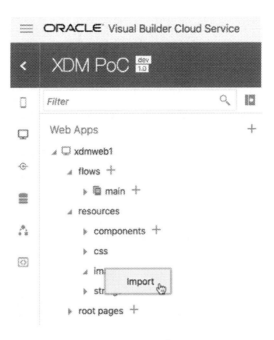

Figure 4-13. *Importing images into your application*

When you click Import, the Import Resources dialog appears as shown in Figure 4-14.

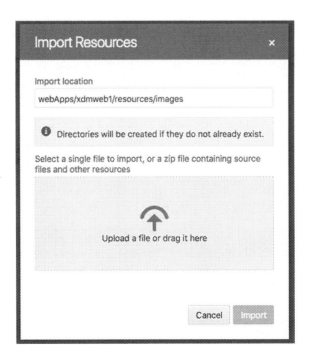

Figure 4-14. *The Import Resources dialog*

Make a note of the *Import* location shown at the top of this dialog. This is where your uploaded image will be stored. You can change this if you want to use subdirectories to organize your images, but don't place them outside the `resources` catalog of your current web application. If you do, your images will not be deployed with the application, so they will be missing when you move from development to staging and production.

When you refer to images in the application in *Image* or *Avatar* component, the *Source URL* (for images) or *src* (for avatars) should start with `resources/images`. For example, if you upload image `803.jpg`, the source of your image is `resources/images/803.jpg`.

The *Avatar* component is intended to show people. It will always be shown as a circle, cropping any image inside. It has an additional property called *Initials* which will be shown as text inside the circle if the *src* property is not set.

Field Components

The field components show one attribute from one record. When you use the quick starts to create pages for creating, viewing, editing, or deleting a single record, VBCS uses field components matching the data type from the underlying business object.

Each field component has a *Data* tab in the property palette where you define a mapping of data in the component to some expression. The most common case is that your component is mapped to a page variable. These page variables can be set with VBCS default functionality, or you can set them yourself using action chains.

In the example used in this book, we have a `Task` business object where one of the attributes is `Description`. If you use the quick starts to create pages for creating, displaying, and editing tasks, you will see that VBCS uses an Input Text component, and the *Value* property on the *Data* tab is `{{ $page.variables.task1.description }}`. You will learn more about variables in a later chapter, but you can see that the VBCS quick start has created a `task1` variable on the page and that record has a `description` property.

Tip   If you want to change a component to another type, you can add a new component from the component palette and reuse the *Value* property from a component added by VBCS.

Most of the field components simply provide a way for the user to interact directly with the underlying data item. Like for layout components, you can point to the question mark next to the component in the component palette to find out which Oracle JET component VBCS is using and then look up the details in the Oracle JET cookbook.

Action Components

The *Common* heading on the component palette also contains action components like *Button* and *Menu*. By themselves, they don't do anything, but they can trigger *Action Chains*. We'll discuss action chains in the chapter on logic in the user interface.

Visualization Components

One of the strong points of modern application development tools like Visual Builder Cloud Service is the ability to create data visualizations easily. VBCS offers two types:

- Charts
- Gauges

All of the visualization components in VBCS are Oracle JET components. Oracle is continually developing new charts and gauges and improving on existing ones, and each version of JET comes with better visualizations.

If you compare the visualizations offered by VBCS to those available in Oracle JET, you will find that not all of the Oracle JET visualizations have made it into the VBCS product. However, since all the visualizations are JavaScript components, you can integrate them into a VBCS application if you really need something that is available in Oracle JET and not in VBCS. To do that, you follow the Oracle JET cookbook for the relevant component.

Charts

A *chart* is a component that displays multiple data points in one or more series of data. If you are familiar with creating charts in desktop products like Microsoft Excel, it will not be hard for you to create graphs in Visual Builder Cloud Service.

The version of VBCS that was current at the time of writing (19.1.3) offers the following charts:

- Area Chart

- Bar Chart

- Box Plot Chart

- Bubble Chart

- Combo Chart

- Donut Chart

- Funnel Chart

- Line Chart

- Line with Area Chart

- Pie Chart

- Pyramid Chart

- Scatter Chart

- Stock Chart

The various charts are described in the following text, grouped by their typical use.

To use the charts, you drop a chart component onto a page. When the chart is selected, the Property Inspector will show an Add Data quick start. When you click this, you will be taken through a three-step data mapping wizard:

1. First, you select your data source (business object, process object, service connection, or raw REST connection).

2. Then you map the fields from the data source to the chosen chart, indicating which field contains the different values the chart needs (e.g., X values, data series values, legends, etc.).

3. The third (optional) step allows you to filter data if you want.

Continuous Data

To present continuous data series (typically values that change over time), you use Line Charts. To use these, you need a data set that represents the X values (typically time periods) and one or more data series that contain the values you want to plot.

Line Charts are most common and allow you to compare values and see trends over time. In *Area Charts*, the area under the line is filled in. To avoid larger values covering smaller values, this is typically used for data sets where it makes sense to accumulate the values, for example, sales by region. *Line with Area Charts* are a hybrid form where the area under the line is semitransparent, allowing you to see through the larger values to smaller values. Figure 4-15 shows a Line, Area, and Line with Area chart.

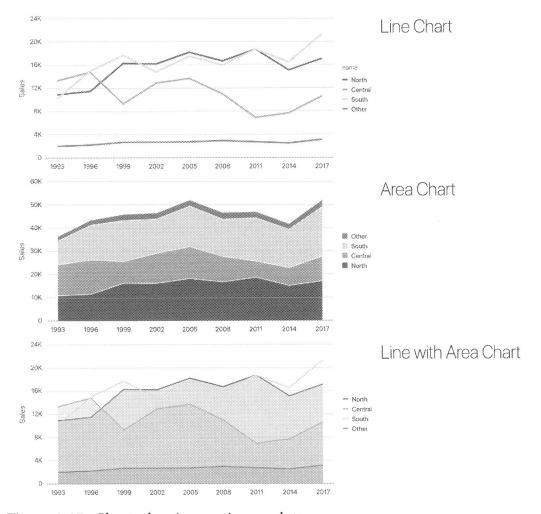

Figure 4-15. *Charts showing continuous data*

The *Combo Chart* can show bars, lines, and area charts together in one component. This is used, for example, for graphs showing the climate in a specific place with lines for average temperature per month and bars for average rainfall.

Discrete Data

When your data set consists of a number of discrete values, you want to compare either absolute or relative values. If you want to compare absolute values, you typically use *Bar Charts*. To compare relative values (how large a part of the whole each part contributes), you use *Pie Charts*, *Donut Charts*, or *Pyramid Charts*. If you are unfamiliar with the last two, their name describes them: a *Donut Chart* is a *Pie Chart* with a hole in the middle (where you can place a label or text), and a *Pyramid Chart* is simply a triangle showing the distribution of values. Figure 4-16 shows a *Bar Chart*, *Pie Chart*, *Donut Chart*, and *Pyramid Chart*.

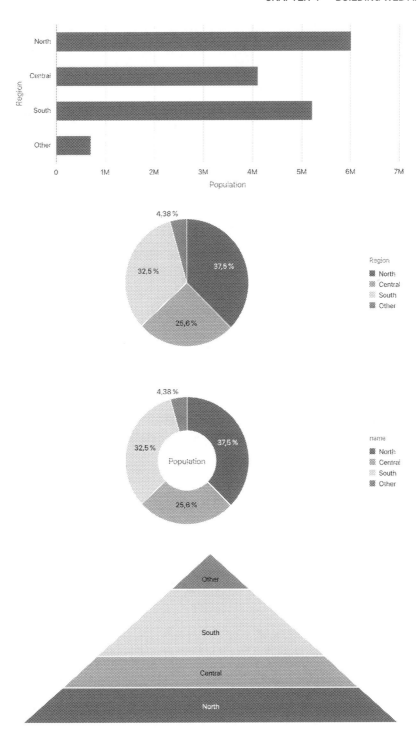

Figure 4-16. *Charts showing discrete data*

The Bar Chart has an *Orientation* property that can be set to *Horizontal* or *Vertical*. The horizontal format is easier to read and allows more space for the text associated with each bar, but the vertical is the default.

Tip   The *Pie* and *Donut* charts have a property that enables a "3D" effect. Don't use this, it distorts the circle and makes the chart harder to read.

Multidimensional Charts

You use multidimensional charts when you want to plot sets of values that all vary freely. Time-bound data has data for every time period, so the distance between data values is constant. Similarly, when you are plotting categories in a bar chart, the distance between the bars does not have any significance.

An example of a multidimensional chart would be to plot life expectancy in years against health cost as a percentage of GDP. You would gather a set of data (e.g., Denmark, 80.9 years, 5.1%) and decide on which value is X and which is Y. To plot two values, you use a *Scatter Chart*. If you want to visualize a third value, you can let the size of the plot point vary, giving you a *Bubble Chart*. Figure 4-17 shows a Scatter Chart of life expectancy vs. health costs and a Bubble Chart where the GDP per person is used as a data source for the size of each bubble.

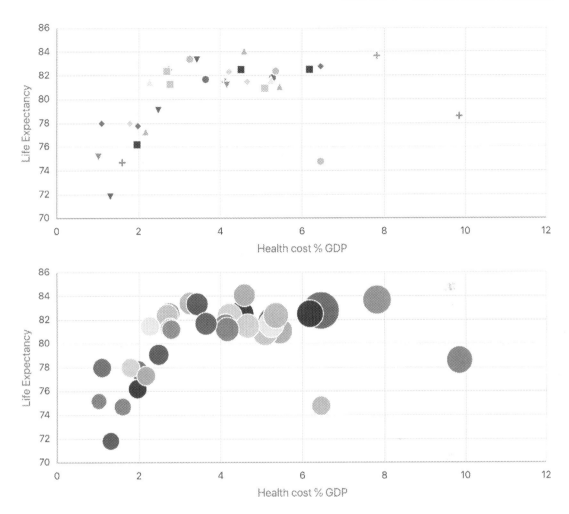

Figure 4-17. *Charts showing dimensional data*

Note   In the preceding charts, the Y-axis does not start at the default zero. To format the axes in a chart, you select the chart and choose *All* in the *Property Inspector*. Some of the properties (e.g., *x-axis* and *y-axis*) have an arrow pointing right, indicating access to more detailed settings.

Specialized Charts

Visual Builder Cloud Service also offers some specialized charts used in specific areas.

A *Box Plot Chart* is a standard way to show statistical values, including median, all four quartiles, as well as any outliers. Figure 4-18 shows an example of a Box Plot Chart.

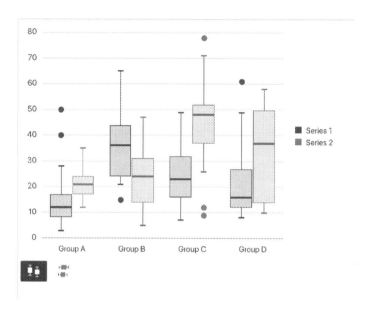

Figure 4-18. *Box Plot Chart example*

A *Funnel Chart* is a standard way of showing stages in a process flow and is very often used in sales organizations. Figure 4-19 shows an example of a Funnel Chart.

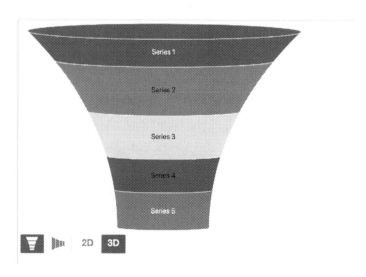

Figure 4-19. *Funnel Chart example*

A *Stock Chart* is a standard way to display the price of a stock. With color coding to show price movement up/down and a symbol showing high, low, open, and close prices, this will be familiar to investors. If you need to show stock prices, VBCS has the right chart.

Gauges

A gauge is a component that displays a single value, possibly comparing it to one or more thresholds. Gauges are typically used in tables of data to provide a quick way to scan a lot of data and find those that are important.

The version of VBCS that was current at the time of writing (19.1.3) offers the following gauges:

- LED Gauge

- Rating Gauge

- Circular Status Meter

- Linear Status Meter

- Progress

The *LED Gauge* is a simple symbol, by default a circle. It is typically used to indicate red/yellow/green status, and you can place the value inside the circle.

The *Rating Gauge* is a series of symbols, some of which are shown in a different color. This is used to indicate a rating as you see in online book and movie reviews. For example, you could show a rating of three out of five as three gold stars and two gray stars. The Rating Gauge can be used as an interactive component if your requirements call for the user to be able to rate something.

The *Circular Status Meter* and *Linear Status Meter* show a small visualization of the value, optionally compared to one or more reference values. The status meters show a bar or an arc where the length indicates the value, while the LED Gauge just shows a symbol of a fixed size.

Figure 4-20 shows some examples of *Linear Status Meter* and *Circular Status Meter*.

Country ⩔	Life expectancy	Indicator threshold color	Indicator bar with all thresholds	Circular gauge
USA	78.6	79		79
TUR	78	78		78
SWE	82.4	82		82
SVN	81.3	81		81
SVK	77.3	77		77
RUS	71.8	72		72
PRT	81.2	81		81
POL	78	78		78
NZL	81.7	82		82
NOR	82.5	83		83
NLD	81.6	82		82
MEX	75.2	75		75

Figure 4-20. *Linear Status Meter and Circular Status Meter examples*

To use a status meter, you set the *Value* property on the *Data* tab in the *Property Inspector*. It is easiest to read the value of this property from a regular text field and then paste it into the Value property for the status meter component.

The thresholds are set with a three-value JavaScript array. You can simply write the value into the *Thresholds* attribute on the *Data* tab (something like [{"max":75},{"max":81},{}]), or you can go to the *All* tab in the *Property Inspector*, find the thresholds field, and click the arrow > to get to the sub-properties. This gives you access to the thresholds properties shown in Figure 4-21.

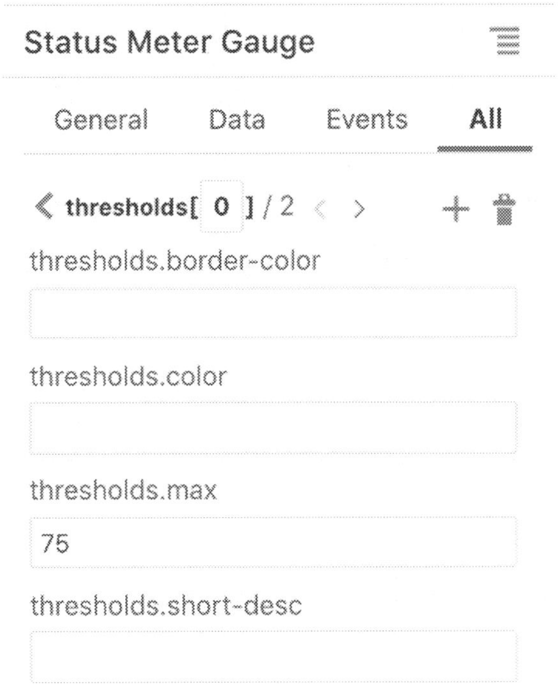

Figure 4-21. *Setting thresholds for a status meter*

From here, you can set the *thresholds.max* value as well as the color. You can also click the plus sign and the trashcan icon to add or remove thresholds. You only need to set the *thresholds.max* value for the first two thresholds to get a default red/yellow/green indicator as shown in Figure 4-20 in this section.

The Component Exchange

Oracle has a vision for a *Component Exchange* feature in Visual Builder Cloud Service. In the version of VBCS current at the time of writing (19.1.3), you can see the basics of how that feature will work, though it is only documented in blog posts and not in the manual.

If your instance is connected to a component exchange, the *Components* area will show a list of additional components you can install into your VBCS environment as shown in Figure 4-22.

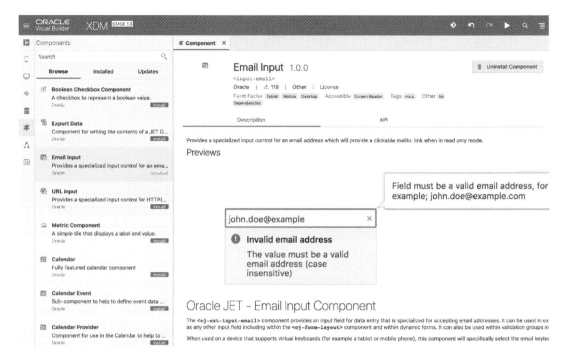

Figure 4-22. *The Components area showing available components*

When you click an available component, its documentation is shown in the main work area. You can click the little *Install* button on the overview or the large *Install Component* button at the top right of the documentation to add it to your VBCS instance. Components you add from the exchange will then show up at the bottom of the *Components* list for use in your VBCS pages.

Note   By default, new instances are currently being configured with a working component exchange URL, username, and password. If this should not be the case for your instance, your VBCS administrator must provide these values under *Tenant Settings* from the instance *Settings* menu. The specific settings for instances in the United States and Europe can be found in the Oracle Administering Oracle Visual Builder manual.

Right now, you can only use the component exchanges Oracle provides, and you can't add your own components to these exchanges. Eventually, you might be able to upload your own components.

Caution   These components are code samples and not supported by Oracle in any way.

Conclusion

In this chapter, you've seen how to build the web pages that your users access to interact with your data. You've learned about the collection components that serve as a starting point, and how to build pages for interacting with data. You've seen many of the components available in Visual Builder Cloud Service, including the powerful and attractive visualizations.

In the next chapter, you'll learn how to manage data in your application, including how to import data into your VBCS instance and how to export it back out of VBCS.

CHAPTER 5

Working with Data

In Chapter 2, you saw how you can create business objects, either manually or by importing an Excel spreadsheet or CSV file, and in Chapter 4 you saw how to create a web application for the user to interact with data. In this chapter, we will discuss how developers and administrators can manage Visual Builder Cloud Service data.

Visual Builder Cloud Service stores all its data internally (in an Oracle database), but you cannot just connect to the VBCS database from a database development tool. Instead, you must use the built-in VBCS features to export and import data to and from comma-separated files and Excel spreadsheets.

VBCS also offers you the ability to edit individual rows and functionality to move data between the development, staging, and production environments. There is even an option to publish your business object data as REST services for other applications to use.

Creating Individual Records

If you want to create a single row of data, you can do so from the *Data* tab in the business object. When you click this tab, you are shown the existing business object instances, as shown in Figure 5-1.

Figure 5-1. *The Data tab for a business object*

© Sten Vesterli 2019
S. Vesterli, *Oracle Visual Builder Cloud Service Revealed*, https://doi.org/10.1007/978-1-4842-4929-1_5

From here, you can create a new business object instance by clicking the *Add Row* button.

If you have a lot of data in your business object, you can click the little triangle next to *Query* to expand the query panel, where you can add query conditions. When a row is selected, you can also edit or delete it.

Note   The drop-down in the toolbar shows which environment you are working on. Initially, you only have the option *Development*, but as you stage and release your application, the options to work with data in the *Staging* and *Live* environments become active.

Exporting Data

To export the data from a single business object, you use the *Export CSV* icon on the *Data* tab of the object (the second from the left, with an up arrow). This downloads a CSV file with the same name as your business object, containing all the data in the business object. There are no decisions to make – you simply get all the values in the business object with one record per line and fields separated with commas. Any Date or DateTime fields are stored in YYYY-MM-DDTHH:MI:SS format (where the time part is 00:00:00 for date fields), and time fields are stored in THH:MI:SS format.

To export all data, you use the *Data Manager*. You access the Data Manager from the menu next to the *Business Objects* heading on the *Business Objects* tab as shown in Figure 5-2.

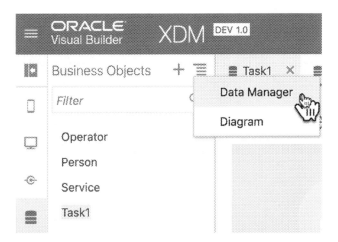

Figure 5-2. *Accessing the Data Manager*

Note   At the top right corner of the Data Manager window is a drop-down showing which environment you work on (*Development*, *Staging*, *Live*).

The Data Manager has an *Export All Data* option, which downloads a ZIP file containing CSV files for all business objects. The file name seems to be your application ID twice, followed by the version number (e.g., XDM-XDM-1.1).

Importing Data

To import data into a single business object, you can click the *Import from File* icon on the Data tab of the object (the leftmost icon, with a down arrow). The *Confirm Import Data* dialog appears, where you can upload a file. You can also choose whether you want to *Append* the records from the file to the data already in the business object, or if you want to *Replace* all existing data.

Tip   The file you import must match the business object exactly. If any column header is misspelled just slightly, that column will be ignored. If you want to import data from a file, it is easiest to start by creating an export file from an empty business object. In that way, you have a file with the right format and all column headings correct.

You can also import data into multiple business objects in one operation from the *Data Manager*. The *Import from File* option will replace all data in your current environment with the data in the file or files.

Caution   Check the value of the environment drop-down at the top right corner of the Data Manager window to make sure you won't accidentally overwrite production data.

You can import

- **An individual CSV file.** This replaces the data in the business object with the same name as the file.

- **An Excel spreadsheet.** This replaces the data in all business objects that have the same names as sheets in the spreadsheet.

- **A ZIP file.** VBCS will unzip it and then process any CSV and/or Excel files as described earlier.

Moving Data Between Environments

As you saw in Chapter 1, one instance of Visual Builder Cloud Service contains development, test, and production environments. Each of these environments has its own database, and VBCS makes it easy to move data between databases.

Like many other data operations, moving data between environments happens in the *Data Manager* found on the business objects menu on the *Business Objects* tab. You can select which environment you want to transfer data *to* from the drop-down list at the top right as shown in Figure 5-3.

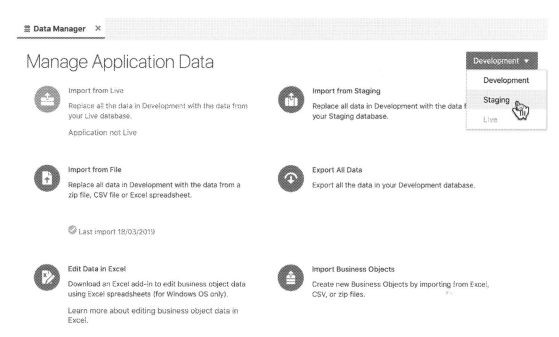

Figure 5-3. *Moving data between environments*

Depending on your selection and the life cycle of the application, VBCS will offer you the data movement options that make sense. In the example in this figure, I have selected the *Development* environment and get the options to *Import from Live* and *Import from Staging*. If you choose *Staging*, you can import from *Live* and *Development*, and if you choose to import to the *Live* environment, you get the options to import from *Staging* and *Development*. If the application is not staged or live, the corresponding option is, of course, grayed out.

If you have changed the data structure, VBCS will show you a warning dialog similar to the one in Figure 5-4.

111

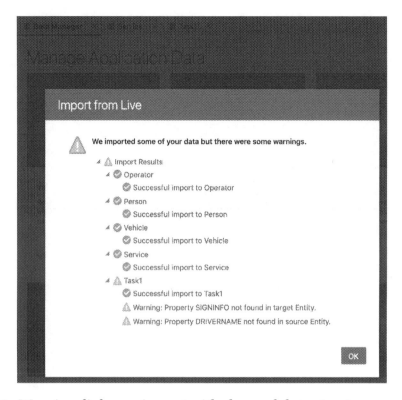

Figure 5-4. *Warning dialog on import with changed data structure*

If you have added or removed fields, you will get a warning, but the import still completes. You will need to decide whether you need to do anything about it. If you have made significant changes to your data structure, it is often easiest to use the *Export All Data* feature to get all your data out into text files, process these text files, change to your target environment, and use *Import from File* to put your data into the new format business objects.

Accessing Business Objects with REST

In addition to the data import and export features from the Data Manager, Visual Builder Cloud Service also allows you to access the REST interfaces it has built for use by VBCS web and mobile applications. This makes it possible for other VBCS applications and even applications outside VBCS to access data in VBCS business objects.

Before you can access the business objects in a VBCS application from outside, you need to change the *Security* settings for your application and enable role-based security for each business object you want to expose to external users. This is described in Chapter 10 on security.

Business Object Endpoints

When you use business objects on the web or mobile pages of a Visual Builder Cloud Service application, you are interacting with REST web services that VBCS has automatically created for you. VBCS normally shields you from having to know about these services in detail, but if you want to access your business objects from outside the VBCS application, you will need to know.

To find the detailed information about a business object, you go to the *Endpoints* tab in a business object tab. As shown in Figure 5-5, there are URLs for Metadata, Data, and Endpoints.

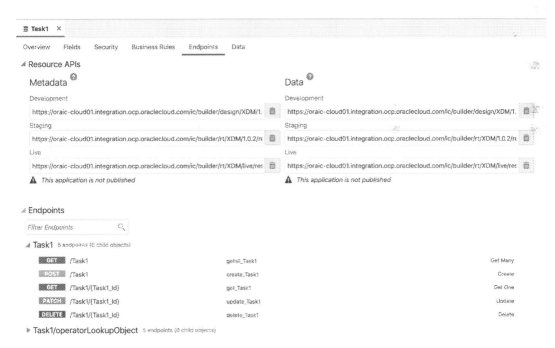

Figure 5-5. *REST endpoints for business objects*

Metadata Endpoints

Connecting to the metadata endpoints will give you a lot of metadata about your business object, including all the attributes and all the operations offered by the REST API. The result of calling the metadata endpoint is a very long JSON file that you would typically not have any use for.

Data Endpoints

Connecting to the data endpoints will give you the actual data for the business object in a JSON response. It will look something like this:

```json
{
    "items": [
        {
            "id": 1,
            "creationDate": "2019-02-16T15:13:01+00:00",
            "lastUpdateDate": "2019-02-16T15:13:01+00:00",
            "createdBy": "sten@vesterli.com",
            "lastUpdatedBy": "sten@vesterli.com",
            "pers": "PF",
            "persLookup": 105,
            "date1": "2016-10-04T00:00:00+00:00",
            "clientGroup": "XYZ Corp",
            "description": "John Smith ",
            "pax": 1,
            "startHour": "T13:25:00+00:00",
            "startWhere": "Airport",
            "flight": "SK 1686",
            "endHour": null,
            "endWhere": "Marriott Hotel",
            "service": "Apt transfer A",
            "serviceLookup": 201,
            "vehicle": "Sedan",
            "vehicleLookup": 305,
            "guide": "no",
            "operator": "Limo",
```

```
"operatorLookup": 407,
"operatorReference": "54549",
"change1": null,
"remarks": null,
"driverName": null,
"links": [
    {
        "rel": "self",
        "href": "https://oraic-cloud01.integration.ocp.
        oraclecloud.com:443/ic/builder/design/XDM/1.0.2/
        resources/data/Task1/1",
        "name": "Task1",
        "kind": "item",
        "properties": {
            "changeIndicator": "ACED0005737200136A6176612
            E7574696C2E41727261794C6973747881D21D99C7619D0
            3000149000473697A6578700000000001770400000001737
            200106A6176612E6C616E672E 446F75626C6580B3C24A296BF
            B0402000144000576616C7565787200106A6176612E6C616
            E672E4E756D62657286AC951D0B94
            E08B02000078700000000000000000000078"
        }
    },
    {
        "rel": "canonical",
        "href": "https://oraic-cloud01.integration.ocp.
        oraclecloud.com:443/ic/builder/design/XDM/1.0.2/
        resources/data/Task1/1",
        "name": "Task1",
        "kind": "item"
    },
    {
        "rel": "child",
        "href": "https://oraic-cloud01.integration.ocp.
        oraclecloud.com:443/ic/builder/design/XDM/1.0.2/
        resources/data/Task1/1/child/operatorLookupObject",
```

```
                    "name": "operatorLookupObject",
                    "kind": "collection"
                },
                {

                    "rel": "child",
                    "href": "https://oraic-cloud01.integration.ocp.
                    oraclecloud.com:443/ic/builder/design/XDM/1.0.2/
                    resources/data/Task1/1/child/persLookupObject",
                    "name": "persLookupObject",
                    "kind": "collection"
                },
                {

                    "rel": "child",
                    "href": "https://oraic-cloud01.integration.ocp.
                    oraclecloud.com:443/ic/builder/design/XDM/1.0.2/
                    resources/data/Task1/1/child/serviceLookupObject",
                    "name": "serviceLookupObject",
                    "kind": "collection"
                },
                {

                    "rel": "child",
                    "href": "https://oraic-cloud01.integration.ocp.
                    oraclecloud.com:443/ic/builder/design/XDM/1.0.2/
                    resources/data/Task1/1/child/vehicleLookupObject",
                    "name": "vehicleLookupObject",
                    "kind": "collection"
                }
            ]
        },
...
    ],
    "count": 25,
    "hasMore": true,
    "limit": 25,
    "offset": 0,
    "links": [
```

116

```
    {
        "rel": "self",
        "href": "https://oraic-cloud01.integration.ocp.oraclecloud.
        com:443/ic/builder/design/XDM/1.0.2/resources/data/Task1",
        "name": "Task1",
        "kind": "collection"
    }
  ]
}
```

The first part is the actual data, followed by some links that allow you to navigate to related items. At the end of all the data, you get some information about the request – in this case, that there were 25 records retrieved (`count: 25`) and there are more (`hasMore: true`).

There are different endpoints for the development, staging, and live environment. A warning will be displayed on the screen if the application has not been staged or made live yet.

Operation Endpoints

For every business object, you get five default endpoints:

- A GET endpoint for retrieving multiple business object instances

- A GET endpoint for retrieving a single business object instance

- A POST endpoint for creating a single business object instance

- A PATCH endpoint for updating a single business object instance

- A DELETE endpoint for deleting a single business object instance

The endpoints are listed in abbreviated form (e.g., /Task1 or /Task1/{Task1_id}). The full endpoint is the one listed as Data endpoint (e.g., `https://oraic-cloud01.integration.ocp.oraclecloud.com/ic/builder/design/XDM/1.0.2/resources/data/Task1`).

Note that the dialog box shows a warning for the staging and/or live URLs if you have not yet staged the application or released it to productions.

Example of Accessing a Business Object Externally

To test REST access to a business object, you can use a tool like Postman (`www.getpostman.com/`).

To get data, you need to enable access in the application security settings, for instance, by obtaining an access token – a long string like you saw in Figure 5-6. Then you need to go to the business object you want to access and get the data endpoint for the business object you wish to access.

In Postman, you then

1. Choose the method (GET, POST, PATCH, DELETE)

2. Enter the data access URL

3. On the Authorization tab, choose Bearer Token and paste in the token value

4. Click Send

See Figure 5-6 for an illustration of how this looks in Postman.

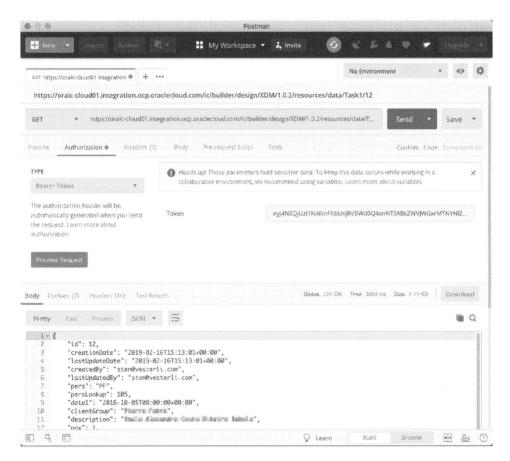

Figure 5-6. *Getting an individual record using Postman*

To create an item, you need to send a POST request with a *Content-Type* of `application/vnd.oracle.adf.resourceitem+json` and JSON payload containing the data you want to create:

```
{
  "id": 123,
  "date1": "2019-02-19T17:35:42",
  "description": "Airport transfer"
...
}
```

To update an item, you need to send a PATCH request to the specific URL for the object you want to change (in the example in this chapter, something like `/Task1/123`) with a *Content-Type* of `application/vnd.oracle.adf.resourceitem+json` and JSON payload containing just the data you want to change:

```
{
  "description": "Airport transfer evening"
}
```

To update an item and create it if it doesn't already exist, you use an "upsert." This is done by sending a POST request to the general business object URL. Do not include an ID in the URL. Use the normal *Content-Type* of `application/vnd.oracle.adf.resourceitem+json`, an additional HTTP Header `Upsert-Mode: true`, and a JSON payload including an `Id` value.

To delete an item, you send a DELETE request to the specific URL for the object you want to remove, that is, the URL should include the ID value.

For more information about how to access business objects through REST, refer to the manual "Oracle Cloud Accessing Business Objects Using REST APIs." You find a link to this on the VBCS documentation page.

Conclusion

In this chapter, you have seen how to work with the data in business objects. You've seen how to create individual records and how to import and export multiple records from and to a business object. You have also seen how to move data between environments and how to access your VBCS data from outside the VBCS application.

In the next chapter, you will see how to add logic to your business objects.

CHAPTER 6

Logic in the Business Layer

You've seen that the default functionality of Visual Builder Cloud Service business objects allows you to do define business objects and create, view, modify, and delete business object instances. A few business rules can be implemented with simple checkboxes, for example, which fields are mandatory or must be unique.

However, most real-life applications require more than that; they require the ability to implement business logic. In this chapter, you will see how to add your own custom logic to VBCS business objects. This is done inside each business object on the *Business Rules* tab shown in Figure 6-1.

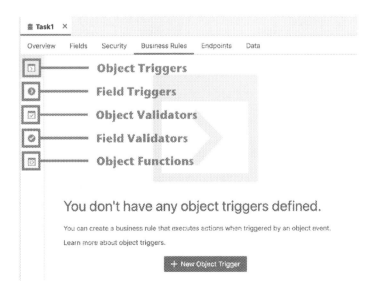

Figure 6-1. *The Business Rules tab*

© Sten Vesterli 2019
S. Vesterli, *Oracle Visual Builder Cloud Service Revealed*, https://doi.org/10.1007/978-1-4842-4929-1_6

There are five types of business rules as shown in Figure 6-1:

- **Object Triggers** are executed when an object-level event happens and can execute any logic.

- **Field Triggers** are executed when a single value changes and can execute any logic.

- **Object Validators** are executed just before a whole object is submitted to the database and can approve or reject the entire object.

- **Field Validators** are executed when a single value changes and can approve or reject the new field value.

- **Object Functions** are pieces of reusable logic.

We'll go through them in a slightly different order, from the simple to the advanced.

Field Validators

The most straightforward business rules on this tab are the *field validators*, which are executed as soon as you make a change to a field. They are used to make sure that the value of a single item adheres to rules you define. To work with field validators, you select the *Field Validators* icon (the fourth from the top) on the *Business Rules* tab for a business object. From this tab, you can see your existing field validators and can create new ones.

Creating a field validator is a two-step process. When you click *New Field Validator*, you are first prompted to provide a validator name, choose a field, optionally provide a description, and provide an error message as shown in Figure 6-2.

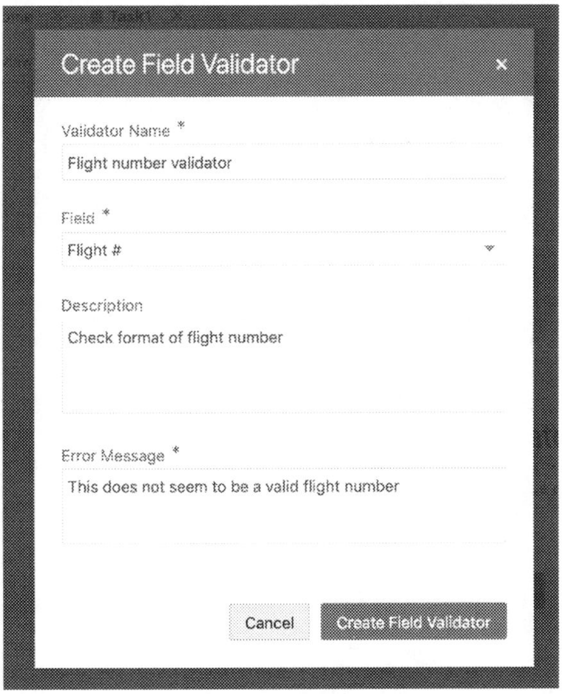

Figure 6-2. *Creating a field validator*

When you create the field validator, you are presented with the field validator editor. As shown in Figure 6-3, this editor has a list of object and field values to the left, a formula editor window in the middle, and the field validator overview information you just entered to the right.

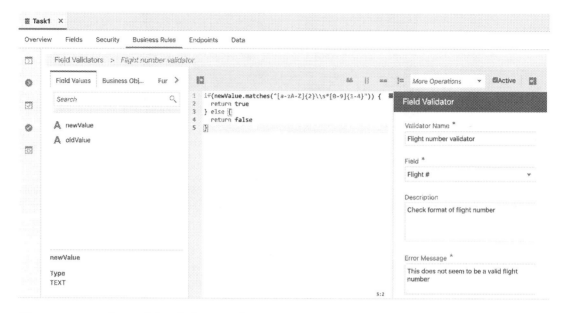

Figure 6-3. *The Field Validator Editor*

Note that the object list pane to the left has multiple tabs. It starts showing the *Field Values* tab, giving you access to *oldValue* and *newValue* variables representing the field value before and after the action by the user. There is also a *Business Object* tab that gives you access to other values in the business object, and (if you scroll right) a *Functions* tab with many useful functions you can click to insert into the editor window, and a *Services* tab where you can select from the service connections you have defined.

Tip   All the business rule code must be written in the programming language *Groovy*. That's how I knew I could use `.matches()` on a *String* object to validate a regular expression as in the preceding figure. To learn more about Groovy, refer to the official Groovy web site at `http://groovy-lang.org/` or find a tutorial online.

In the editor window, you must write an expression that returns a *Boolean* value. You can have multiple validators for a single field; if any of them returns `false`, the validation of the field has failed, and it cannot be saved.

Once you have defined a field validator, it appears on the *Field Validators* tab. For each field validator, there is a menu in the lower right-hand corner as shown in Figure 6-4.

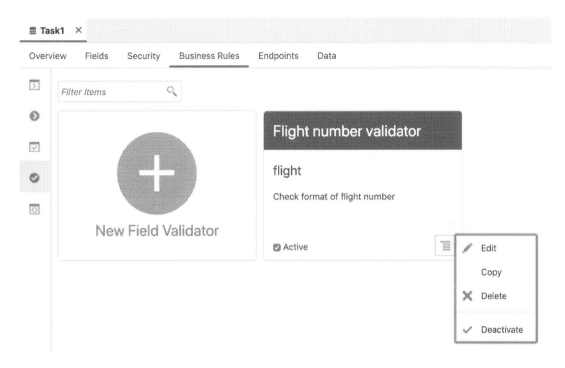

Figure 6-4. *Field validator Edit menu*

This allows you to edit, copy, or delete it. If you want to disable it temporarily, you can also deactivate it by removing the checkmark in the *Active* checkbox or choosing *Deactivate* from the menu.

Object Validators

For validations that must be executed when you submit the whole object, you use *object validators*. They are similar to field validators, but since they work at the whole object level, you do not have access to the old and new values of fields. To work with object validators, you select the *Object Validators* icon on the *Business Rules* tab (the third from the top). From this tab, you can see your existing object validators and can create new ones.

Creating an object validator is similar to creating a field validator. When you click *New Object Validator*, you are first prompted to provide a validator name and provide an error message. Then, you are presented with the object validator editor shown in Figure 6-5.

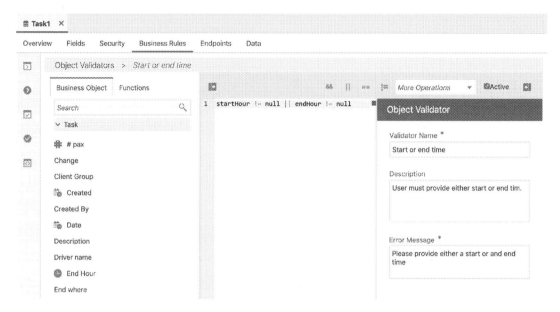

Figure 6-5. *The object validator editor*

You might notice that there are only *Business Object*, *Functions*, and *Services* tabs. There is no tab giving access to the old and new values. An object validator is written in Groovy like a field validator and must similarly return a *Boolean* value to indicate if the validation is successful.

As for field validators, you can also edit, copy, deactivate, or delete it using the menu and/or checkbox.

Field Triggers

A *field trigger* is executed like a field validator: when the field value changes. However, VBCS can implement much more complicated business logic than just checking the value of a field. To work with field triggers, you select the *Field Triggers* icon (the second from the top) on the *Business Rules* tab for a business object. From this tab, you can see your existing field triggers and can create new ones.

Creating a field trigger is a two-step process. When you click *New Field Trigger*, you are first prompted to provide a trigger name, choose a field, and optionally provide a description as shown in Figure 6-6.

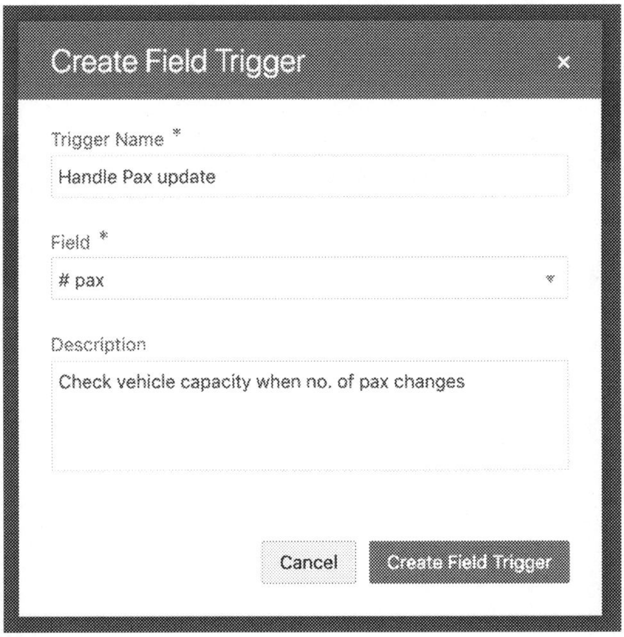

Figure 6-6. *Creating a field trigger*

When you click *Create Field Trigger*, you are presented with the *Visual Trigger Designer* described in a later section, where you can define your trigger logic using drag and drop.

Object Triggers

An *object trigger* is executed when a selected object-level event happens. Object triggers are different from object validators in several ways.

Object Validator	Object Trigger
Triggering event is given (just before committing object to the database)	A selection of triggering events available
Logic can decide to accept or reject the record	Any logic is possible, but not possible to reject record

To work with object triggers, you select the *Object Triggers* icon on the *Business Rules* tab (the top one). From this tab, you see your existing object triggers and can create new ones.

Creating an object trigger is also a two-step process. When you click *New Object Trigger*, you are first prompted to provide a trigger name and an optional description and select the start event as shown in Figure 6-7.

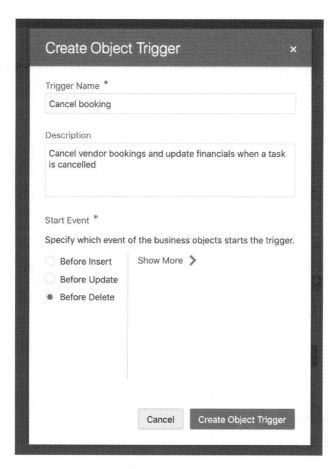

Figure 6-7. *Creating an object trigger*

Triggers executing before insert, update, and delete are the most common and are always presented as options. You can click *Show More* to see the additional available trigger events (*On Initialize, On Invalidate, On Remove, Before Commit, Before Rollback*).

When you click *Create Object Trigger*, you are presented with the Visual Trigger Designer described in the next section.

Visual Trigger Designer

When you have created a field or an object trigger, you are presented with the visual trigger designer. Figure 6-8 shows the designer with an object trigger open; for field triggers, only the property inspector to the right is different.

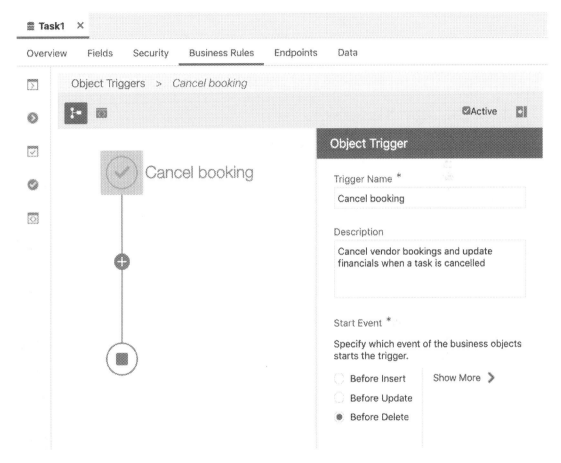

Figure 6-8. *The visual trigger designer*

The trigger initially shows a visual representation of the entry and exit points and a plus sign to define a branch of the trigger. A trigger can have multiple branches, each with their own *trigger criteria*, controlling when the trigger executes. When you click the plus sign, you will be given the following options:

- Execute Conditionally

- Always Execute

- Custom Code

Always Execute

The most common type of trigger is the kind that always executes. When you choose *Always Execute*, your trigger gets one branch with an *Add Actions* box for you to add the triggering actions as shown in Figure 6-9.

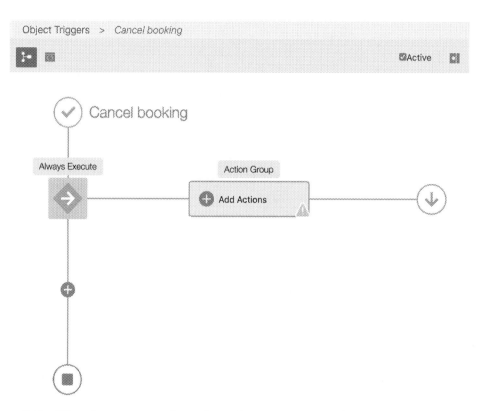

Figure 6-9. *Visual representation of an always execute trigger*

Now you can click *Add actions* to define the actions of the trigger as described later in this chapter. Note that the icon to the far right (after the *Action Group* box) is a green *Continue evaluating the next criteria* icon. This indicates that after the action, the flow continues with the next trigger branch below.

Execute Conditionally

You can also create triggers where the logic does not always execute. These are created by choosing an *Execute Conditionally* criterion.

When you select the *Execute Conditionally* node in the visual designer, the detail window to the right contains an *Add Conditions* button as shown in Figure 6-10.

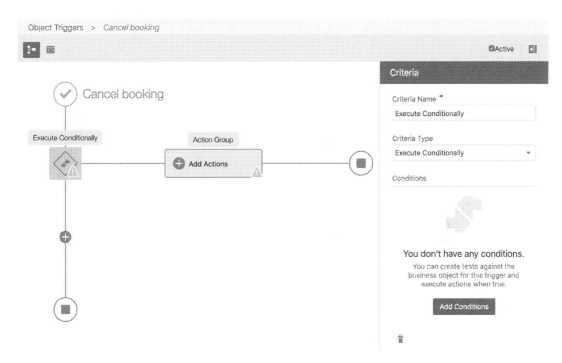

***Figure 6-10.** Visual representation of a conditional trigger*

Notice that the icon at the end of the branch is now a red *End of the workflow*. This means that if the condition is satisfied, the action is taken and the trigger ends. If you want your processing to continue, you can click the red stop icon and change it to a green *Continue evaluating the following criteria*.

When you click the *Add Conditions* button in the property palette for the *Execute Conditionally* action, the full-screen *Build Conditions* dialog appears as shown in Figure 6-11.

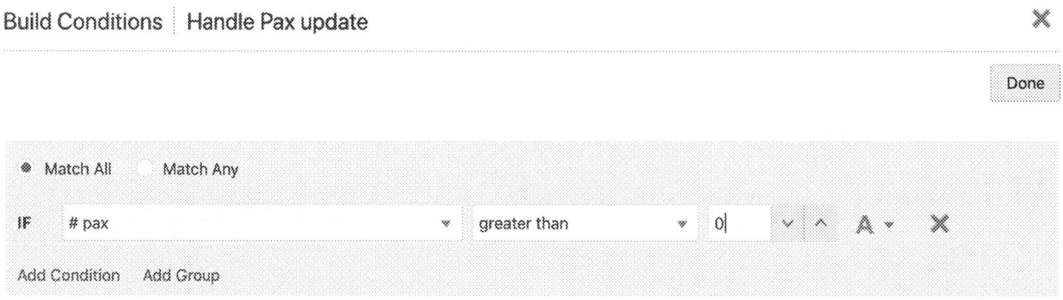

Build Conditions ┆ Handle Pax update   ✕

Done

● Match All   ○ Match Any

IF   # pax   ▾   greater than   ▾   0│   ▾ ∧   A ▾   ✕

Add Condition   Add Group

Figure 6-11. *Creating trigger conditions*

This dialog allows you to define when the trigger is executed. This can avoid unnecessary trigger invocations and is useful especially if your trigger logic is complex or long-running (e.g., because it has to access an external system).

When you have defined your trigger criteria, you can click *Add actions* to define the actions of the trigger as described later in this chapter.

Custom Code

The final option for trigger criteria is *Custom Code*. When you choose this option, you get an *Add Custom Code* button that brings up a code editor. The code editor is already filled in with the skeleton of your code, like this:

```
if (/* enter your condition here */) {
    return true;
} else {
    return false;
}
```

You can write any Groovy expression here, referring to fields in business objects like in other code editors. If your code returns `true`, the action to the right of the condition executes.

Adding Actions to Triggers

Once you have defined your trigger actions, you can click *Add Actions* to define the actions of that branch of your trigger. This brings up the full-screen *Configure Actions* dialog box as shown in Figure 6-12.

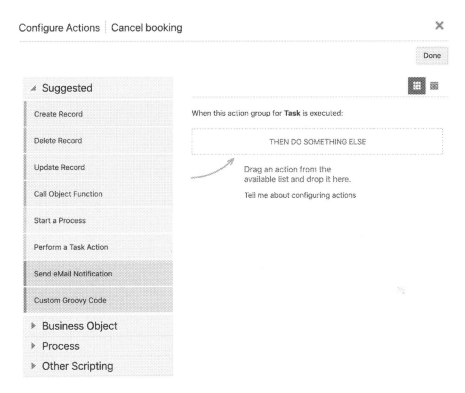

Figure 6-12. *Configuring trigger actions*

From this dialog, you can visually construct your trigger logic by dragging in actions from the palette to the left. You can drag in multiple actions in the order you want them executed. For each action, fields and drop-down list boxes appear as shown in Figure 6-13.

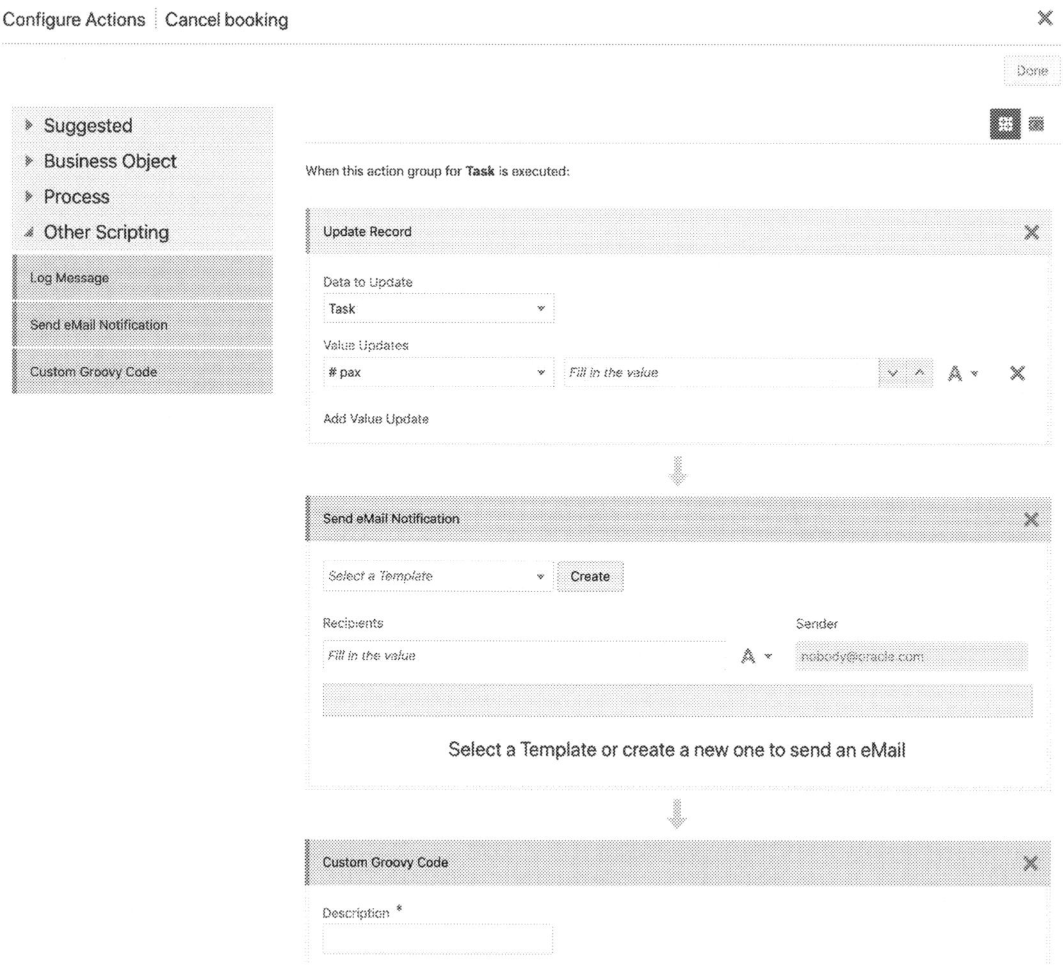

Figure 6-13. *Defining action details*

This allows you to specify the details for each action you have selected.

Using Email Actions

One of the common actions is sending an email when something happens. This is easy to do in VBCS – you just drag a *Send eMail Notification* onto the work area. The second action in Figure 6-13 is an empty email notification action.

All the emails you send must be based on email *templates*. To create one, click the *Create* button next to the *Select a Template* drop-down. This brings up the eMail Template dialog shown in Figure 6-14.

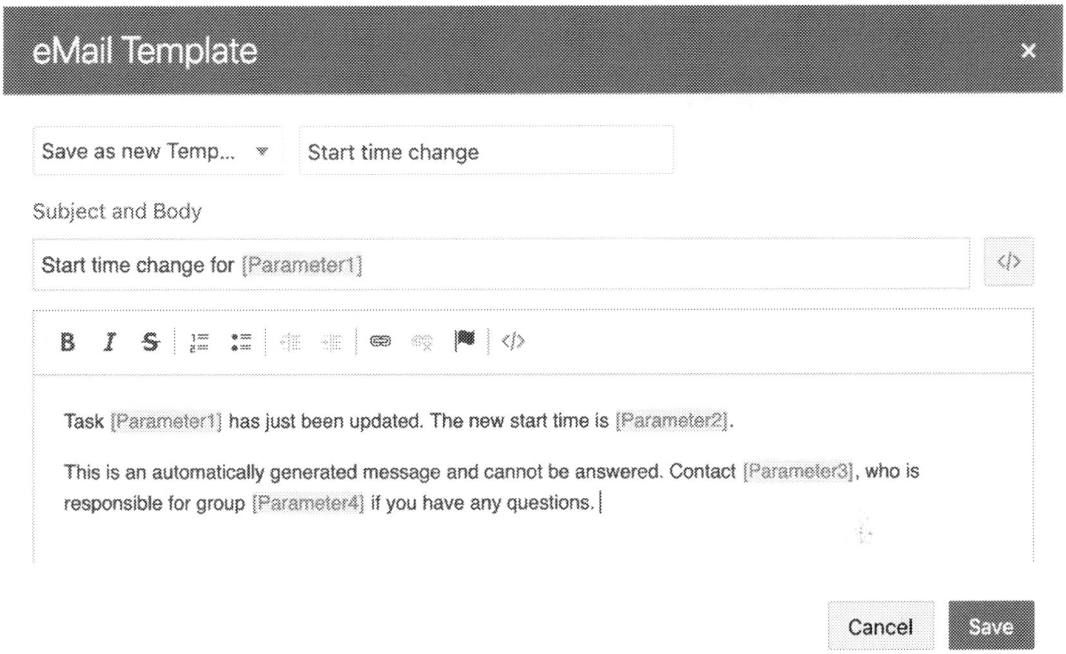

Figure 6-14. *Creating an email template*

You can click the </> buttons (to the right of the subject field and at the right end of the body toolbar) to insert parameters into your template. When you are done, you can either choose *Save as a new Template* and provide a name (to create a reusable email template) or choose *Save for this Action only*.

When you have saved your template, you can select it in the *Send eMail Notification* and provide values for the parameters as shown in Figure 6-15.

When this action group for **Task** is executed:

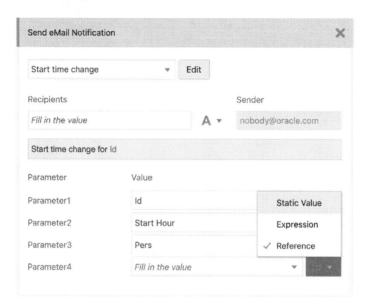

Figure 6-15. *Defining parameter values for email notification action*

The *Recipients* field and any of the parameter fields can be set to either a *Static Value*, an *Expression,* or a *Reference*. The most commonly used choice is *Reference*, which allows you to choose among the fields in the business object. For more complicated cases, you can also choose *Expression* which opens the VBCS expression builder.

Converting to Custom Code

The visual editor is just a helper, making it easier for you to define your triggers. Behind the scenes, the visual editor is actually writing code for you. To see that code, you can click the *code editor* icon in the toolbar above the visual representation of your trigger. This shows the actual code as illustrated in Figure 6-16.

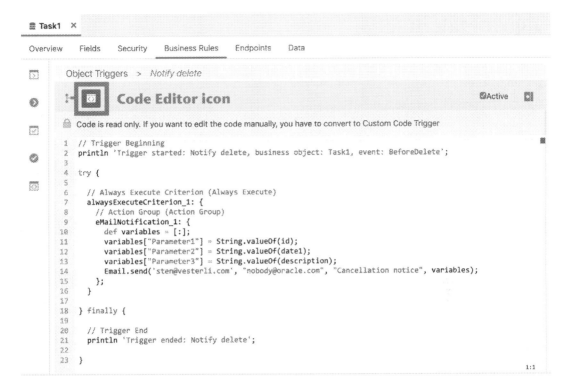

Figure 6-16. *The code editor*

Note the message above the code, saying that the code is *read-only*. If you want to edit the code, you can click *convert to Custom Code Trigger*. You will get a warning telling you that you are now taking responsibility for maintaining this code in the code editor from now on. Once you convert to a custom code trigger, there is no way to go back to the visual editor.

Tip   If you have complicated requirements that you cannot implement in the visual editor, click together as much as you can before converting to a custom code trigger.

Object Functions

If you find you have reusable snippets of code that might be used in several places in your logic for a business object, you can create *Object Functions* using the bottom-most icon on the *Business Rules* tab.

When you click *Create Object Function* and have given your object function a name and optionally a description, a code editor opens. This works like the code editors for triggers but has the additional feature of allowing you to define the input parameters your function takes, as well as a return type.

By default, your object function can only be called by other scripts that work on the same business object. So, if you create a function on the `Task1` business object, it can be called by all triggers and other object functions on that business object.

Object functions have two unique properties:

- **Callable by External System**. Checking this checkbox indicates that you allow external systems to run your object function. This is relevant if you expose your business object externally. By default, only your internal logic can run your object function.

- **Privileged**. Checking this checkbox indicates that the code should run with access to all data. Typically, your object function runs with the privileges of the current user. If you have placed restrictions on access to data, and your logic requires access to data that the user is not allowed to see, check this checkbox.

Logging Business Logic

Visual Builder Cloud Service does not have a debugger to step through your business object code, but it does offer logging statements.

You can create log entries by putting `println` statements in your trigger code, or in the visual trigger editor by dragging in *Log Message* actions.

To see your log statements, you click *Logs* in the status bar at the bottom of the VBCS window to open and close the *Logs* panel. In this panel, you need to check the *Enable* checkbox to actually write any log entries. There is also a search function, and you can refresh the log, export it, and clear it. Figure 6-17 shows the default logging VBCS writes when a trigger is executed.

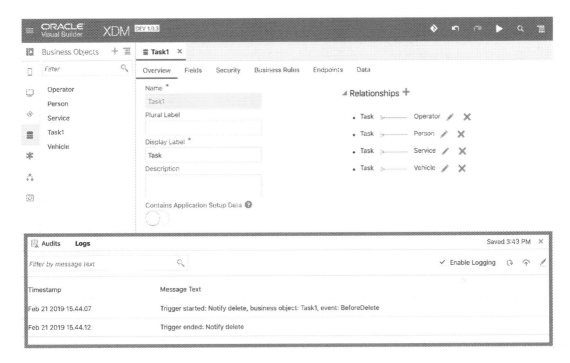

Figure 6-17. *VBCS Trigger logging*

Tip   In the version of VBCS available at the time of writing, the *Logs* window always opens with log entries sorted with the oldest log entries at the top. You can click the *Timestamp* heading to reverse the sort to show the latest messages at the top.

Conclusion

In this chapter, you learned how to add logic to your business objects, both for simple data validation and to implement more complicated logic. You saw how you can quickly click together triggers to implement common requirements and how to break out of the visual editor and write Groovy code.

In the next chapter, you will see how to add logic to the user interface layer of your application.

CHAPTER 7

Logic in the User Interface

In the last chapter, you saw how you can add your own logic to business objects. In this chapter, we will discuss how to implement logic in the user interface layer of the application.

You've seen that the VBCS drag-and-drop features combined with the Quick Starts allow you to build a complete application that can handle query, insert, update, and delete. If that is enough for your needs, you don't have to read this chapter unless you are curious how VBCS works behind the scenes. But if you want to understand the internals of VBCS and make full use of its power, you need to be able to write your own user interface logic.

How VBCS Really Works

If you examine what Visual Builder Cloud Service builds for you when you run the Quick Starts, you will see that the Quick Starts are just a convenient way for you to build the basics of your application quickly. When you need something more than the default, you can either adapt the logic built by the Quick Starts or create new logic from scratch.

A VBCS application consists of three elements: *UI components*, *action chains*, and *variables*. UI components can raise events that trigger action chains. Action chains can read and write variables, calling REST web services as necessary. The variables store the values and are used by the UI components to present the data and user interface to the end user. This circle is illustrated in Figure 7-1.

© Sten Vesterli 2019
S. Vesterli, *Oracle Visual Builder Cloud Service Revealed*, https://doi.org/10.1007/978-1-4842-4929-1_7

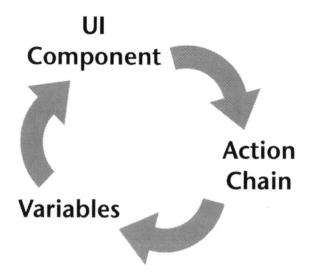

Figure 7-1. *The VBCS processing circle*

This chapter provides an overview of this process. For more details, refer to the long "Understand the Page Model" chapter of the *Developing Applications with Oracle Visual Builder* manual.

Examples from the Quick Starts

To see how these parts work together, you can build a simple application based on a business object. If you drop a collection component on the main-start page and then use Quick Starts to map that component to data and create an edit page, you have examples of much of the logic that a VBCS application uses.

Getting Data

When you have run the *Add Data* Quick Start on the main-start page, you can look at the *Variables* tab on that page. You will see a variable for holding the ID of the selected record and a variable of type xxxListSDP. The *Types* tab shows the definition of the type – we'll discuss variable types in more detail later in this chapter. See Figure 7-2.

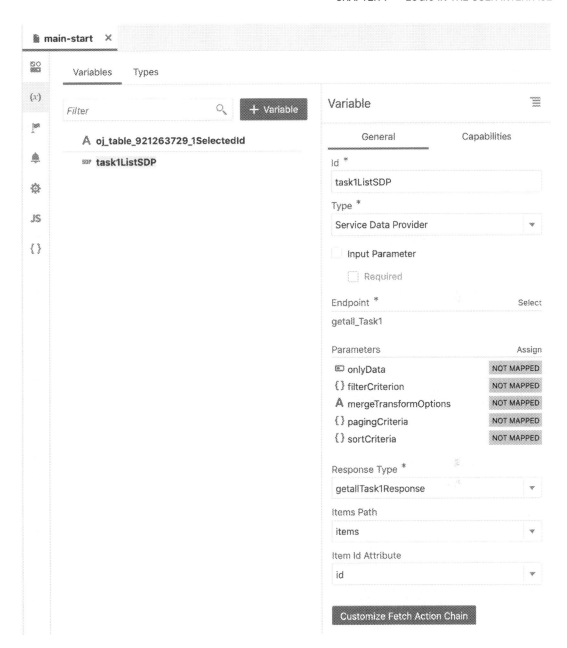

Figure 7-2. *The variables created by the Add Data Quick Start*

The variables are automatically populated by VBCS. If you want to see how this happens, and possibly override the default functionality, you can click the *Customize Fetch Action Chain* button at the bottom of the properties for the variable. Figure 7-3 shows the *Customize Fetch Action* dialog which tells you that you are overriding default functionality and will have to take responsibility for keeping the action chain and the variable in sync.

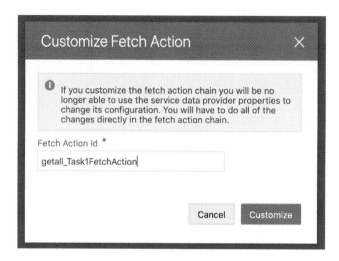

Figure 7-3. *Customizing the fetch action chain*

When you click *Customize* in this dialog, you will be shown the action chain the Quick Start has created to handle the call to the REST endpoint to retrieve the data. See Figure 7-4.

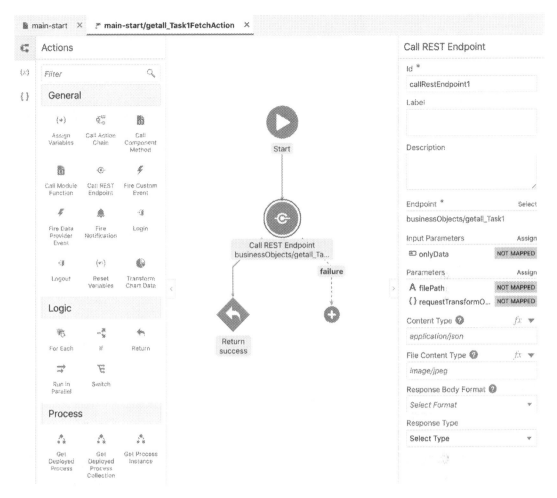

Figure 7-4. *The default fetch action chain*

This action chain is automatically triggered when you load the main-start page. You can click the Call REST Endpoint action and investigate its properties. There is an *Endpoint* property pointing to the specific REST service to call as well as some parameter mappings that define how to call the service and how to map the result back to VBCS variables.

Editing Data

When you have run the *Add Edit Page* Quick Start on the main-start page, you will find that the main-start page has acquired a new button to edit a record. If you select this button in *Design* mode and examine the *Events* tab in the *Property Inspector*, you will find an ojAction event mapped to an action chain called navigateToEditXxxChain. See Figure 7-5.

145

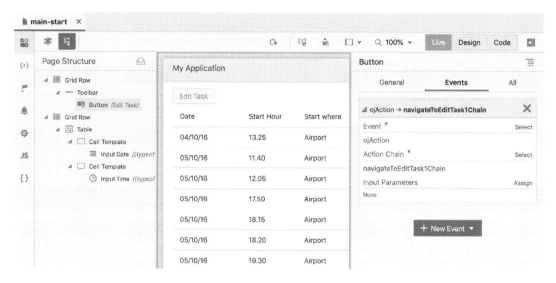

Figure 7-5. *An event and its action chain*

From here, you can click *Select* next to *Event* to see what the possible events are and *Select* next to *Action Chain* to see the available action chains. From the *Select Action Chain* dialog, you can even create a new action chain. You can also click the action chain name itself (`navigateToEditXxxChain`) to open the automatically created navigation action chain. This action chain is more straightforward than the one to fetch data and merely include the necessary navigation step.

If you open the `main-edit-xxx` page created by the Quick Start, you will see that it has its own action chains to load data (`loadXxxChain`), save data (`saveXxxChain`), and go back (`goBackChain`).

UI Components

Now that we've seen some example of how VBCS default functionality is implemented, let's look at the different moving parts in detail. We'll start with the *UI components*.

When you have a UI component selected in the *Page Designer*, you can see and edit the events associated with the component on the *Events* tab in the *Property Inspector*.

Note   Remember that you must be in *Design* mode (not *Live* mode) to change the properties of UI elements.

To add a new event, you click the + *New Event* button. You are presented with a choice between a relevant *Quick Start* event and a *New Custom Event*. See Figure 7-6.

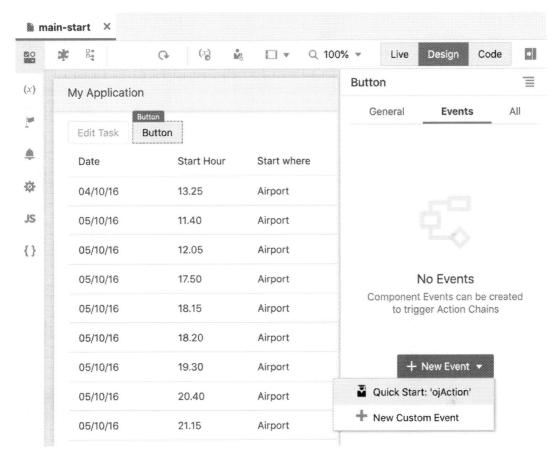

Figure 7-6. *Creating a new event for a UI component*

The *Quick Start* depends on the component you selected. For example, when adding an event to a *Button* component, the Quick Start will suggest an `ojAction` event (triggered by clicking the button). An input field will offer a `value` event (triggered when the value in the field is changed), and other components will offer other Quick Starts.

If you select New Custom Event, you will be presented with a dialog where you can select the event as shown in Figure 7-7.

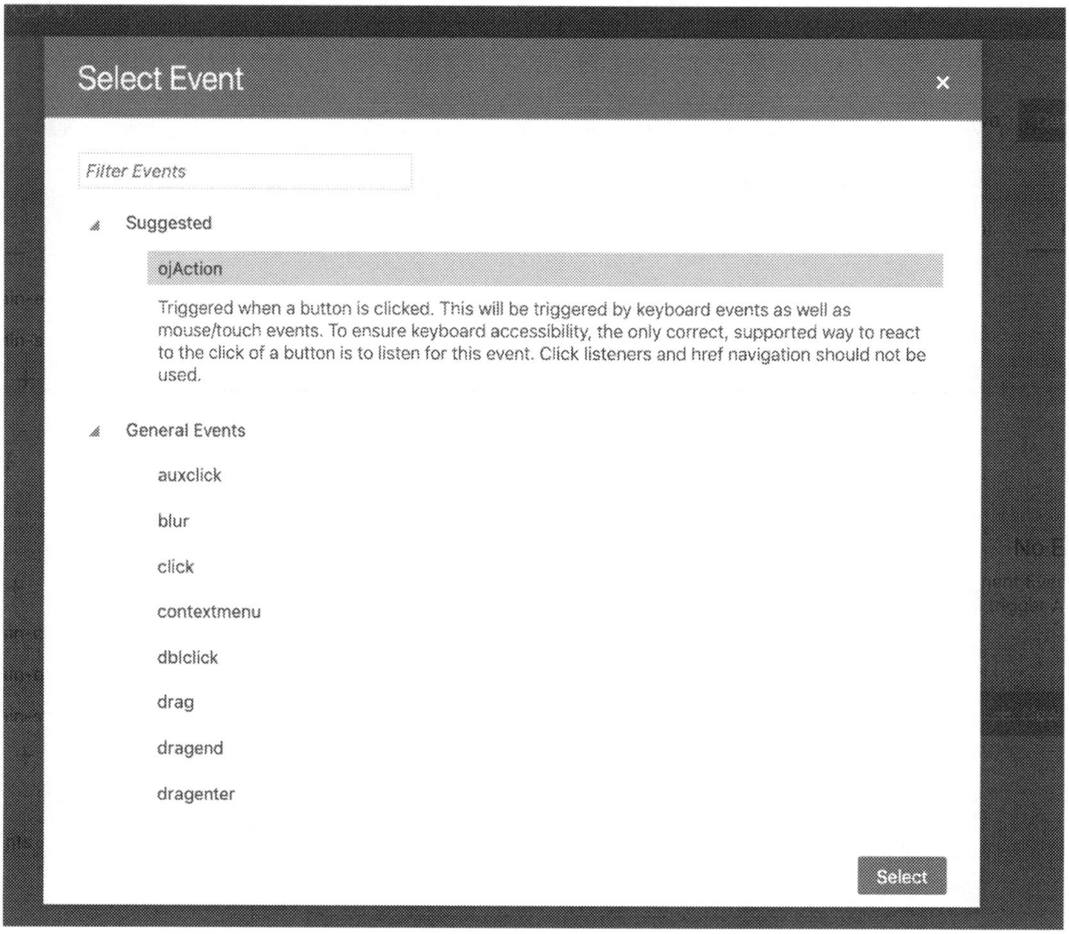

Figure 7-7. *Creating a custom event*

The *Suggested* heading will show the most commonly used event for that component, but the *General Events* heading allows you to react to double-click, mouse enter/leave, and much more. If you scroll down, there are more headings with more events you can react to.

The Quick Start automatically creates, connects, and opens a new action chain as described in the section on action chains later in this chapter. If you create a custom event, you will be prompted to select an existing action chain, or you can create a new one.

Once you have created events, you can access them either from the *Property Inspector* for the specific component or from the *Events* tab of the page.

Lifecycle Events

Some events are not tied to a specific component but are automatically triggered as the user works with the application. These are called *lifecycle events* and belong to pages or flows.

Visual Builder Cloud Service version 19.1.3, which was current at the time of writing, offers the following lifecycle events:

- **vbBeforeEnter** is triggered before navigating to a page.

- **vbEnter** is triggered when all flow or page variables have been initialized, but before the flow or page is shown.

- **vbBeforeExit** is triggered before leaving a page. This event can be canceled, allowing you to force a user to, for example, decide on saving data before leaving.

- **vbExit** is triggered when leaving a flow or page.

- **vbNotification** is a standard event that can be triggered by the application when it needs to notify the user of something.

- **vbAfterNavigate** is triggered when navigation to this page is complete.

Associating an action chain with one of these events allows you to intercept and augment the default VBCS page and flow processing.

Note   The fetch action chain that populates a screen with data when the user first enters it is implicitly triggered by a vbEnter event.

You add a lifecycle event to a flow or a page on the *Events* tab. This tab shows all the lifecycle and component events for the page or flow, and you can add a new lifecycle event by clicking the + *Event Listener* button.

Variables and Types

Like other applications, a Visual Builder Cloud Service application holds its data in variables. These can either be simple variables or larger data structures that VBCS calls *types*. Data retrieved from REST services are stored in variables, and the value of the variables is displayed to the user. When the user enters or changes data, this change is made to the variable and then made persistent by calling the underlying REST service.

Note   When you use the Quick Starts, VBCS automatically creates all the necessary variables and types for you. To learn about variables and types, you can use a Quick Start to create, for example, an *Edit* page and inspect the variables and types created for you.

VBCS variables belong to one of four *scopes*, and they are automatically created and destroyed when the application enters and leaves a specific scope.

- *Application scope* variables are accessible everywhere in the application. They are created when the application starts and exist for the lifetime of the user session (until the user closes her browser or the session times out).

- *Flow scope* variables are accessible from all pages within their flow. They are created when entering the first page in the flow and exist until the user navigates to another flow or exits the application.

- *Page scope* variables are only accessible from a specific page. They are created when the user enters the page and are destroyed when the user leaves the page.

- *Action scope* variables are only accessible within a specific action chain. They are created when the action chain starts and automatically destroyed when the chain completes.

You access variables from the *Variables* tab. When you have the entire application selected in the navigator, you can see and work with application scope variables. When you have a flow selected or are on the tab showing the flow, the *Variables* tab show flow variables. Similarly, when you select a page in the navigator or have the tab for the page selected, you see page variables. Action scope variables are only accessible from the tab showing the relevant action chain.

When you have a specific variable selected, the *Property Inspector* allows you to set various properties, for example, the default value.

Variable Types

At the top of the *Variables* tab, you can see both a *Variables* and a *Types* sub-tab as shown in Figure 7-8.

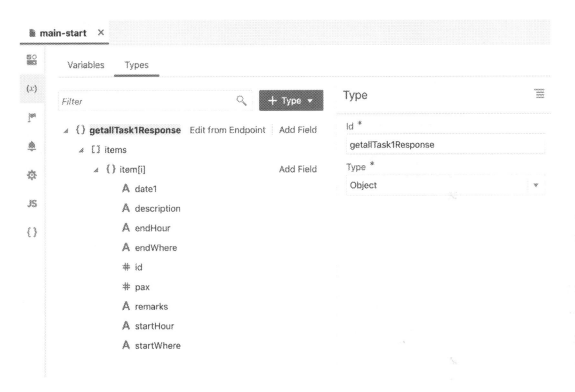

Figure 7-8. *Variable types*

You can create new types by clicking the + *Type* button and selecting either a *Custom* type or a type based on a REST service by selecting *From Endpoint*. If you create a type from an endpoint, the *Create Type From Endpoint* dialog in Figure 7-9 is shown.

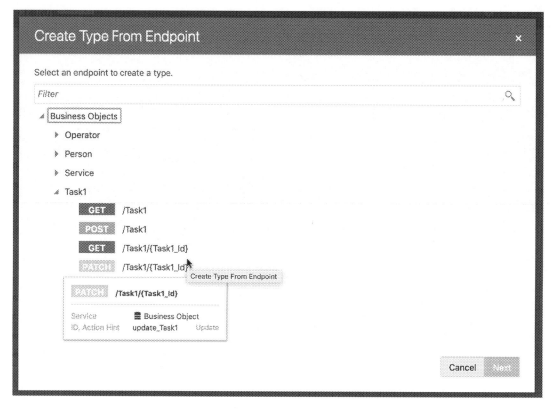

Figure 7-9. *Create Type From Endpoint*

Here you select the specific REST service you want to use as the basis for your type. You can point to one of the services to get more details about what that service does. When you click *Next*, you are given the option to select which attributes from the endpoint you want to include in your type.

Using the Quick Starts normally saves you from having to worry about variables and types, but you do need to work with the types if you afterward decide you need another attribute from the REST endpoint. To edit an existing type created from a REST endpoint, you click the *Edit From Endpoint* link next to the type. If you refer back to Figure 7-8, you find this link next to the getAllTask1Response heading.

The *Edit Type From Endpoint* dialog looks like the step in the Quick Start where you select attributes. You have the option to check the checkbox for additional attributes, adding them to the type. The action chains use the type, so the logic to retrieve and store values does not need to be changed if you add additional attributes.

Action Chains

Action chains are visual representations of the UI logic in your application. They are mapped to events triggered by something in the user interface, whether a button click or the loading of a page. Similar to variables, action chains also have a scope. Usually, your action chains will be created at the page level, but if there are chains you might want to use in several places in your application, you can also create action chains at the flow level or the application level.

The *Action* tab for an object (application, flow, or page) shows a list of all action chains at that level. You can click + *Action Chain* to create a new action chain. After you have provided a name, the *Action Chain editor* appears as shown in Figure 7-10.

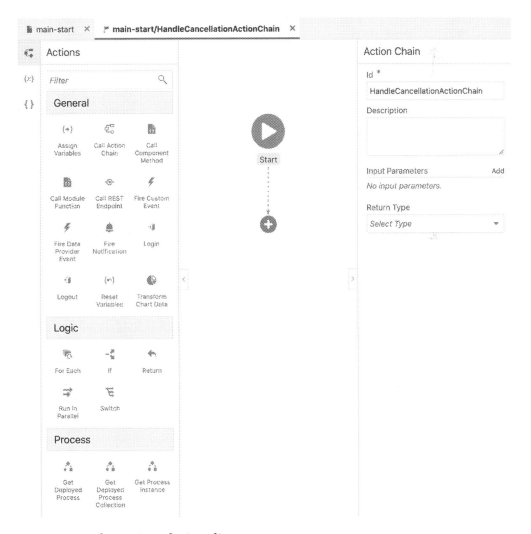

Figure 7-10. *The action chain editor*

In this editor, you can drag and drop elements from the action palette to the left onto the visual representation of the flow. If you drop it on a line or a plus sign at the end of a line, the action is added to the flow at that point.

The actions in the *General* category all have two possible outcomes success and failure. If you drag a new action on the plus sign below a general action, that action goes on the success branch, that is, it will happen if the general action was successful. This is the default and is not indicated in the diagram. Note, however, that when you start dragging an action, a plus sign appears at the lower right corner of the general actions already in the diagram. If you drop the new action onto that plus sign, it will be added to a new failure branch. Figure 7-11 shows both failure and success branches and shows the plus signs being shown while dragging an action.

Figure 7-11. *Dragging a new action in*

Different actions have different properties you can set. If you refer back to Figure 7-4, you see a *Call REST Endpoint* action step selected. The *Property Inspector* shows some properties to select the endpoint to call and various assignment of parameters. If you click the *Assign* hyperlink next to a parameter property, the visual assignment editor shown in Figure 7-12 appears.

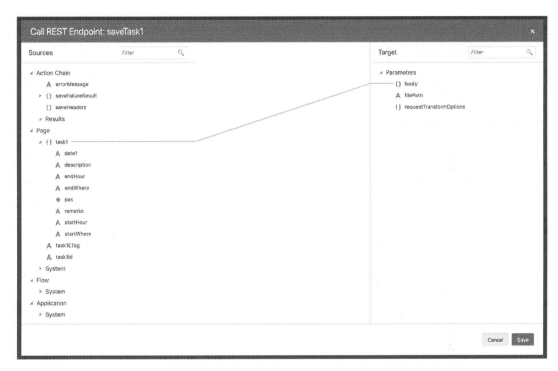

Figure 7-12. *Assigning variables in an action chain*

Here you can drag and drop to connect value sources on the left with targets on the right.

Adding JavaScript

The visual action chain builder can handle many simple requirements, but for more complicated requirements, you are likely to have to write your own JavaScript functions.

You do this on the *Functions* tab for the application, the flow, or the page. When you open the tab, you will see the default define() function that you need to insert your logic into. At the application level, there is already an AppModule definition; at the flow level, there is a `FlowModule` definition; and at the page level, there is a `PageModule` definition. You use the `prototype()` function from the module VBCS has already defined to add your logic. For example, to add a function to a page, you add the following:

```
PageModule.prototype.stenGreeting = function(str) {
  return "hello " + str;
}
```

In the editor, it looks as shown in Figure 7-13.

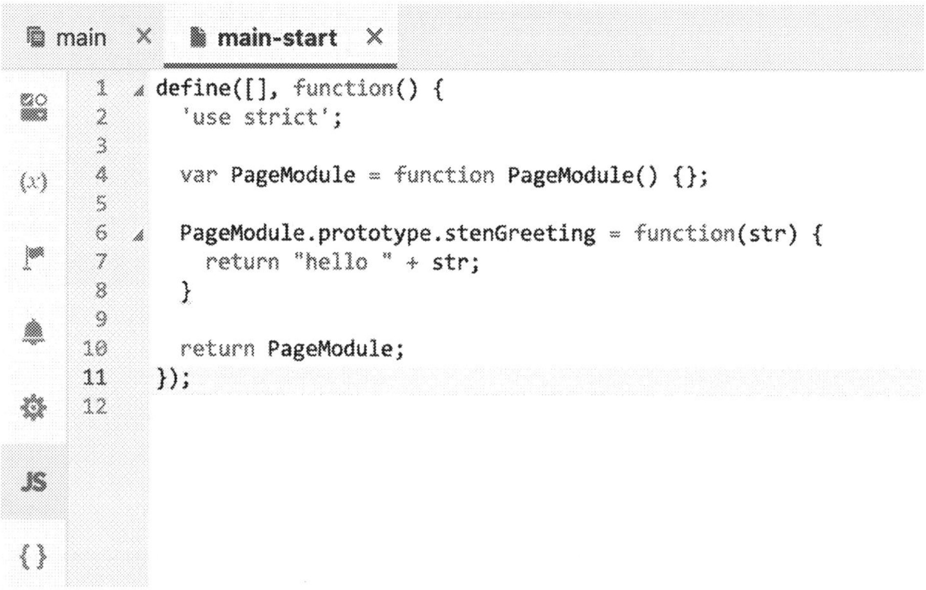

```
main  ✕    main-start  ✕

 1   ▲ define([], function() {
 2        'use strict';
 3
 4        var PageModule = function PageModule() {};
 5
 6   ▲    PageModule.prototype.stenGreeting = function(str) {
 7          return "hello " + str;
 8        }
 9
10        return PageModule;
11   });
12
```

Figure 7-13. *Adding a function to a VBCS module*

If you want to refer to your variables in your JavaScript, you can refer to them by scope and name. For example, to refer to a page scope variable, you use `$page.myVar`. Similarly, you can use `$application` and `$chain` to refer to application level and action chain level variables. The shortcut `$variables` refers to variables in the current scope, that is, in a page-level module, `$variables` is the same as `$page`.

To use your module in an action chain, you drop a *Call Module Function* action onto your flow. You use the *Select* link to select your function and the *Assign* link to assign variables as shown in Figure 7-14.

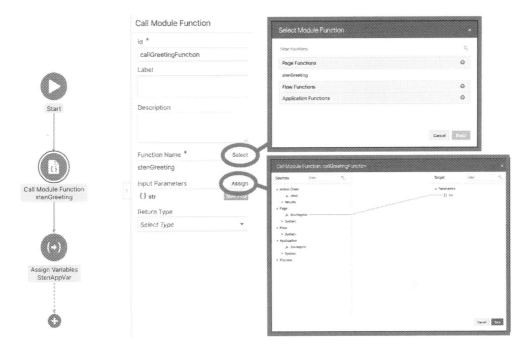

Figure 7-14. *Calling a module from an action chain*

The return value from your function can be mapped in a subsequent *Assign* action. The result of your module call will appear in the source section to the left under the *Id* of the *Call Module Function* action as shown in Figure 7-15.

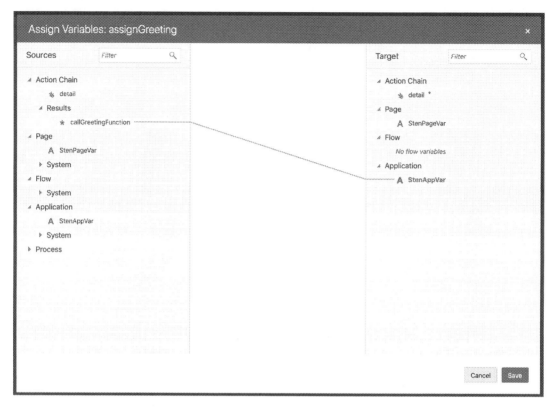

Figure 7-15. *Assigning the result of calling a module*

Conclusion

In this chapter, you learned about the way Visual Builder Cloud Service implements the functionality that magically appears in your application when you use the Quick Starts. You also saw how UI components, action chains, and variables work together to allow you to implement complex UI logic, and how to add your own JavaScript logic when the visual action chain builder doesn't offer you enough functionality.

In the next chapter, you will see how to use the Visual Builder for Excel plugin, which is another way for your users to interact with data in your VBCS application.

CHAPTER 8

Using the Visual Builder Add-in for Excel

So far, you have seen how to build web and mobile applications to interact with data from REST web services. But Oracle also offers another way to interact with this data: using the Visual Builder Add-in for Excel. Using this add-in, your users can simply download REST data into an Excel spreadsheet, work with it, and upload it back to the REST service.

The Visual Builder Add-in for Excel is currently only officially supported for 32-bit versions of Microsoft Excel 2016, but I have found it to work in newer versions as well.

Installing the Visual Builder Add-in for Excel

The Visual Builder Add-in for Excel is installed by running an .exe file you download from the *Data Manager*. To access the download, open the *Business Objects* tab and select *Data Manager* from the business objects menu. In the Data Manager window, select Edit Data in Excel. See Figure 8-1.

159

S. Vesterli, *Oracle Visual Builder Cloud Service Revealed*, https://doi.org/10.1007/978-1-4842-4929-1_8

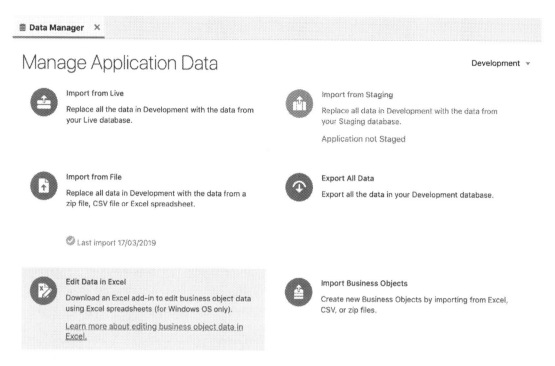

Figure 8-1. *Downloading the Visual Builder Add-in for Excel*

Clicking the box downloads the `vbcs-excel-addin-installer.exe` file; clicking the "Learn more..." link takes you to the *Using the Oracle Visual Builder Add-in for Excel in Oracle Integration* manual.

When you run the downloaded installer, it might install some required additional Microsoft software. While you don't need administrator rights to install the add-in itself, you might need them to install the required support software.

When you have installed the add-in, it should automatically appear as a new ribbon tab in Excel as shown in Figure 8-2.

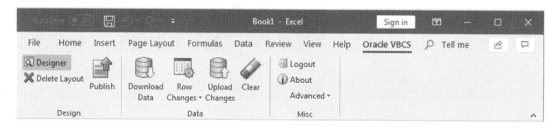

Figure 8-2. *The Visual Builder Add-in for Excel on the Excel ribbon*

If you don't see the *Oracle VBCS* tab, check the add-in settings in Excel under *File* ➤ *Options* ➤ *Add-ins.* If the Oracle Visual Builder Add-in for Excel has been installed correctly but is not active, it will be listed under *Inactive Application Add-ins.* In that case, click the *Manage* drop-down at the bottom of the *Excel Options* dialog as shown in Figure 8-3.

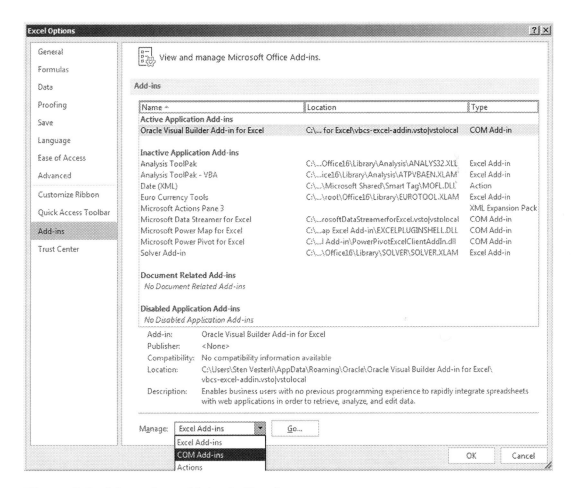

Figure 8-3. *Managing add-ins in Excel*

When you select *COM Add-ins* and click *Go*, you will be shown a dialog box where you can select which COM Add-ins to activate. Make sure there is a checkmark next to *Oracle Visual Builder Add-in for Excel.*

Connecting an Excel Spreadsheet

Once you have the add-in active, you can connect an Excel worksheet with a REST service.

Start by creating a blank standard Excel format workbook (.xlsx format). Place the cursor in the A1 cell and click Designer on the Oracle VBCS tab in Excel. You will be prompted to provide the Metadata API URL as shown in Figure 8-4.

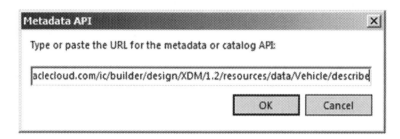

Figure 8-4. *The prompt for Metadata API in Excel*

You get this URL from the *Endpoints* tab in a business object under the *Resource APIs* heading in the *Metadata* column. See Figure 8-5.

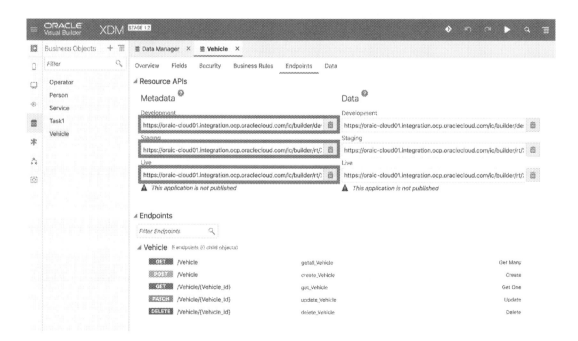

Figure 8-5. *Getting the metadata URL from VBCS*

Depending on which environment (Development, Staging, Live) you want your users to access from Excel, choose one of the three URLs. The icon next to the URL copies it to the clipboard. They have one of the following formats:

- `https://<server>/ic/builder/design/<app name> /<vers>/ resources/data/<obj>/describe`

  (development)

- `https://<server>/ic/builder/rt/<app name> /<vers>/ resources/data/<obj>/describe`

  (staging)

- `https://<server>/ic/builder/rt/<app name> /live/resources/ data/<obj>/describe`

  (development)

For example, the URL to the `Vehicle` business object in the staging environment for version 1.2 of the XDM application looks like this:

`https://<server>/ic/builder/rt/XDM/1.2/resources/data/Vehicle/describe`

When you paste this URL into the *Metadata API* dialog and click OK, you will be prompted to sign in to the Oracle Cloud (unless you have enabled anonymous access to your data). When you have signed in, you see a formatted table matching your REST service with an empty placeholder row. See Figure 8-6.

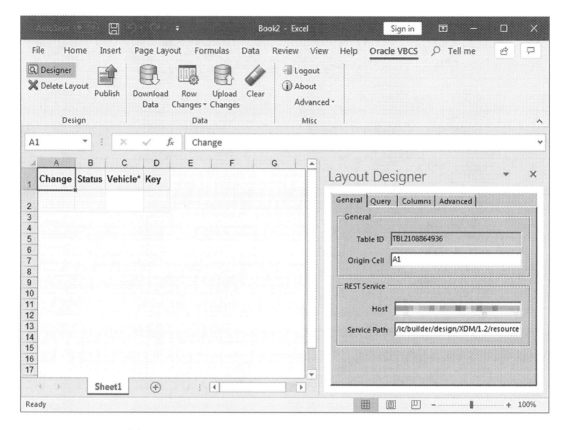

Figure 8-6. *A table in Excel connected to a REST service*

Working with Data

Once you have the connection established, you can click *Download Data* to get the data from your REST service into Excel and work with them. As you work with data, you will see the *Change* column indicate the operation to be done.

- Update data by just changing the values. The *Change* column shows *Update*.

- Create new data by inserting a new row between the existing rows. The *Change* column shows *Create*. If the row contains mandatory fields, the *Status* column will show *Invalid* until you have provided all the values.

- Delete data by selecting the row and choosing *Mark for Delete* from the *Row Changes* drop-down. The Change column will show *Delete*.

Caution   Don't use standard Excel functionality to delete a row. If you do, the add-in loses knowledge about the row and can't send a delete instruction.

When you are done, click *Upload Changes*. This will send your changes to the REST service to be effectuated. If you have deleted records, you will receive an extra confirmation prompt "The table has pending deletions. Do you wish to continue?" Afterward, the status column is updated with the result of the operation. See Figure 8-7.

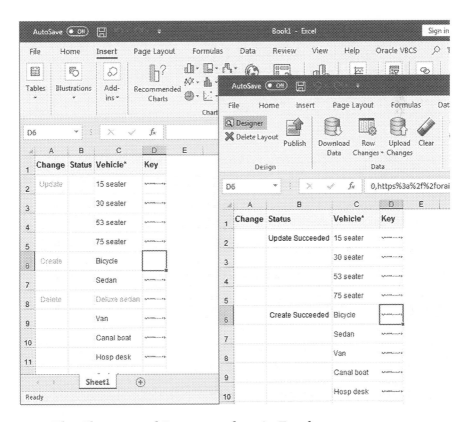

Figure 8-7. *The Change and Status markers in Excel*

Note that there is no feedback for deleted rows – because the rows are gone, there is no place for Excel to show feedback.

Limiting Data

If you want to limit the data you download, you can use the *Query* tab in the layout designer. When you click the pencil next to the *Search* field, a list of all fields in the object is shown. Select one and click *OK* to add it to the *Search* dialog shown in Figure 8-8.

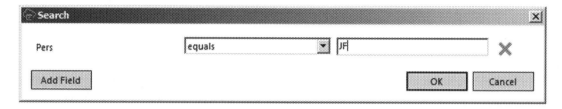

Figure 8-8. *The Search dialog in Visual Builder Add-in for Excel*

If you want to limit by multiple fields, click *Add Field* to select another field and then add a criterion for that field. When you have defined a search, the *Search* dialog appears each time you click *Download Data*, allowing you to download different subsets of the data from the REST service.

If your REST service supports *Finders*, you can also use these to limit the number of rows returned. Refer to Chapter 5 of the *Using the Oracle Visual Builder Add-in for Excel in Oracle Integration* manual.

Resetting Excel

If you have made changes in Excel that you don't want to apply, you can select the row and choose *Clear* from the *Row Changes* drop-down.

If you want to clear the whole table in Excel, you can click the *Clear* button on the Oracle VBCS tab. You will be asked to confirm you want to clear the table, and then all data is removed and can be redownloaded.

Publishing a VBCS Excel Workbook

When you have verified that your workbook functions as you wish, you can decide to *publish* it. When you click *Publish* on the Oracle VBCS tab in the Excel ribbon, you are prompted for a name, and your published workbook is saved.

The idea of publishing a VBCS-connected Excel workbook is that the published workbook doesn't have the design tools. It is also protected using standard Excel functionality so your users can't make changes outside the VBCS-connected table.

They can still download data, work with row change markings, and upload changes.

Caution   Only users who have the Visual Builder Add-in for Excel installed will be able to work meaningfully with a published VBCS Excel workbook. While the Excel file is an ordinary Excel file and can be edited without the add-in, any changes can't be handled once you move the file back to an Excel instance with the add-in.

Troubleshooting the VBCS Excel Add-in

If you are unable to connect to your REST service, try one of the other environments. Note that all the URLs are valid, but, for example, the Live URL doesn't make sense until you have set the application live.

To see the communication between Excel and your REST service, you can choose *Advanced* and then *REST Console* from the Oracle VBCS tab on the Excel ribbon. This will show you the HTTP communication and will look something like this:

```
Sending POST request to https://.../ic/builder/design/XDM/1.2/resources/data
Headers:
User-Agent: Oracle VBCS (1.5.0.18452) .NET
Authorization: Basic c3RlbkB2ZXN0ZXJsaS5jb206YmFzMDNESzQ=
REST-Framework-Version: 4
accept-language: en-US
Content-Type: application/vnd.oracle.adf.batch+json; charset=utf-8
Content-Encoding: gzip
Host: ...
Content-Length: 288
```

```
Accept-Encoding: gzip
Connection: Keep-Alive
Request Body:
```

```
{"parts":[{"id":"part1","path":"/Vehicle","operation":"create",
"payload":{"vehicle":"Kayak"}},{"id":"part2","path":"/Vehicle/310",
"operation":"update","ifMatch":["ACED0005737200136A6176612E7574696C2E417
27261794C6973747881D21D99C7619D03000149000473697A65787000000001770400000
001737200106A6176612E6C616E672E446F75626C6580B3C24A296BFB040200014400057
6616C7565787200106A6176612E6C616E672E4E756D62657286AC951D0B94E08B0200007
8703FF000000000000078"],"payload":{"vehicle":"On foot"}}]}
```

```
---

Response: 200: OK
...
```

The log is much longer than this, even for a single update operation. If you have someone on your team who is skilled at HTTP and REST troubleshooting, this can be very useful.

For more technical troubleshooting of the add-in itself, you will want to open a Service Request with Oracle support. To help them, you can choose *Enable Logging* from the *Advanced* drop-down. You can also click the *About* icon and then click *Diagnostic Report* to save a file with your configuration and version numbers of various components.

Conclusion

In this chapter, you learned how to install and use the Visual Builder Add-in for Excel to maintain data in a familiar Excel environment. You also saw how it is possible to publish an Excel sheet without the configuration information so that it can be distributed to end users who prefer to maintain data using Excel.

In the next chapter, you will see how to build mobile applications as yet another way to interact with REST data.

CHAPTER 9

Building Mobile Applications

You've seen how to create business objects, work with web services, and build web applications to allow the user to interact with data. However, in many cases, users want to interact with data on the go through a mobile application. Visual Builder Cloud Service also allows you to build mobile applications, and this chapter describes how to do this.

Creating a Mobile Application

To get started building a web application, you select the *Mobile Applications* icon in the left-hand menu and then click the plus sign next to the *Mobile Application* heading. This will bring up the *New Mobile Application* dialog shown in Figure 9-1.

© Sten Vesterli 2019
S. Vesterli, *Oracle Visual Builder Cloud Service Revealed*, https://doi.org/10.1007/978-1-4842-4929-1_9

Figure 9-1. *Creating a new mobile application*

You will be prompted to provide a name for your application and to choose a navigation style.

- If you are building a simple application, choose the *None* layout. This gives you a simple application without navigation items at the bottom.

- If you know your application will contain a number of different screens for different use cases, choose the *Horizontal* or *Vertical* layout and provide labels for your navigation items.

In the next step of the *New Mobile Application* wizard, you are prompted to select a layout for the home screen of your application, as shown in Figure 9-2.

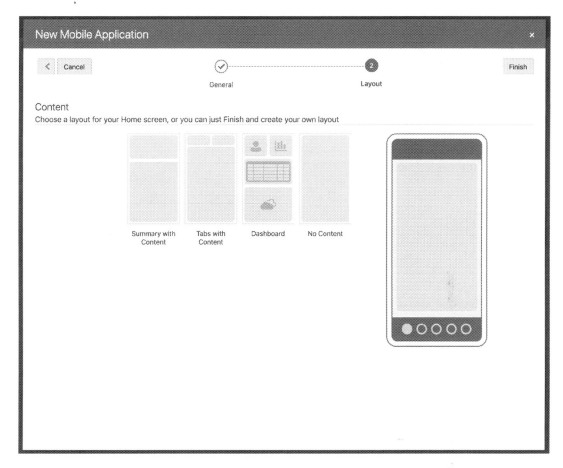

Figure 9-2. *Creating initial content for a new mobile application*

On this screen, you can choose if you want your mobile layout prepopulated with some components. If you choose *No Content*, you simply get a blank mobile screen to work with. If you choose one of the other options, VBCS will add some initial components on your home screen to achieve the layout you selected.

A VBCS web application has a very similar structure to a web application, and the navigator to the left shows you *flows, resources,* and *root pages* in the same way they appear in a web application.

Working with Pages

You open a mobile page like you open a web application page by double-clicking it in the *Mobile Apps* navigator or in the visual representation of its flow. The page opens in a dedicated page tab in the VBCS main work area like for web applications.

Along the left edge of the page tab, you find icons for the usual seven different views of a page:

- Designer

- Variables

- Actions

- Events

- Settings

- Functions

- Metadata

The Mobile Page Designer

The *Mobile Page Designer* view contains a page canvas with an illustration of a mobile device and the same three additional areas as web applications. This is shown in Figure 9-3.

The puzzle piece icon shows and hides the *component palette*, and the navigation tree icon shows and hides the *Page Structure* panel.

Tip   On the small screens of mobile devices, you might need quite a few layout components to control the layout to the level of detail you want. When you have many nested components, it is often easier to select and reorder them in the page structure panel.

The rightmost icon shows and hides the *Property Inspector*, where you can make changes to the properties of the selected component. The *Quick Start* wizards also appear in the *Property Inspector* pane.

Selecting the Mobile View

When working with mobile applications, you will also want to work with the *Mobile View* button marked on Figure 9-3 (above the work area canvas). This button allows you to select different mobile devices to see what your application will look like on various mobile devices.

Figure 9-3. *The Page Designer view for a mobile application*

The options in VBCS 19.1.3, which was current at the time of writing, are

- iPhone

- iPhone X

- Samsung S8

- Samsung S8 Plus

- Samsung Note 8

- iPad

Oracle provides you with a representative sample of current mobile devices (both iOS and Android) in various sizes, and you can expect this list to change over time as new devices are released and older ones fade from view.

If you try out the different options, you will see that VBCS not only uses a different device outline but also uses different visual representations of components in accordance with the User Experience standard for that device. Figure 9-4 shows the same application as iPhone (iOS) and Samsung Galaxy S8 (Android 7.0 Nougat).

Figure 9-4. *A VBCS mobile application shown in iOS and Android*

Obviously, VBCS makes an effort to present your mobile application in a way that meets your users' expectation for the platform. This also applies when you deploy the application to iOS or Android devices as explained later in this chapter.

At the bottom of the list, you might see the message *Device orientation locked to Portrait in Application Settings*. By default, VBCS applications are locked to portrait mode. This makes your work as a developer easier because you will not have to consider what will happen when your user turns her device sideways and suddenly has a wider, but shorter, screen. If you want your application to change when the user rotates the device, you need to uncheck the checkbox *Lock Portrait Mode* in the application settings. The words "Application Settings" in the message are a hyperlink to the page with the application settings, where you find this checkbox. When you uncheck the *Lock Portrait Mode* checkbox, the mobile view menu acquires a *Landscape/Portrait* toggle at the bottom. This lets you see what your application will look like in both vertical and horizontal mode.

Mobile Page Canvas

The page canvas shows the contents of your page inside a representation of your chosen mobile device. Mobile applications have the same two types of layouts available as web applications: *Grid* and *Flex*. When the entire page is selected, the property inspector shows you the two types and allows you to choose your preferred layout.

Tip   To select the entire page, either choose it in the *Navigator* or select the top-most item in the *Page Structure* panel, right-click and choose *Select Parent*.

The grid layout with its 12 predefined columns is normally not a good choice for the constrained space on a mobile device. Instead, choose the flex layout, which allows you to add components in rows of any size.

Collection Components

As for web applications, you connect your mobile application components to the underlying REST services through a VBCS collection component. For small mobile screens, you will normally choose a *List View* component. *Table* components are rarely used in mobile applications unless you are specifically building an application for an iPad (possibly even in landscape mode).

When you have placed a collection component on the page, the property palette contains a *Quick Start* icon to the right (the "graduate" icon).

To connect data to your *List View* component, use the *Add Data* wizard.

The first step in this wizard lets you select an endpoint for your data source like you saw in Chapter 4 for web applications.

The second step of the wizard lets you select a template that will be used to display the items on your list as shown in Figure 9-5.

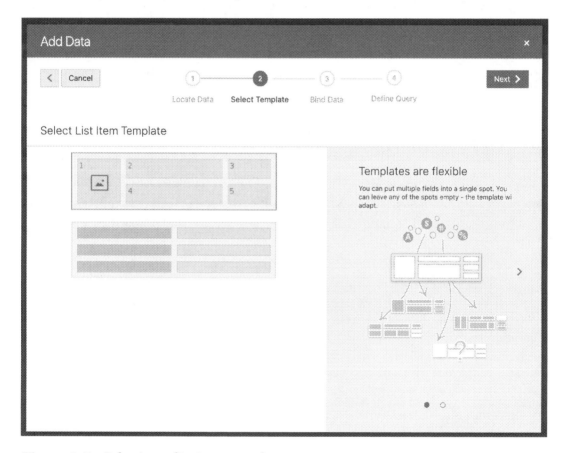

Figure 9-5. *Selecting a list item template*

Here, you select one of the available templates. VBCS version 19.1.3, which was current at the time of writing, offered two templates: one with space for an icon and up to four fields in a two-by-two grid, and one with space for any number of fields shown as a vertical list within the item.

The third step allows you to map data fields from the chosen data source to the individual locations in your chosen template. You can also drop multiple items into one slot and let VBCS try to arrange them within the location, and you don't have to drop something in all slots. You can reorder the fields later in the mobile page designer.

The fourth and final step of the wizard allows you to define query parameters. You use query parameters if the endpoint for your service offers a way to limit the result set of rows returned.

When you finish the wizard, the page canvas will show your *List View* component with real data returned by the endpoint you selected.

Creating Standard Pages

After creating the overview page, typically with a *List View* collection component, you can use the Quick Starts to add additional pages to your application. The quick starts are available when you have the *List View* component selected.

Adding a Create Page

If you want to allow the user of your mobile application to create records, you use the *Create Page* quick start to select the data source for your create operation and then select the fields you want to allow the user to provide values for.

You are also prompted for a label for the button to invoke the page, the title of the create page, and its internal name. Note that because of the small size of mobile devices, the button to invoke the create page will be a plus sign, and the label you provide will become a mouseover help item.

Note   Be aware of the limitations of mobile devices. Only add a create page to your mobile application if users really need to capture data on the go. If you decide you do need it, capture only the most important data.

When you complete the wizard, a new page is added to your flow, and a button to invoke the create page is added to your overview page.

As was the case for web applications, you can change to *Live* mode to test your create page. In *Live* mode, clicking the create button will execute its associated navigation item and take you to the create page. In *Design* mode, clicking the create button will just select it and not navigate to another page.

To test the application in VBCS's simulation of the chosen mobile device, you click the white triangular *Run* icon. This will run your application in a new browser tab. To test your application on an actual device or a more realistic emulator, you need to *build* the mobile application as described at the end of this chapter.

Adding an Edit Page

To allow your mobile users to edit data, you use the *Add Edit Page* quick start to add an edit page.

This process to create an edit page for a mobile application is similar to the process for creating an edit page for a web application. First, you select the read endpoint, then you select the update endpoint, and then you select the fields you want to allow your mobile user to update. You will be prompted for a button label and a title and internal name for the edit page.

The button label you provide does not seem to be used in the mobile application.

When you complete this quick start, the edit page is added to your mobile application and to the navigation flow.

If you look at the *Page Structure* panel, you will see that a *Swipe Tile* action has been added to the *Right Side Tiles* node as shown in Figure 9-6.

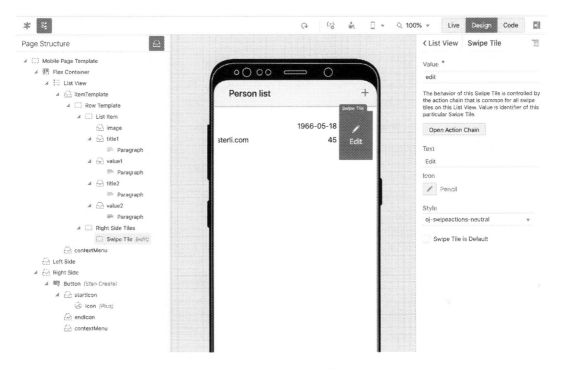

Figure 9-6. *Swipe action to edit in a mobile application*

Caution   This feature seems to be more aspirational than real in the version of VBCS current at the time of writing (19.1.3). VBCS does create a `performSwipeOperationChain`, but it is not triggered when you tap the swipe icon. There is no way to add a click event on the swipe tile to activate it, and the entire VBCS documentation does not contain the word "swipe" even once. Hopefully, this feature is fully implemented by the time you read this book. If not, you will have to create your own navigation flow, create a click event, and map the current ID to flow in order to get to the edit page for the right record.

If you add an *Edit* page to a mobile application using a *Table* collection component, you also get an *Edit* page, but no way to activate it. You will have to add a button and an action chain with a navigation item yourself.

Adding a Detail Page

If you need to provide detailed information in a mobile application, you should use a detail page. The *Add Detail Page* quick start helps you do that.

Using the quick start, you simply select the endpoint for reading one record and then select the fields you want to be displayed on the detail page. You are also prompted for a button label and the title and internal name of that page.

The button label you provide does not seem to be used in the mobile application.

When you complete this quick start, the detail page is added to your mobile application and to the navigation flow. If you examine the *List View* component, you will find that a select action has been added and that it triggers a new action chain called `navigateToPersonDetailChain`. If you open this action chain, you will find it performs the navigation to the detail page.

You can test the edit page in *Live* mode or by running the application. The navigation to the detail page is triggered by a `selection` event which happens when you tap or click an item in the list. Since the detail page uses click and not swipe, it does work.

Adding Delete Functionality

To allow your users to delete records from the mobile application, you can use the *Add Delete Action* quick start.

This quick start only requires you to select the endpoint for deleting a record.

When you complete this quick start, a *Swipe Tile* action is added to your *List View* component. This one has the value `delete`, and the styling is `oj-swipeactions-danger`. If you select the *Swipe Tile* action, you can click *Open Action Chain* in the *Property Inspector* to see what happens on this action.

If you have added both *Edit* and *Delete*, your action chain looks as shown in Figure 9-7.

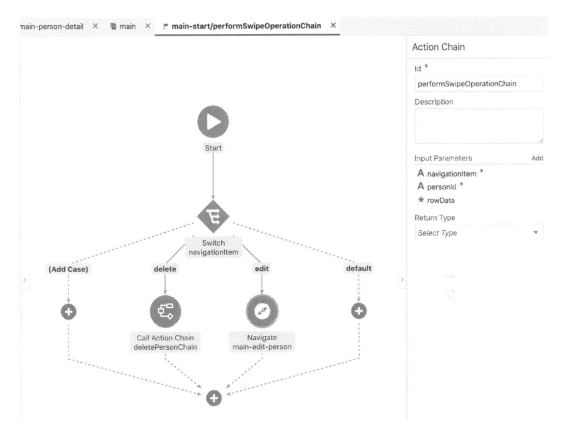

Figure 9-7. *Action chain for Edit and Delete*

The idea is that depending on whether you select *Edit* or *Delete* when you swipe, the flow either takes the navigation branch to the Edit page or calls the `deletePersonChain`. You can drill into this chain to see how VBCS does the delete, including notification of success or error.

If you test the page in *Live* mode or by running the application, swiping left will now show a *Delete* action as shown in Figure 9-8.

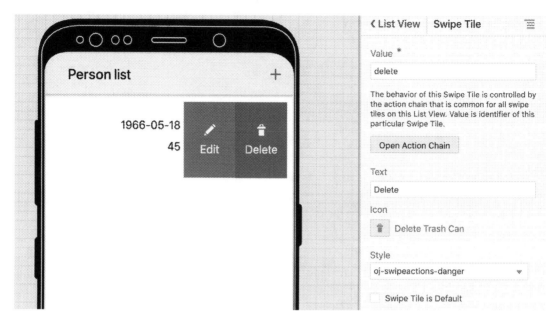

Figure 9-8. *Swiping left to edit or delete*

The figure shows what a swipe looks like if you have added both Edit and Delete.

Caution   Swipe to delete also doesn't work in the current version of VBCS. However, if you have implemented a detail page (based on a selection, which does work), clicking either swipe button instead triggers the action chain to show the detail page.

Layout Components

To control the layout of your mobile application, you have the full selection of layout components from the *component palette* at your disposal. All of the components are mobile-capable Oracle JET components, and you can look them up in the Oracle JET documentation.

When building mobile applications, you should be especially careful not to overload the small screens with content.

Static Components

The *Common* heading in the component palette contains standard components like *Heading*, *Text*, *Label*, and others.

You can also use *Image* and *Avatar* components. We discussed these in Chapter 4, where we also saw how to import and use images in a web application. They work in the same way in a mobile application.

Field Components

You can also use the normal field components in your mobile applications to show one attribute from one record. These are the components VBCS uses for create, edit, and detail screens.

As you saw in Chapter 4 about web applications, each field component has a *Data* tab where the component is mapped to some expression that defines the data (normally a page variable). When you first get started with VBCS, it is a good idea to use quick starts to have VBCS set this property, but as you become more proficient with VBCS, you can also set them yourself using action chains.

The field components are Oracle JET components, so you can point to the question mark next to the component in the component palette to find out what component it is, and then find more information in the Oracle JET cookbook.

Action Components

The *Common* heading also contains action components like *Button* and *Menu*. Due to the small screen on mobile devices, you are not likely to use these much in mobile applications. But if you need to allow the user to run some logic, you can add a component like a button and let it trigger an action chain. Refer to the chapter on logic in the user interface for more.

Visualization Components

You can also use all of the VBCS visualization components in your mobile applications. It is common to present data both in list form and with some kind of visual overview. Gauges can be used to good effect in List View components, while charts are normally presented on their own tab where they can use the entire screen of the mobile device.

Gauges

Gauges show a graphical representation of a single value, possibly comparing it to one or more thresholds. In mobile applications, they are typically used in List Views to let the user quickly identify which items she wants to examine in more detail.

VBCS 19.1.3, which was the current version when this book was written, offers the following gauges:

- LED Gauge

- Rating Gauge

- Circular Status Meter

- Linear Status Meter

- Progress

The *LED Gauge* is a simple colored symbol, typically used to indicate red/yellow/green status. On a small mobile screen, it is very useful to present data that can be meaningfully compared to some threshold as an LED Gauge with the actual data value inside the circle. In this way, you take up very little space more than just the number and can provide a good quick overview.

The *Rating Gauge* is a series of symbols (e.g., stars), some of which are shown in a different color. You will be familiar with this from star ratings in online reviews. If you are gathering coarse-grained data in your mobile application, you can use a Rating Gauge as an interactive component to allow the user to rate something.

The *Circular Status Meter* and *Linear Status Meter* show small visualizations of the value and can compare the value with one or more reference values. For mobile applications on small screens, simple linear status meters work well. The circular status meters can also be useful, but they tend to take up too much space vertically.

Chapter 4 on web applications gives examples of how to use VBCS gauges, including how to set up the *Value* property and threshold values. Gauges work in the same way in mobile applications as in web applications.

Charts

Charts display multiple data points in one or more series of data. For mobile applications designed for small screens, you should show no more than three data series. If you are explicitly targeting tablets, you should think of your application like a web application and follow the advice in Chapter 4 on web applications.

The latest version of VBCS when this book was written was 19.1.3, which offers the following charts:

- Area Chart

- Bar Chart

- Box Plot Chart

- Bubble Chart

- Combo Chart

- Donut Chart

- Funnel Chart

- Line Chart

- Line with Area Chart

- Pie Chart

- Pyramid Chart

- Scatter Chart

- Stock Chart

The following sections briefly describe how these charts can be used in VBCS mobile applications. You use them in mobile applications like in web applications: drop a chart component onto a page and run the *Add Data* quick start. For examples of the charts, refer back to Chapter 4, which contains some figures showing the different types.

Continuous Data

Continuous data series (typically representing values changing over time) should be shown with line charts. They need X values (typically time periods) and one or more data series to be plotted. In mobile applications displayed on small screens, do not show more than three different series.

Line Charts are most common and are good for seeing trends over time. *Area Charts*, where the area under the line is filled in, can be easier to read on small screens, but they should only be used for data sets where the total of the different data series has a meaning, for example, sales by region.

Line with Area Charts are a hybrid form, but the semitransparent fill doesn't work well on small mobile screens. The *Combo Chart* can show bars, lines, and area charts together, but should be used with care in mobile application because they tend to be overloaded with more data than can reasonably be decoded.

Discrete Data

Discrete values are typically visualized with *Bar Charts* or *Pie Charts*. To compare absolute values, *Bar Charts* are good, but don't put too many values on the small screens of mobile applications. If you allow the mobile application to respond to device rotation, you should add logic to the *Orientation* property so your bar chart changes between *Horizontal* and *Vertical*.

To show how large a part of the whole each data point represents, you normally use *Pie Charts*. For mobile devices, don't try to display more than six slices to avoid cluttering up the visualization, and always (in both web and mobile applications) avoid using the "3D" effect.

VBCS also offers *Donut Charts* and *Pyramid Charts* for plotting discrete values – refer back to Chapter 4 for an illustration of all four types of charts.

Other Charts

To plot sets of values that all vary freely, you use multidimensional charts. If you have sets of X and Y values, you can use a *Scatter Chart*. These can be hard to decode for the user on a small mobile device, so consider if some simpler visualization fits better to mobile. *Bubble Charts*, where the size of the marker indicates some third data value should be avoided on mobile.

Finally, Visual Builder Cloud Service also offers some specialized charts like *Box Plot Charts*, *Funnel Charts*, and *Stock Charts*. These are very detailed charts – too detailed for most mobile applications.

Many of these charts are illustrated in the section on visualizations in Chapter 4 that covers web applications.

Building Apps

During development, Visual Builder Cloud Service does its best to simulate what the application will look like on an actual mobile device. However, once you are done with development and are ready to test your app, you will want to deploy it to a real mobile device or a high-fidelity simulator.

VBCS allows you to build real apps for both iOS and Android – applications that can be deployed to the app stores and downloaded by your users like all other apps. Your VBCS code is not magically converted to Objective-C or Java – instead, VBCS builds an app that contains a properly configured web view to display your application. You can also build *Progressive Web Apps* (PWA), which are web applications with some app-like capabilities.

Building on-device mobile applications is tricky, and VBCS cannot isolate you from the challenges of getting the various certificates you need for your application to be accepted by your device and the app store. If you have someone in your organization with experience building mobile applications with other tools, it will be a good idea to involve these people in the mobile app build process. PWA applications come with a different set of limitations and challenges.

Setting Up

Before you start building your mobile app, you need to set some application settings and create at least one build configuration or configure your application for Progressive Web Apps.

Application settings are accessed from the *Settings* menu (the gearwheel icon) when you have the entire application selected. See Figure 9-9.

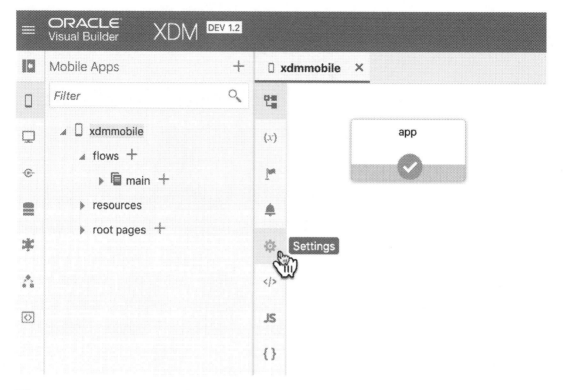

Figure 9-9. *Accessing application settings*

In the *Application Settings* window for a mobile application, you set the mobile application name to be shown on the device, as well as the name of your organization and a default Bundle ID. See Figure 9-10.

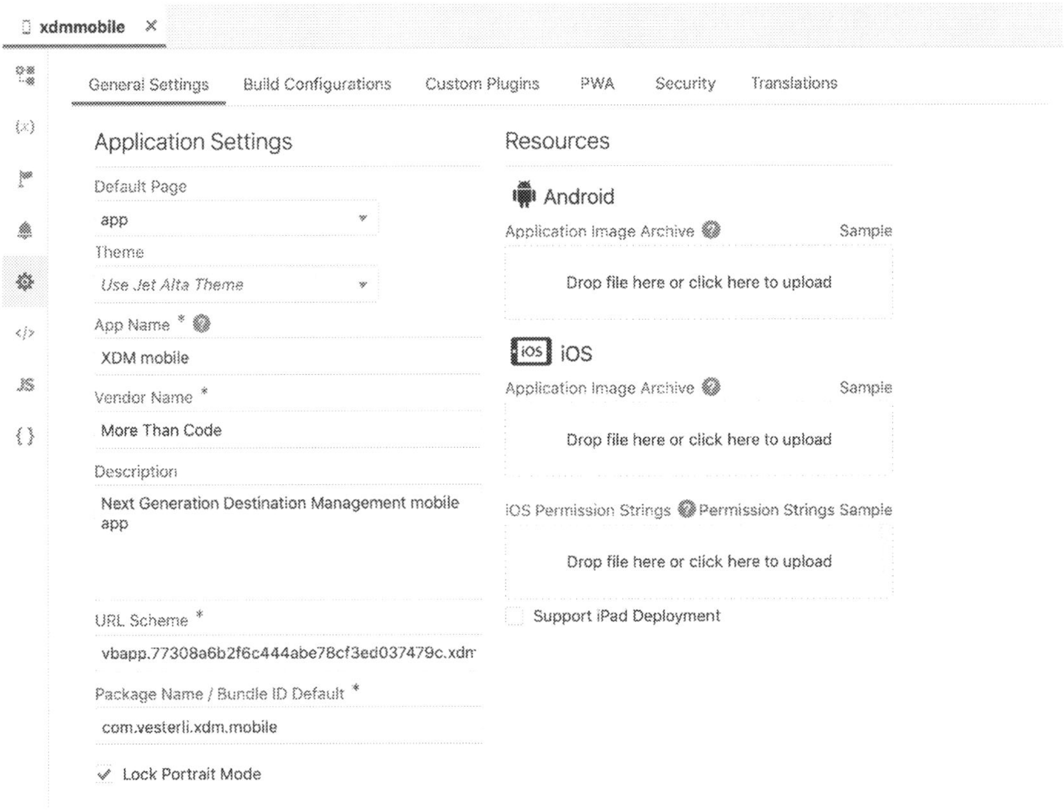

Figure 9-10. *Application settings for a mobile application*

You can upload custom images to be used for the splash screen and the icon of your application in various resolutions; click the *Sample* link next to both Android and iOS to download a ZIP file with examples of the files the respective platforms expect. If you don't upload anything, VBCS will build your application with the default logos.

There is also an option to upload a file of custom iOS permission strings ("The camera may be used to take pictures that may be uploaded to a server," etc.).

Note there is a checkbox at the bottom of the right column to indicate whether you will allow this application to be installed on iPad tablets. iOS makes a distinction between phone and tablet apps – if you have not designed your application for large tablet screens, you can prevent it from being installed on iPads.

There is no option to prevent users from installing your app on Android tablets –
with the plethora of Android screen sizes, it doesn't make sense for Android to
make a distinction between "small" and "large".

When you have set your mobile application settings, you need to create one or more
Build Configurations or configure your application for Progressive Web Applications.

Building for iOS

To build an iOS application, you need to have access to a MacOS computer. You must
run the *Xcode* development environment and the *Keychain Access* application to get the
certificates you need, and both exist only for MacOS.

You first create an iOS build configuration on the *Build Configuration* tab, then you
build the iOS app, and finally install it on your device.

Preparing to Build for iOS

When you click *New Configuration* and choose *iOS*, the *iOS Build Profile* window
appears as shown in Figure 9-11.

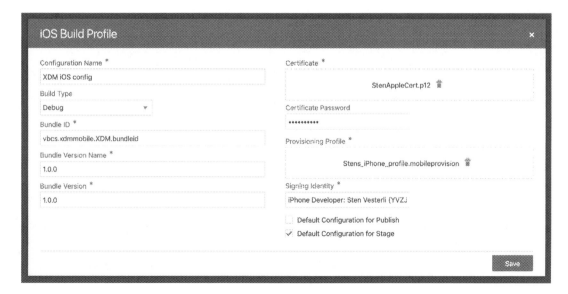

Figure 9-11. *Creating an iOS Build Profile*

The *Build Type* should be *Debug* as long as you are developing and testing your application. Do not choose *Release* until you are ready to deploy your final application to an app store for download by end users.

The *Bundle ID* identifies your application on the device. It must be unique on the device; it is a good idea to include the domain of your organization in the Bundle ID to prevent collision with apps from other developers.

The *Bundle Version Name* and *Bundle Version* must be in numeric x.y.z format and start with 1.0.0. You must increment this each time you upload to an App Store.

The *Certificate* field is where you drag and drop or upload the certificate associated with the provisioning profile you will drop into the *Provisioning Profile* field. This must be a .p12 file, not a .cer file. You can download this from the Xcode application under *Preferences* ➤ *Accounts*.

The *Certificate Password* field is where you write the password you set when you exported the provisioning certificate from the *Keychain Access* app on your Mac.

The *Provisioning Profile* field is where you drag and drop or upload the provisioning profile.

The *Signing Identity* field is where you enter the name of the developer or distribution certificate that will be used to sign the code. You need to enter the whole *Common Name* from the certificate as shown in Figure 9-12.

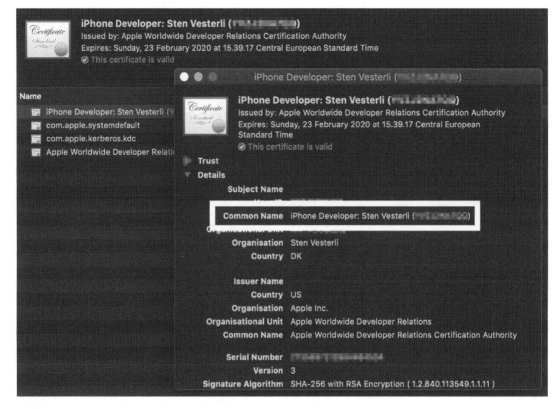

Figure 9-12. *Identifying Common Name for a certificate*

Check one of the checkboxes for either *Default Configuration for Publish* or *Default Configuration for Stage.* You should have separate build configurations for a test build (Stage) or a final deployment build (Publish).

When you are done with all of this information, click *Save.*

Executing Build and Installing on iOS

When your build configuration is set up, you can build the application. To do so, you run the application with the white triangle *Run* button. This brings up the VBCS run environment for mobile showing your application. Here, you can select *iOS* and click *Build my App* (or *Rebuild my App* after the first build) to actually generate a functioning mobile app for iOS. You will be shown the usual prompt about whether to copy development data into the staging environment and then the application is built. This will take a while.

If the build is successful, you will see a QR code to download and run the application as shown in Figure 9-13.

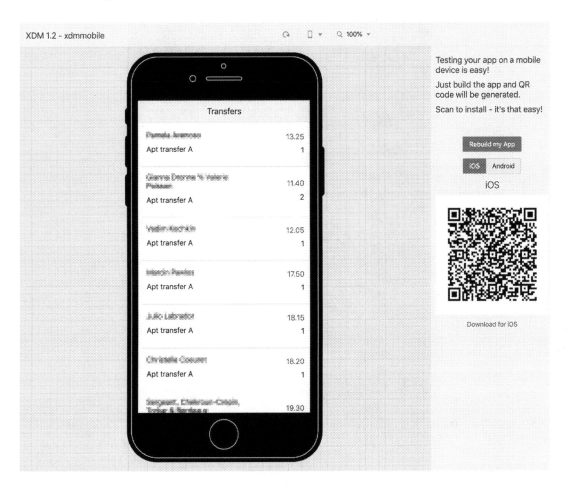

Figure 9-13. *A mobile application ready to install*

From this page, you can either click *Download for iOS* to get an installable `.ipa` file or use the device camera to scan the QR code. As shown in the device screenshot in Figure 9-14, your device will prompt you to use iTunes to install the app. When you tap *Open in iTunes*, your application will be installed on the device.

Figure 9-14. *Installing a VBCS mobile application on an iOS device*

When you run the application, if you have not enabled anonymous access, you will first see a VBCS login screen where you provide your username and password. After you have logged in, your application runs on your mobile device.

Building for Android

To build an Android application, you need the Android SDK. This can be installed on Windows, MacOS, and Linux computers.

You first create an Android build configuration on the *Build Configuration* tab, then you build the Android app, and finally install it on your device. You can also run it on the Android emulator that is part of the Android SDK.

Preparing to Build for Android

When you click *New Configuration* and choose *Android,* the *Android Build Profile* window appears as shown in Figure 9-15.

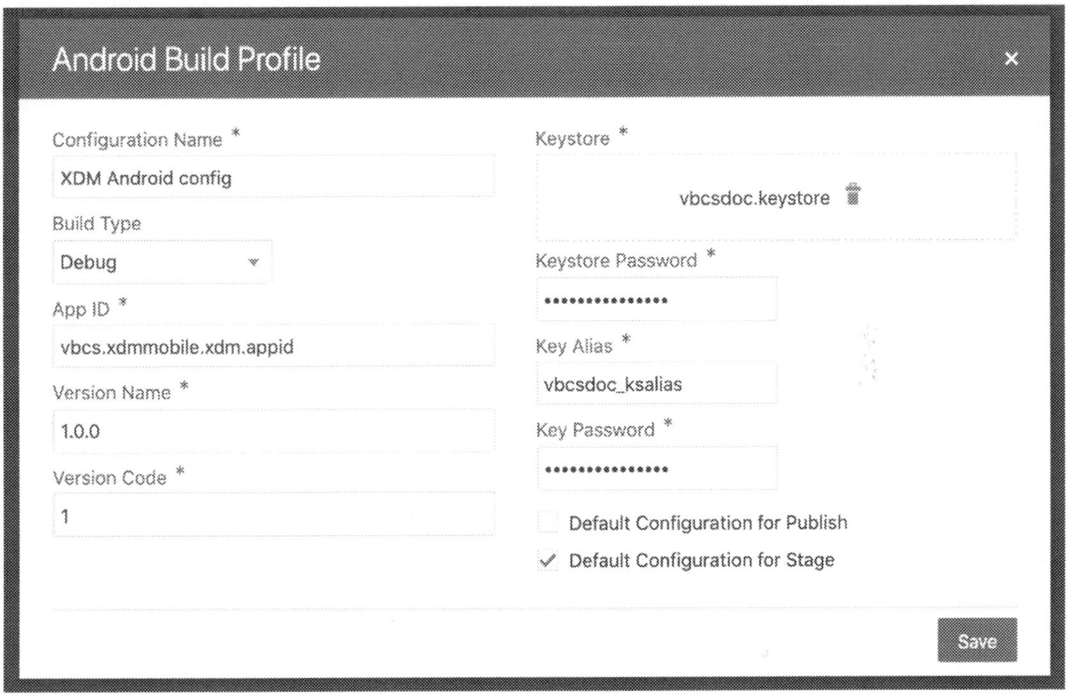

Figure 9-15. *Creating an Android Build Profile*

Build Type should be *Debug* as long as you are developing and testing your application, and *Release* when you are ready to deploy your final application to end users.

The *App ID* identifies your application on the device. It must be unique on the device; it is a good idea to include the domain of your organization in the App ID to prevent collision with apps from other developers.

The *Version Name* is the release version shown to users. It is a good idea to use a standard semantic versioning number in numeric x.y.z format.

The *Version Code* is an integer that allows the OS to determine if a new version is available. Normally, you would start with 1 and increment by one for each new version.

The *Keystore* field is where you drag and drop or upload the keystore for the application. Android allows an application to be self-signed. To do this, you can generate your own key using the `keytool` command-line tool.

The *Keystore Password* field is where you enter the password for the entire keystore.

The *Key Alias* field is where you enter the key alias (set with the alias parameter when running keytool).

The *Key Password* is where you enter the password for the specific key identified by the alias within the keystore.

Check one of the checkboxes for either *Default Configuration for Publish* or *Default Configuration for Stage*. It is recommended to have separate build configurations for a test build (Stage) or a final deployment build (Publish).

When you are done with all of this information, click *Save*.

Executing Build and Installing

You build an Android application like an iOS application. First, you run the application with the *Run* button to see the application run in the VBCS run environment for mobile. Then you select *Android* and click *Build my App* or *Rebuild my App*. After the prompt about copying data into the staging environment, VBCS will build for a while and then display a QR code and a *Download for Android* link.

You can use the camera on your device to download the app to your device, or you can download the `.apk` Android application file.

If you want to run the application in the emulator that is part of the Android Studio, you can start a virtual device from the *AVD Manager* and then use the adb command to install it. In my example, my application file is called `xdmmobile.apk`, so I run this command:

```
adb install xdmmobile.apk
```

It will look something like Figure 9-16 in a Google Pixel 2 virtual device.

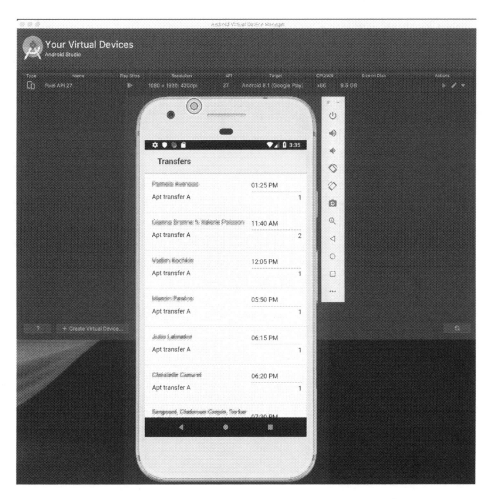

Figure 9-16. *Running an Android app in an Android Virtual Device*

If you have not enabled anonymous access, you will first see a VBCS login screen, and then your application running.

Building Progressive Web Apps

In the latest versions of VBCS (from 19.1.3 onward), you also have the possibility to create *Progressive Web Apps* (PWA). These are web applications with enhanced functionality to make them more "app-like." For example, a PWA might offer access to device features or the ability to work offline.

To turn a mobile Visual Builder Cloud Service application into a Progressive Web App, you go to the *PWA* tab in the mobile application settings and select *Enable Progressive Web App (PWA)* as shown in Figure 9-17.

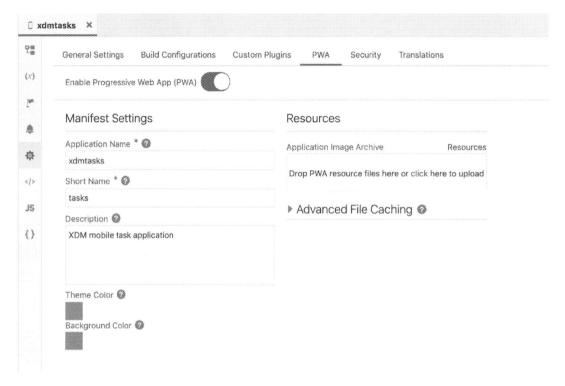

Figure 9-17. *Enabling Progressive Web Apps*

When you have activated PWA, the run page for the mobile app gets a *Launch in Browser* link when you have built the application. Additionally, when you scan the QR code on the run page with a mobile device, the application is opened in the mobile device browser.

If the application is run in Google Chrome on a laptop or desktop computer, the user will see a dialog box asking if the application should be installed locally as a Chrome app.

If the application is run on an Android device, the user will be asked if it should be added to the home screen. If the user selects this, an icon for the application appears on the user's device, and it can be run from this icon just like a native application.

If the application is run on an iOS device, it is opened in Safari, but there is no prompt to install it on the home screen (though it is possible from the normal Share icon in iOS Safari).

> **Caution**   Apple is offering support for Progressive Web Apps only slowly and reluctantly. If your user is on iOS, it must be the latest version (12.3 or later), and there are many limitations and restrictions. Follow the link "Learn more about PWA support" from the mobile app run page in VBCS to the VBCS documentation to learn more about the current limitations. Obviously, Apple prefers developers to build native apps and deploy them through their App Store.

Conclusion

In this chapter, you have seen how to build mobile VBCS applications. The development experience is very similar to building web applications, though you need to keep the small screens on mobile devices in mind when you design pages. You have also seen how to create build configurations for both iOS and Android devices and how to build for both platforms.

In the next chapter, we will discuss VBCS application security.

CHAPTER 10

VBCS Security

You've seen how easy it is to build a fully functional application with Visual Builder Cloud Service. Of course, while we want our applications to provide value for our users, we often don't want just anybody to access them.

Users and Roles

You as the developer decide if you want to allow unknown users into your application, or whether you require everyone to identify themselves with a valid Oracle Cloud username and password.

Note Anonymous access is only possible if your VBCS service administrator has allowed anonymous access under *Tenant Settings*.

Anonymous and Authenticated Users

Users who have not identified themselves are automatically assigned the *Anonymous User* role. By default, they don't have access to anything, but you can explicitly grant access to specific web applications and business objects to users with the *Anonymous User* role.

Users who have identified themselves by logging in are automatically assigned the *Authenticated User* role. By default, these users have full access to your web applications and business objects unless you specifically restrict certain items.

201

© Sten Vesterli 2019
S. Vesterli, *Oracle Visual Builder Cloud Service Revealed*, https://doi.org/10.1007/978-1-4842-4929-1_10

Other User Roles

For more complicated access management, you can create your own application roles. This is done on the *User Roles* tab under application settings. To define and manage user roles, you first choose *Settings* from the *Application* menu (at the right end of the horizontal menu bar at the top of the VBCS window). Then choose the User Roles tab as shown in Figure 10-1.

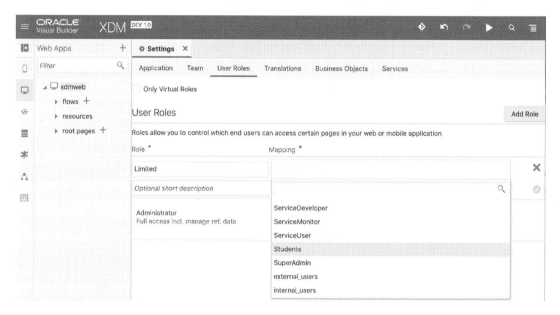

Figure 10-1. *Application user roles*

On this tab, you provide a role name in the *Role* field, optionally a description, and then map that role to a user role or group defined in Identity Cloud Service (ICS).

The name you provide is the one you can use in your application. When you define access to an object in your application, the roles you define here will show up as possible roles when deciding on access.

The name you select in the *Mapping* field is the name of a group or role *that is already defined.* As a VBCS developer, you cannot change the options that appear on this list. Your Identity Cloud Service administrator has defined these groups, and you can only select from them.

This architecture separates the access definition work nicely:

- The VBCS developer just needs to know that some users should have limited access and can choose a name (e.g., `limited_access`).

- The Identity Cloud Service administrator doesn't know about the application but can assign users to roles that make sense to the organization. For example, a group of student helpers can be assigned the ICS `student` role.

- Either VBCS developer or ICS administrator can map these together, for example, mapping the ICS `student` role to the VBCS application role `limited_access`.

Testing Role-Based Security

To test your application with users with different roles, you can use the *Who Am I?* button in the top toolbar, shown in Figure 10-2.

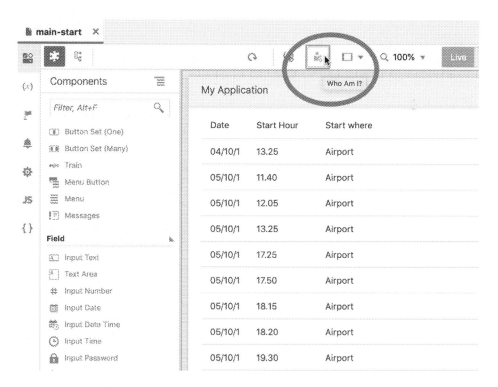

Figure 10-2. *The Who Am I? button*

This button brings up a dialog with all the roles in the application as shown in Figure 10-3.

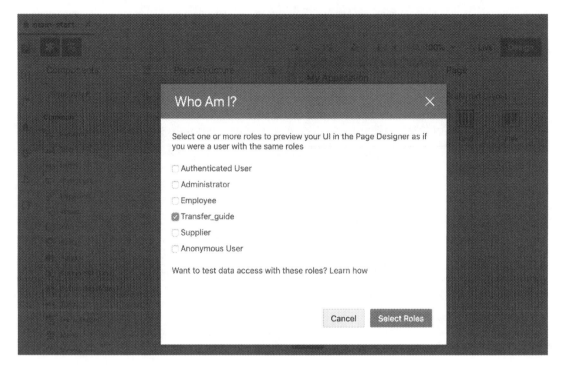

Figure 10-3. *Who Am I? role selection dialog*

You will always see *Authenticated User* and *Anonymous User* in this dialog, as well as any application user roles you have created. By making selections in this dialog, you can see how the application will look and behave for users with different roles.

Web Application Security

Security for a web application is handled at the application level. VBCS does not currently offer you the ability to restrict access to specific pages in an application, so if you have different security requirements for different classes of users, you must build separate web applications.

You find the web application security settings on the *Security* sub-tab on the application settings tab as shown in Figure 10-4.

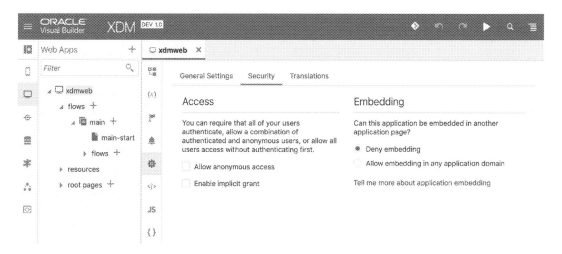

Figure 10-4.   *Web application security settings*

On this tab, you can select that users have access to your application without authenticating by checking the *Allow anonymous access* and *Enable implicit grant* checkboxes.

If you check these boxes, a user will not be presented with a login screen and will get access to the application as user anonymous and the *Anonymous User* role.

Note   Unless you also grant access on your business objects or service connections, your anonymous user will see the application, but it will look like it doesn't contain any data.

Application Embedding

On the Security tab, you also find the *Embedding* settings. The default is *Deny embedding,* which means that the application won't run if you try to embed it inside a web page that runs on another domain than your Oracle Cloud instance.

If you want to use your VBCS application inside an existing web site, you need to choose *Allow embedding in any application domain.*

> **Tip** When embedding a VBCS application, you should show only the functionality and not the surrounding artifacts. Edit your shell page to remove the page header and footer.

Changing Security Settings

Changes you make to the security settings for your web application do not take effect until you stage or publish the application. If you have already staged or published the application with specific security settings, you must create a new version and stage and publish that for the new settings to take effect.

Mobile Application Security

Security for VBCS mobile applications is also handled at the application level. To change security settings for your mobile application, open the *Security* sub-tab on the mobile application settings tab as shown in Figure 10-5.

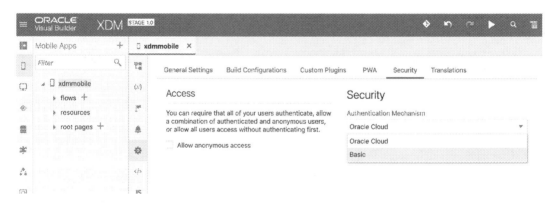

Figure 10-5. *Mobile application security settings*

Here you have a similar option to allow mobile users to access your application without authentication.

You can also choose the *Authentication Mechanism*. The default setting is *Oracle Cloud,* which means that the mobile user will have to log in with a valid Oracle Identity Cloud Service account.

If you choose *Basic*, you will see a warning and two additional fields *Login URL* and *Logout URL*. With Basic authentication, your user will be prompted for a username and password, and this information will be sent to the *Login URL* as a basic authentication header. If the login service accepts the authentication, the home page of your mobile application is shown to the user.

Caution   Basic authentication has some limitations, and you need to consider how to pass authentication to any REST services your mobile application needs. Refer to the section "Configure Basic Authentication for a Mobile Application" in the *Developing Applications with Oracle Visual Builder* manual.

Business Object Security

Some business object security settings apply to all business objects in a Visual Builder Cloud Service application, and some control access to operations on specific business objects.

General Business Object Security Settings

The general business object security settings are set under application settings on the *Business Objects* tab as shown in Figure 10-6.

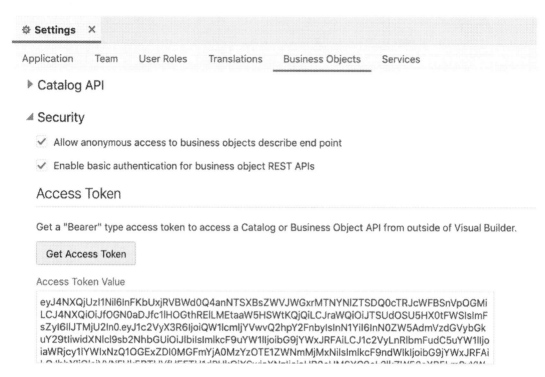

Figure 10-6. *General business object security settings*

The *Enable basic authentication for business object REST APIs* checkbox allows external services to access the REST endpoint that describes the operations if they authenticate with a valid VBCS username and password. If you plan to access your business objects from outside the VBCS application, and the development tool you use can understand the extra metadata VBCS provides, you can consider allowing anonymous access to the describe endpoints.

Note   Even if you allow anonymous access to the describe endpoints, the request must still contain an authorization header (`Authorization: public`).

For more secure access, you can click the *Get Access Token* button. This fills the *Access Token Value* field with a long text string you can give to developers who are building applications that need to access the REST endpoints of your business objects.

Role-Based Security for Business Objects

Access to VBCS business objects is handled at the individual business object level with *role-based security*. By default, this is not active. This means that users with *Authenticated User* role have full access and users with *Anonymous User* role have no access. To enable role-based security for a business object, you go to the *Security* tab in the business object and click the top-hat-and-key icon as shown in Figure 10-7.

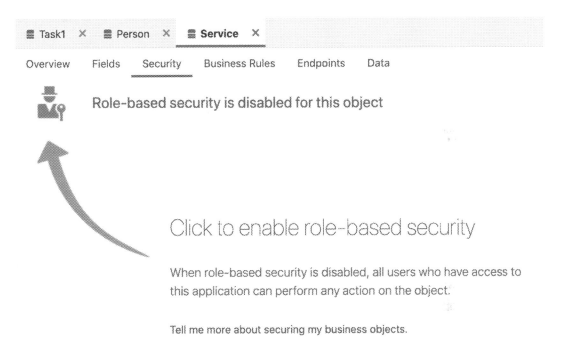

Figure 10-7. *Enabling role-based security for a business object*

This is done object by object so that you can have role-based security for some business objects and standard security for others within the same application.

When you click the icon, you are presented with a matrix showing the capabilities of the object (view, create, update, delete) and the roles available in your application. The standard roles *Authenticated User* and *Anonymous User* are always available. If you have defined additional application user roles, these are also shown as illustrated in Figure 10-8.

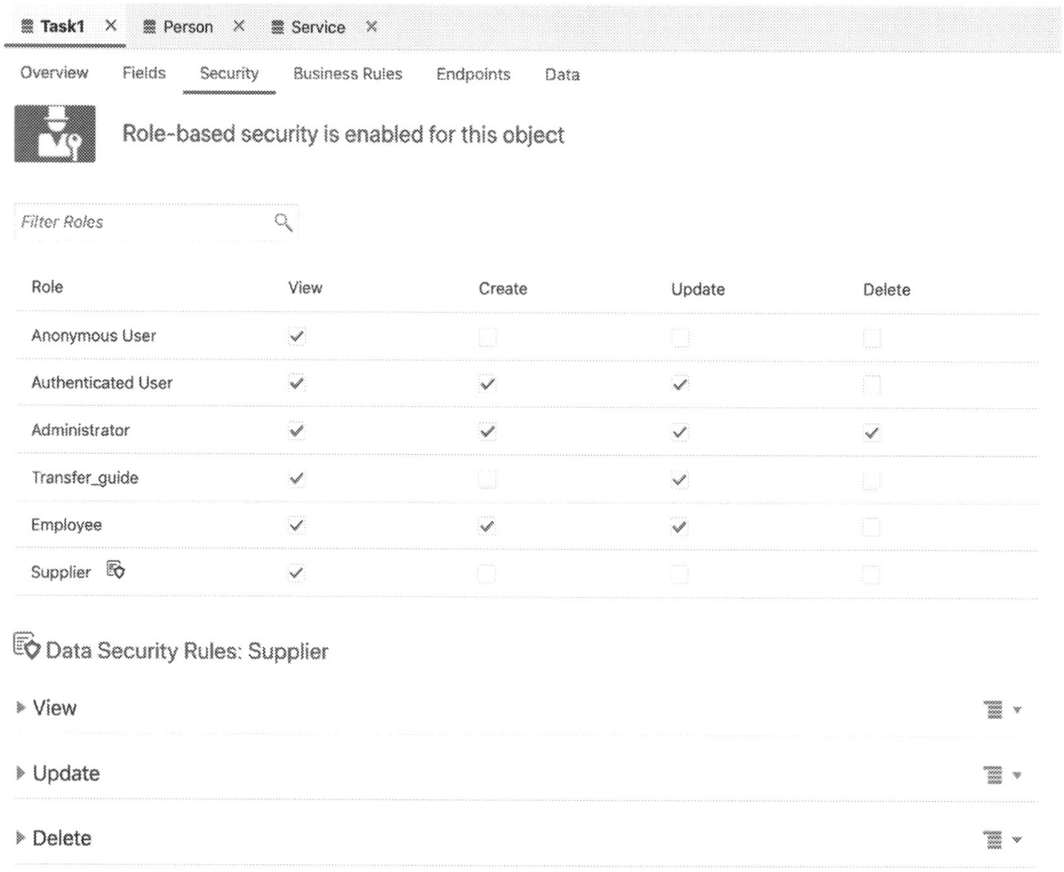

Figure 10-8. *Role-based security for a business object*

To grant a role the unconditional privilege to perform an operation, you just check the corresponding checkbox in the matrix. For example, users with the role Transfer_ guide are allowed to *view* and *update* records in the Task1 business object, but cannot *create* new records or *delete* records.

Tip   The little icon with the shield (e.g., next to Supplier in the preceding figure) indicates that detailed data security rules have been defined for that role.

For more fine-grained control, you can select a role in the table and use the lower part of this tab. The *Data Security Rules* heading changes to indicate which role is selected. For example, in Figure 10-9, the developer is defining detailed data security rules for the *Administrator* role.

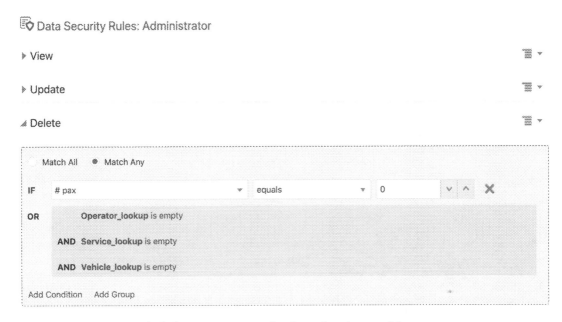

Figure 10-9. *Detailed data security rules for a business object*

Using a combination of *Match All* and *Match Any* together with individual conditions and groups of conditions, you can specify very detailed rules. For example, in Figure 10-6, users with the *Administrator* role can delete records if either the # pax field has the value zero or all of the fields `Operator_lookup`, `Service_lookup`, and `Vehicle_lookup` are empty.

Naturally, you will often want to apply similar conditions to different business objects and operations. To save time doing this, the menu to the right of each operation heading (*View, Update, Delete*) offers you the option to *Cut, Copy, Paste,* and *Clear* conditions.

One specific requirement that occurs often is to allow users only to manipulate their own records. VBCS lets you easily define this with the menu item *Allow if user created the row* on the condition menu. This is simply a shortcut for the condition

IF **Created By** equals $current_user.username

Cross-Origin Resource Sharing (CORS)

For security reasons, your REST services are by default only accessible from approved domains. If the application that needs access is not a VBCS application, it will not be in the same domain as the VBCS REST services, and your administrator has to add each domain that needs access to the *Allowed Origins* list. This is done from the *Tenant Settings* screen that is only accessible to VBCS administrators.

If you are an administrator of your VBCS instance, you will find a menu item called *Settings* on the VBCS main menu accessible from the menu icon next to the Oracle Visual Builder logo at the top left of the screen. See Figure 10-10.

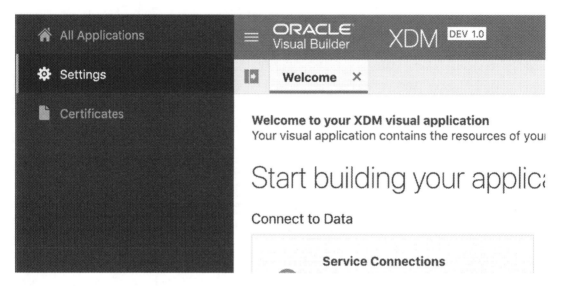

Figure 10-10.   *Accessing VBCS instance settings*

Note   If you do not see this menu item, it means you do not have administrator rights on your instance, and you will have to work with your administrator to change this setting.

Service Connection Authentication

Service connections exist outside Visual Builder Cloud Service and handle their own security. However, for services that require authentication, you need to define this in VBCS on the *Authentication* tab for each service as shown in Figure 10-11.

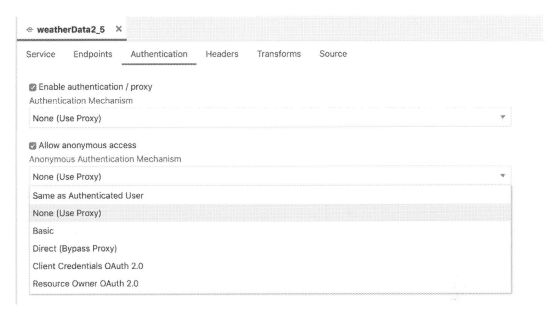

Figure 10-11. *Authentication settings for a service connection*

The *Enable authentication/proxy setting* is used to define the authentication for services when the user has logged in to the application. It has the following options:

- Propagate Current User Identity

- None (Use Proxy)

- Basic

- Direct (Bypass Proxy)

- Oracle Cloud Account

- User Assertion OAuth 2.0

- Client Credentials OAuth 2.0

Depending on your choice, more fields might appear asking you for additional information.

You only need to check these checkboxes and select an authentication mechanism if your service requires authentication or you have issues accessing services in another origin (protocol/server/port).

The option *Direct (Bypass Proxy)* is a direct call that VBCS does not process in any way. You have to provide all necessary authentication headers and so on. If the service is set up to limit where it receives requests from, you might have to work with the service provider to set up CORS.

The option *None (Use Proxy)* is a call passed through the VBCS authentication proxy. It works only for services that do not require authentication, but because the call comes from the VBCS server, it might prevent issues with same-origin policies restricting access. This is the default setting.

Basic is a simple username/password authentication and should only be used for development.

Client Credentials OAuth 2.0 can be used for OAuth services that can provide fixed values for *Client Id, Client Secret,* and *Token URL.*

The options *Propagate Current User Identity, Oracle Cloud Account,* and *User Assertion OAuth 2.0* all pass the current user identity from the application to the service. The *Oracle Cloud Account* is the best choice when your service is running somewhere else in the Oracle Cloud, for example, a web service that is part of an Oracle SaaS solution, or a web service from Integration Cloud Service or Process Cloud Service.

Tip   You might want to use a simple authentication scheme like *Basic* while developing and only change to a more secure (and possibly more cumbersome) scheme when you stage and deploy your application.

The *Allow anonymous access* setting is used to define the authentication for services for anonymous users. This is only relevant when you allow anonymous access to the application that uses the services. It has the following options:

- Same as Authenticated User

- None (Use Proxy)

- Basic

- Direct (Bypass Proxy)

- Client Credentials OAuth 2.0

- Resource Owner OAuth 2.0

The *Same as Authenticated User* option doesn't provide much value for anonymous access, because the user name will always be the string `"anonymous"`.

None (Use Proxy), Basic, Direct (Bypass Proxy), and *Client Credentials OAuth 2.0* all work as described earlier. The option *Resource Owner OAuth 2.0* is similar to *Client Credentials OAuth 2.0* but offers you the option to provide a username and password as well.

Security-Related Programming

Much of the security in Visual Builder Cloud Service application can be handled declaratively, but you might want to add programming in a few places to improve the user experience. This section describes how to disable items for unauthenticated users and how to add login and logout functionality.

Removing Unauthorized Functionality

If you have implemented detailed security restrictions in your business objects, you probably want your user interface to reflect those restrictions. If, for instance, you have created a page for creating new records, but only authenticated users can create records, anonymous users will by default see a confusing `403 Forbidden` error.

To control which user interface elements are shown, you can set the *disabled* or *hidden* properties. For example, if you want to show the button to create a record, but not allow it to be active for unauthenticated users, you can set disabled to

```
{{ !$application.user.isAuthenticated }}
```

Note the exclamation mark, indicating a "not" condition. That is, the button is disabled if the user is *not* authenticated. You can use the drop-down list above the property field to navigate to the user variable by expanding first *Application* and then *System* to see the `user` built-in variable.

If you want to hide the button altogether, you can set the *hidden* property instead.

For more sophisticated logic, you can query `$application.user.roles.<rolename>`, which will return true if the user has a specific role. You can also access the `$application.user.roles` variable, which is a string array of all the roles the current user has.

Adding Login and Logout Functionality

When you look at an application built using the default *Empty Application* template, you will notice that the shell root page contains email of the logged in user at the top right. You can click this email address to pull down a menu, showing a *Sign Out* item as shown in Figure 10-12.

Figure 10-12. *The default shell page with user email and Sign Out button*

In the current version of VBCS, this menu item is just a placeholder – it doesn't actually log the user out. However, you can add the functionality to log in and out using action chains.

If you look at the *Page Structure* window, shown in Figure 10-13, you will see that there is a *Menu Button* where the text is `$application.user.email`, and below that there is a single *Option* with the value `out`.

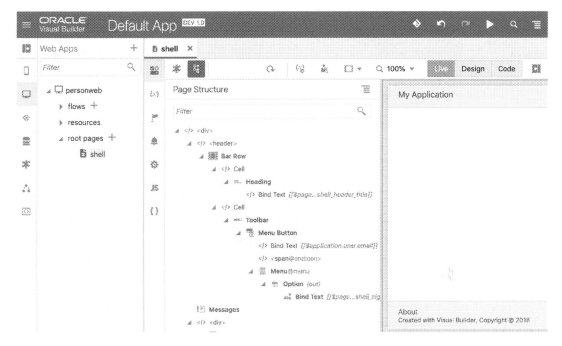

Figure 10-13. *The page structure of the default shell page*

To create real login and logout functionality, you need to add an extra option (for logging in) and to create an action chain to handle user selection from the menu.

Options are added from the *Property Inspector* when you have the *Menu* item selected. Click the + sign next to the *Slots* heading to create another *Option* and then click the corresponding Option hyperlink and set the *Value* property (e.g., to `signin`).

Then go to the *Events* tab for the *Menu* item and click + *New Event*. Use the quick start to create a new action chain as shown in Figure 10-14.

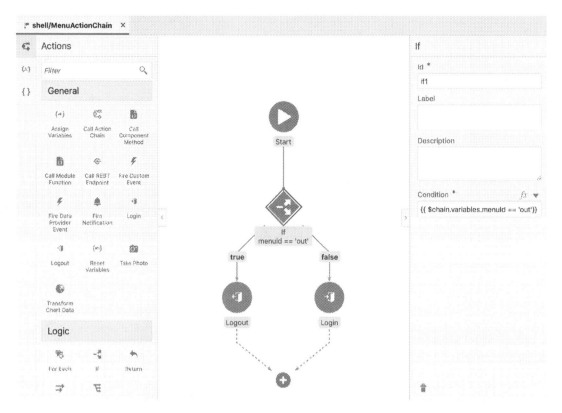

Figure 10-14. *An action chain for handling login and logout*

It has an `If` event with two branches and the condition

```
{{ $chain.variables.menuId == 'out'}}
```

If that is true (i.e., the user chose the default *Sign Out* option which has the value out), the chain takes the branch with a *Logout* action. Otherwise, the chain takes the branch with the *Login* action.

Note   The reason you can refer to `$chain.variables.menuId` for the menu selection is that the VBCS Quick Start automatically creates that variable and sets it to `$event.target.value`, that is, the value of the item that caused the triggering event. You can see this in the *Input Parameters* property for the event.

Conclusion

In this chapter, you have learned how to define user roles and set security on web applications, mobile applications, and business objects. You also saw how to define authentication for service connections to external services.

In the next chapter, we will discuss how to manage your Visual Builder Cloud Service applications.

CHAPTER 11

Managing Applications

The previous chapters have described how to build applications. Applications are the largest building blocks in Visual Builder Cloud Service, and within one VBCS instance, you can have many applications. This chapter is about how to work with and manage entire applications.

Application Overview

When you open VBCS, you start on the application overview page. This page lists all your applications and the applications where you are a team member. There is one row for each version of each application, though by default each version is collapsed to one line showing only the latest version. The number after the plus sign next to the version indicates how many other versions of the application exist. You need to expand that node to see older versions.

Note By default, you see only VBCS applications using the most recent architecture. You can click the little triangle next to the *Visual Applications* heading and change to *Classic Applications* if you have very old VBCS applications that have not been migrated.

Next to each line, you see the status and the application menu for that application version. See Figure 11-1.

© Sten Vesterli 2019
S. Vesterli, *Oracle Visual Builder Cloud Service Revealed*, https://doi.org/10.1007/978-1-4842-4929-1_11

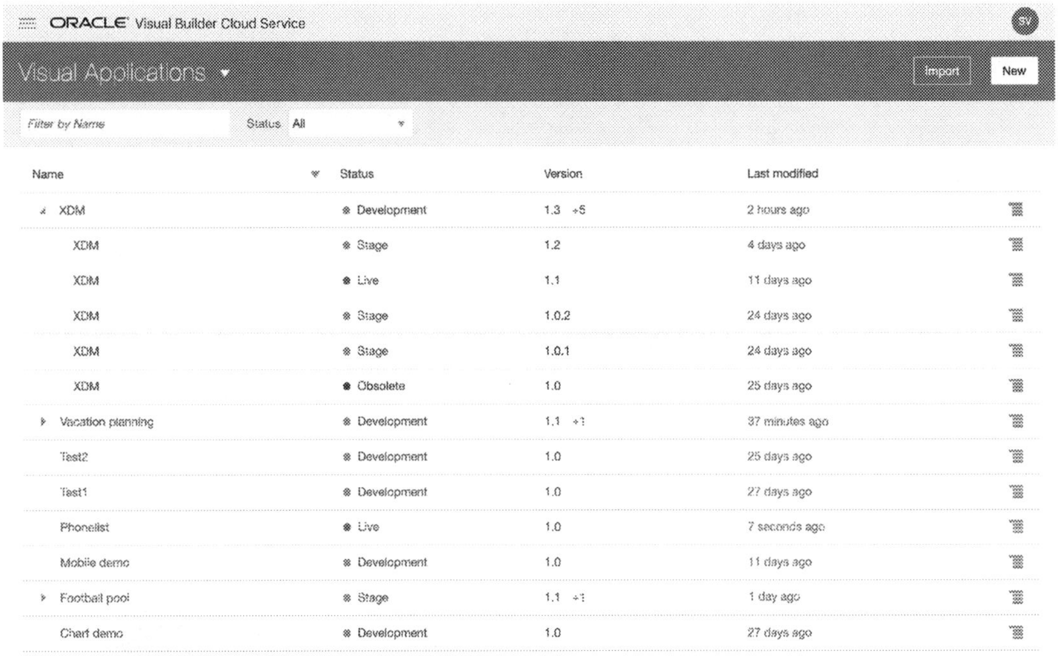

Figure 11-1. *Application overview*

The possible values for application status are

- Development

- Staging

- Live

- Live Locked

- Pending Push Request

- Obsolete

Development is the default status for new applications.

Staging is the status for applications that have been released to test.

Live indicates the version that your end users are currently working with.

Live Locked is a special status for an application that used to be live, but currently cannot be accessed. This is used for maintenance, for example, if you want to export the live database.

Pending Push Request is another specialized status. It indicates that you have asked for a staged version of the application to be deployed to another environment, but there has not been a response to the push request yet.

Obsolete is the status acquired by older versions of the application when a newer version is published. Obsolete applications are read-only.

At the far right on each application line, you find the application menu (a small icon with four horizontal lines). This is where you perform most actions on complete applications.

Creating Applications

You can create a new application from scratch by clicking *New* to open the *Create Application* dialog shown in Figure 11-2.

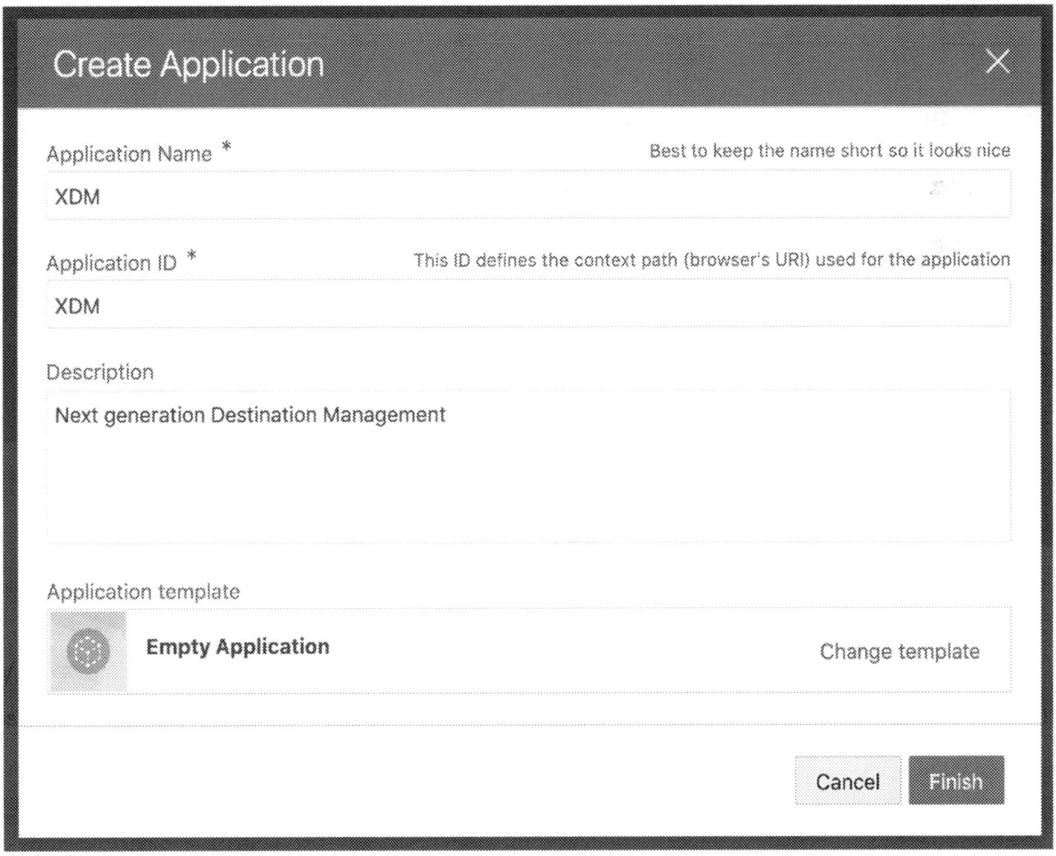

Figure 11-2. *The Create Application dialog*

Here, you provide an application name, an ID (which becomes part of the URL), and a description. If your Visual Builder Cloud Service instance is connected to a Component Exchange as described in Chapter 4, you might also see a *Change template* link in the *Application template* box. If you click this link, you will be presented with the application templates available from that exchange as shown in Figure 11-3.

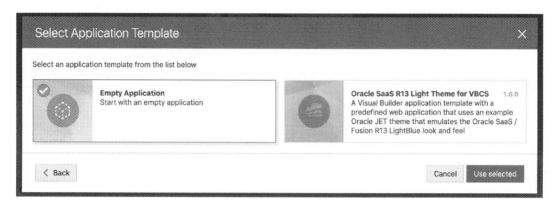

Figure 11-3. *Selecting an application template*

As a demonstration of the application template functionality, VBCS version 19.1.3 contains a template that looks like an Oracle SaaS application as shown in Figure 11-4.

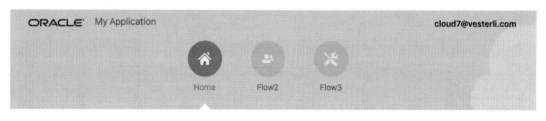

Figure 11-4. *The Oracle SaaS R13 Light Theme for VBCS*

This template contains three flows with basic navigation plus styling to look like the most recent Oracle SaaS applications and will be useful if you are building Oracle SaaS extensions with VBCS.

If you already have an application that does something similar to what you want your new application to do, you can also copy an existing application version by selecting *Duplicate* from the application menu for that version. Irrespective of the version of the application you copy from, your duplicate always starts from the beginning with a version 1.0.

Duplicating an application creates a copy of everything – business objects and service connections as well as web and mobile applications. It usually is not cost-effective to try to connect a copy of an existing application to a new data source – there are many moving parts that have to be changed in exactly the right way to connect to new business objects or service connections. However, it can save you time to copy an application and reuse the business objects even if you are not reusing any part of the user interface.

If you are continuing development on an existing application, you choose *New Version* from the application menu for an existing version. By default, VBCS will suggest you a version number in major-minor-patch `x.y.z` format, incremented by one on the last part (the `z`). Depending on the magnitude of the change you are planning to implement, you might decide to change the major or minor version.

Tip   It is recommended to follow the rules of semantic versioning for your VBCS application. See `https://semver.org/`.

Exporting and Importing Applications

Your Visual Builder Cloud Service applications live in the VBCS instance where you create them. If you want to keep a local backup copy or you want to move your application to another VBCS instance, you can *export* them. To take an export file and place it into the same or a different VBCS instance, you use the *import* function.

Exporting a VBCS Application

To export an application, you choose *Export* from the application menu. You are given a choice to export the application with or without data. When you click one of the choices, a ZIP file is downloaded to your browser download directory. This file contains your application (and data if you asked for that). If you unpack it, you find the following directories:

- webApps
- settings
- services
- process
- mobileApps
- emailTemplates
- businessObjects

Inside the `businessObjects` directory, there is a subdirectory for each business object in your application. If you did not export data, there is just an `entity.json` file defining the structure of your business object. If you have defined business rules for the object, there will also be a `businessrules.json` file. If you decided to export data, the directory for the business object also contains an `entity-data.csv` file with your data.

Note   Credentials for external services are not exported. If you are using external REST services, you will have to reenter the credentials when you import the application.

You can also export an application from within the application itself. While you are working on an application, the application menu is displayed at the far right of the VBCS menu bar as shown in Figure 11-5.

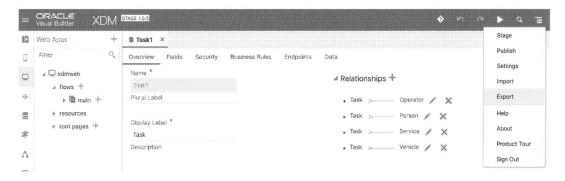

Figure 11-5. *The application menu inside an application*

Importing a VBCS Application

To import an application into a VBCS instance, you use the *Import* button in the toolbar above all the existing applications (next to the *New* button).

Note   There is also an *Import* item on the application menu, both inside the application and on the application overview. That function imports resources (e.g., images) into an existing application. To import a whole application, you need to use the import button on the overview screen.

You are given a choice between importing an application from GIT version control or from an export file. See Figure 11-6.

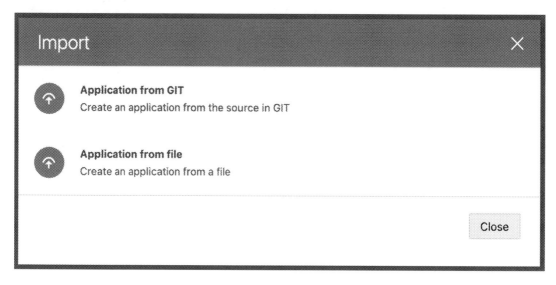

Figure 11-6. *Importing a VBCS application*

In this chapter, we'll discuss importing from a file. The next chapter on enterprise development with VBCS will cover working with GIT version control as part of your VBCS application development workflow.

When you select to import from a file, the *Import Application from File* dialog opens. Here, you can drag and drop your export file or click the *Upload a file* field and select it. The default value for the application name and ID will be the name of the file, but you don't have to reuse the application name. Of course, the ID cannot be the same as any existing application in the VBCS instance you are importing into. When you click *Import*, the application file is imported as a new application. It starts with status *Development* and version 1.0 just like an application created from scratch.

You can also import an application from the application menu inside an existing application.

Importing a VBCS Classic Application

If you have an export file containing an old VBCS application (known as a "VBCS Classic" application), you can import the business objects from it.

Because of the many changes to the user interface layer, it is not possible to convert web or mobile applications in a VBCS Classic application to the modern VBCS style. If you try to import a VBCS Classic application, you are also given a warning that only business objects and data will be imported.

Staging and Publishing

A Visual Builder Cloud Service instance actually includes three complete environments, corresponding to the typical DEV-TEST-PROD flow. In VBCS, the test environment is called *Staging*, and the production environment is called *Live*.

Staging an Application

When you are ready to release a version of your application to test, you move it to the staging environment by selecting *Stage* from the application menu, either on the application overview screen or from the application menu inside the application.

You will be presented with a choice of whether to include a copy of your development data into the staging environment as shown in Figure 11-7.

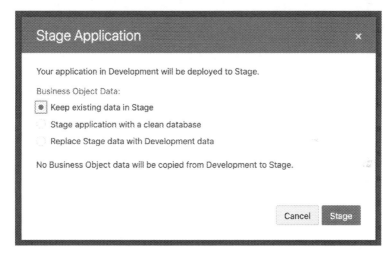

Figure 11-7. *Staging an application*

The first time you stage an application, you are only presented with the last two options because there is no existing data to keep. If your application does not contain any business components, the dialog does not contain any choices but just the *Stage* button.

When you click the *Stage* button, your application is copied into the staging environment.

Note   If you have created a mobile application in your VBCS application and haven't created at least one build configuration or configured the application as a Progressive Web App (PWA), staging will fail. If your application contains a mobile app, you must create a mobile build configuration or configure PWA as described in Chapter 9.

You are returned to the application overview screen, where you can see your application now has status *Stage*. You can click the word *Stage* to see a popup listing all the web and mobile applications inside the staged VBCS application as shown in Figure 11-8.

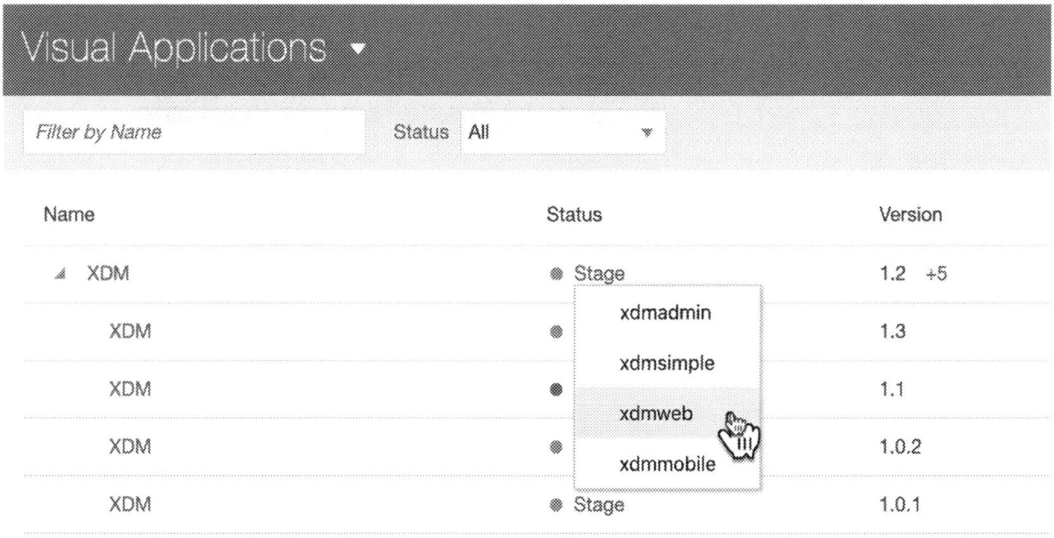

Figure 11-8. *The URLs to staged applications*

You can click each application to open it in a new tab. For web applications, you are taken to the running staged application, and you can copy the URL from the browser and give it to the people who will be testing your application. If you click a mobile application, you will be taken to the simulated mobile run environment inside VBCS. From here, you can click *Build my App* to produce the QR code that your testers will need to install the mobile app on their devices.

Caution   There is nothing that prevents you from continuing to work on an application that has been staged. However, the purpose of staging an application is to release it to test, so you should stop working on it once you have given the URL of the staged application to your testers. Create a new version as described earlier in this chapter to continue development.

Publishing an Application

When you are ready to release your application to your end users, you move it to the production environment by selecting *Publish* from the application menu, either on the application overview screen or from the application menu inside the application. The *Publish* option is only available for applications that have status *Stage*.

You are presented with a dialog box similar to when you stage an application, asking you if you want to copy data from the staging environment to the live production environment.

If you already have data in your production environment and select to copy from staging or to deploy with a clean database, you will have to check a checkbox confirming you understand that existing live data will be lost.

When you click the *Publish* button, your application (and data if you requested it) is copied to the production environment.

You are returned to the application overview screen, where you can see your application now has status *Live*. You can click the word *Live* to see a popup listing all the web and mobile applications inside the live VBCS application. To get the URL for the live application that you are going to distribute to your end users, click the web application to open it in a new tab, and copy the URL from the browser.

To build the live version of a mobile application, you will first need to run it in the simulated mobile run environment and click *Build my App*. When your application is built, you can download the iOS `.ipa` file or the Android `.apk` file and submit it to the relevant app store using the standard procedure for publishing mobile apps.

Note   A published application is locked and cannot be changed. If you open it, you will see that the *Design* button on pages is grayed out, and you can only run the application in *Live* mode. In other places in the development environment (e.g., in the business objects), you can attempt to make changes, but you will immediately receive an error message saying your changes could not be saved.

A published application is also cached in the web browser of your users. Because the HTML, JavaScript, and other resources that make up the application cannot be changed, there is no reason for the browser to access the server for anything other than data retrieval and manipulation REST calls.

When you publish a VBCS application the second time, the previous version changes to status *Obsolete*. You can no longer run it from the application overview page, but you can still open it and run it from within the development environment if you need to test how something worked in the old version.

Locking an Application

To temporarily restrict access to a *Live* application, for example, because you are migrating data, you can *Lock* it. This can only be done from the application menu on the overview screen, not from the menu inside the application. If you also click *Lock* in the confirmation dialog, your application changes status to *Live Locked*.

Note   Locking an application does not activate any previous version of the application. If previous versions of the application were live, these remain in status *Obsolete*.

If users try to access the application while it is locked, they will be shown the *Application Locked* screen in Figure 11-9.

Application Locked

This application is temporarily locked for maintenance, please try again later.

Figure 11-9. *The Application Locked screen*

You unlock the application by selecting *Unlock* on the application menu on the application overview screen. After clicking *Unlock* again in the confirmation dialog, your application is unlocked.

Deleting an Application

If you want to remove an application version completely, you can choose *Delete* from the application menu on the overview screen. After clicking *Delete* in the confirmation dialog, that version of the application is irrevocably removed together with all its data. Deleting one version of an application does not affect other versions of the application.

Note   Deleting the latest *Live* version of an application does not activate any earlier version of the application. Old versions that were made obsolete by a new version remain *Obsolete*.

Application Settings

The application menu from both the overview and inside an application gives you access to the application *Settings* shown in Figure 11-10.

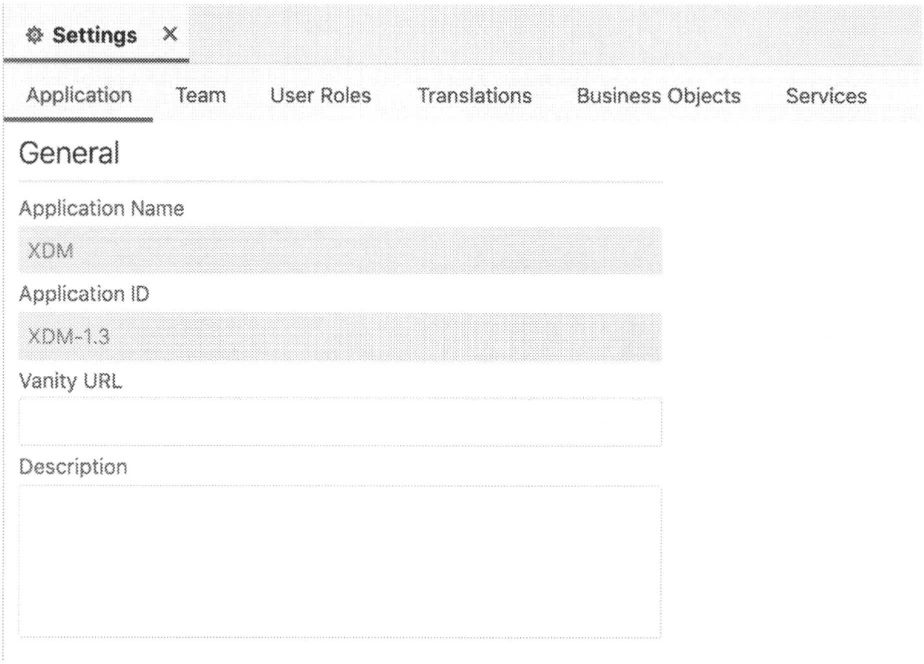

Figure 11-10. *Application Settings*

Vanity URL

On the *Application* tab, you can define a nice-looking ("vanity") URL for your application. This is not a trivial task and will involve the developer, your own DNS management, and Oracle.

If you have decided that your application should be live at `https://timereporting.company.com`, you need to enter this URL in the *Vanity URL* field.

You then need to work with the person or team who manages the DNS records for `www.company.com` and create a new CNAME record pointing the vanity URL to the IP number of your instance.

Finally, you need to open a Service Request with Oracle to allow the Oracle DevOps team to configure your VBCS environment to respond to requests for the vanity URL.

Other Settings

On the *Team* tab, you can give other developers access to work with the application.

The settings on the *User Roles* and *Business Objects* tabs relate to application security and were discussed in Chapter 10.

The *Services* tab is used to configure access to integrations and an Oracle SaaS service catalog and was discussed in Chapter 3.

The *Translations* tab allows you to manage the user interface strings of the application. You can download these strings in several formats, have them translated, and upload translated resource bundles to make your application multilingual. This is outside the scope of this book, but you can find examples of how to do this on Oracle blogs.

Conclusion

In this chapter, you learned how to manage applications, including the transitions from development to test (staging) and production (live). You also learned about other application status options and how to import and export applications.

In the next chapter, we will discuss the workflow for enterprise application development with VBCS.

CHAPTER 12

Enterprise Development with VBCS

If you've been reading this book from the beginning, by now you have learned how to use all the building blocks of Visual Builder Cloud Service. This chapter is about some of the tasks and procedures that make you and your team more productive with VBCS.

Team Work

Much VBCS development happens as an individual effort. By default, only the person who creates an application can work on it.

If you want to involve others in building your VBCS application, you can include them in your development team. This is done from the Application settings screen on the Team tab. Here you can see which users are currently part of the team, and add other users as shown in Figure 12-1.

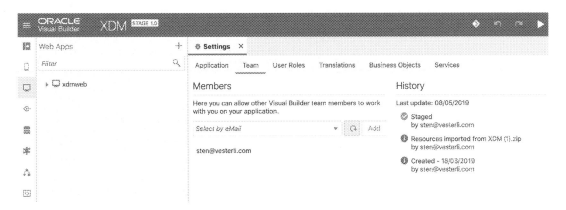

Figure 12-1. *Adding people to your team*

© Sten Vesterli 2019
S. Vesterli, *Oracle Visual Builder Cloud Service Revealed*, https://doi.org/10.1007/978-1-4842-4929-1_12

237

The drop-down list shows all users who have access to your Visual Builder Cloud Service instance, but you can also just start typing the email address of the developer you want to add.

Setting Up Developer Cloud Service

If you want more powerful versioning than the simple one-user versioning built into Visual Builder Cloud Service, you can use the Git repository that is part of Oracle Developer Cloud Service (DevCS). This service is a free add-on for all users who have an account using Oracle's PaaS or IaaS services. It comes with 20GB of storage, which is enough for a lot of VBCS applications. If you want more storage, or you want to use DevCS functionality to build your code, you will need to buy storage or computing resources in the Oracle cloud.

You access DevCS from your *Oracle Cloud My Services* dashboard. You worked with this dashboard in Chapter 1 when you set up your VBCS instance, and you similarly have to set up a Developer Cloud Service instance.

To do that, you click *Create Instance*, choose the *All Services* tab, and scroll down to the *Developer* item (not *Developer Classic*) and click *Create*. See Figure 12-2.

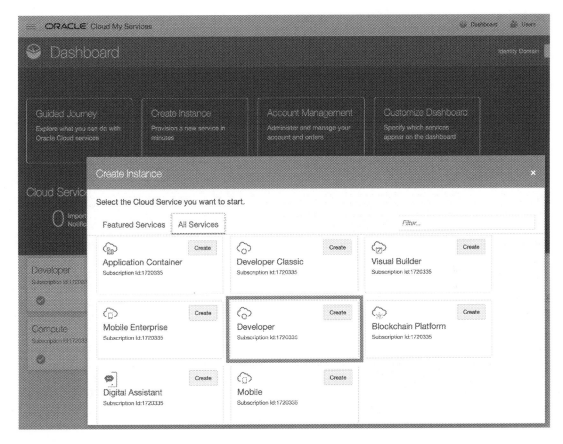

Figure 12-2. *Creating a Developer Cloud Service instance*

You will be taken to the Developer Cloud Service instance overview, where you can click *Create Instance*.

Note   You can only have one Developer Cloud Service instance (but you can have any number of projects inside that instance). If you already have a service, simply click *Access Service Instance* from the application menu to the right of the instance name.

You provide a name for your instance and an email account to receive notifications and select a region. Select the one closest to you for best performance. When you click *Create,* the Oracle cloud starts provisioning your service. This is faster than creating a VBCS instance and should only take a few minutes.

Once your instance is created, you can choose *Access Service Instance* from the application menu to the right of the instance name. This will take you to the Developer Cloud Service home page. You will probably see a message *"You must configure Compute & Storage before your projects will be fully functional."* If you intend to use the build capabilities of Developer Cloud Service, you must configure an Oracle Compute Infrastructure (OCI) connection in order to have compute resources available. If you just want to use basic DevCS functionality like the Git repository, issue tracking, Wiki, and so on, you don't have to create an OCI connection and can dismiss this message.

Developer Cloud Service is very insistent that you create an OCI connection. The message will reappear often when you work with DevCS. If you decide to establish the OCI connection, click the *OCI Credentials* link in the message and fill in the dialog box. Note the *Help me find this information* link to the right, which will take you to the relevant documentation.

Creating a DevCS Project

Inside Developer Cloud Service, you can have any number of projects. For VBCS development, you should have one DevCS project for each VBCS application.

Click *Create* and go through the wizard. In step 2, you should select *Initial Repository* as shown in Figure 12-3.

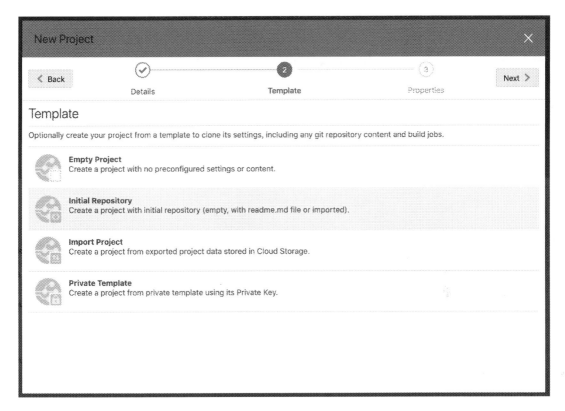

Figure 12-3. Creating an initial repository in a new project

In step 3, you should choose *Initialize repository with README file* and click *Finish.*

You will see the "Project is being provisioned" message for a few minutes as DevCS sets up all the different features it offers. Then you will be returned to the project home page.

Note   This book only describes the DevCS Git repository and how to use that together with VBCS. Developer Cloud Service has many other features that can be relevant to your projects. Refer to the documentation to learn more about Developer Cloud Service (https://docs.oracle.com/en/cloud/paas/developer-cloud/index.html).

On the project home page, the right-hand box contains three tabs *Repositories*, *Statistics*, and *Team*. Select the *Team* tab and add the other developers that are part of your team. They must already be Oracle Cloud users and have been granted the role DEVELOPER_USER (Developer Service User) on the specific Developer Cloud Service instance you use.

Note   You have to add your team members here if you want to be able to use enterprise development functions like code review (merge requests).

Getting the Connection Information

Once you have created a project with a repository, you need to gather the information you need to connect VBCS to that repository. The elements you are looking for are the URL of your developer cloud instance and the URL to the Git repository in the project inside that instance.

In Developer Cloud Service, choose the *Git* tab. The header shows the current project as shown in Figure 12-4.

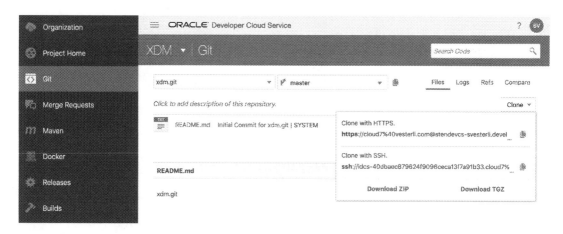

Figure 12-4. *The Git tab in Developer Cloud Service*

If the right project is not selected, click the triangle next to the project name and select the right one.

Then choose the *Clone* drop-down to the right and click the copy icon next to the `https://` line. This copies the entire URL of your project repository to the clipboard. It will look something like this:

`https://sten%40vesterli.com@stendevcs-svesterli.developer.ocp.oraclecloud.com/stendevcs-svesterli/s/stendevcs-svesterli_xdm_2383/scm/xdm.git`

From this, you can extract both the URL of your developer cloud and the Git URL you need in VBCS.

- The Developer Cloud Service URL is the part after the @ and up to the second following slash. For the preceding URL, the DevCS URL is `https://stendevcs-svesterli.developer.ocp.oraclecloud.com/stendevcs-svesterli`.

- The repository URL you need in VBCS is the whole URL but without the username at the start. That is, you want everything after the @. For the preceding URL, the Git URL is `https://stendevcs-svesterli.developer.ocp.oraclecloud.com/stendevcs-svesterli/s/stendevcs-svesterli_xdm_2383/scm/xdm.git`.

Connecting VBCS to DevCS

Armed with these URLs, you can now connect Visual Builder Cloud Service to Developer Cloud Service. You do this from the Git menu (the leftmost of the icons to the right in the VBCS main menu), as shown in Figure 12-5.

Figure 12-5. *The Git menu in VBCS*

The first step is to connect VBCS to DevCS using the menu item *Configure DevCS Credentials*. This brings up a dialog box where you can click *Add Credentials* and enter your DevCS URL and the username and password you use to log in to DevCS. See Figure 12-6.

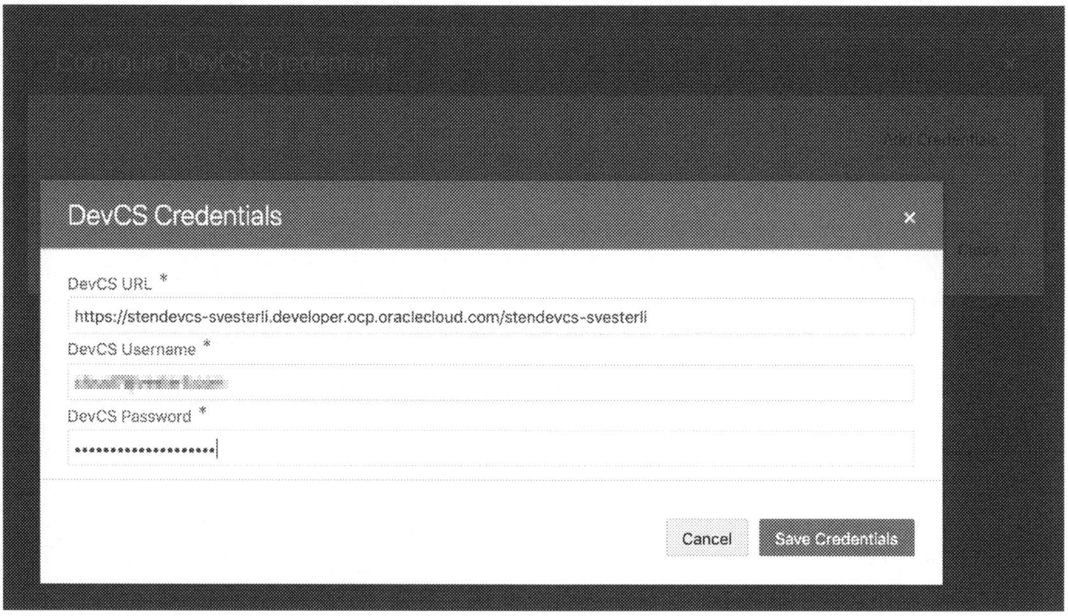

Figure 12-6. Entering DevCS credentials

When you have saved your DevCS credentials, the next step is to link your VBCS project to a specific Git repository in the DevCS instance. To do this, you use the *Link DevCS GIT Repository* menu item. While your application is not linked, you will be shown a dialog box with a message "Your Application is not linked with a Developer Cloud Service Repository." Click the *Add Link* button in this box to bring up the *Link DevCS GIT Repository* dialog shown in Figure 12-7.

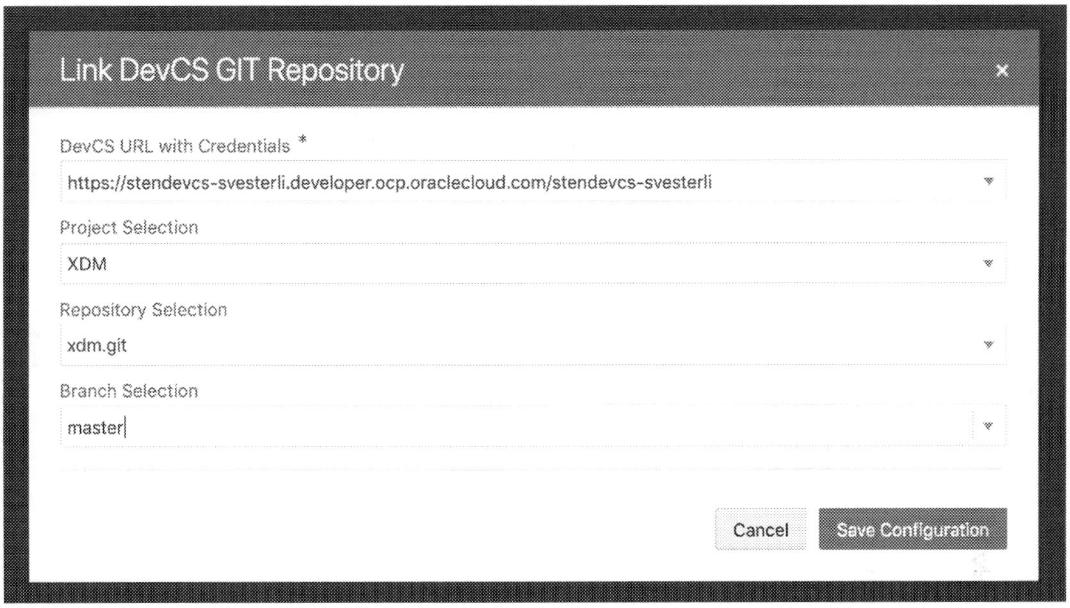

Figure 12-7. *Linking a VBCS application to a DevCS repository*

First select your DevCS instance from the *DevCS URL with Credentials* drop-down list. Then select a project in that instance, select a repository in that project, and finally select a branch. Initially, you will only have a `master` branch. When you have saved the configuration and closed the dialog box, you are ready to start working with Git version control in your application.

Working with Git in VBCS

When you work with Git, the repository in DevCS becomes your source of truth. The application code in VBCS should be considered a temporary working copy, and the code version in Git is the true version.

Caution   Your *data* is not stored in Git. If your VBCS application contains business objects, the data from these are *not* stored in DevCS.

Saving Changes

To save changes to your code in the DevCS Git repository, use *Push to Git* from the *Git* menu. You will be prompted for a mandatory message to go together with this version of the code. When you click *Push to Git* in the dialog, your code changes are sent to the DevCS Git repository. The dialog box provides some logging of what has happened as shown in Figure 12-8.

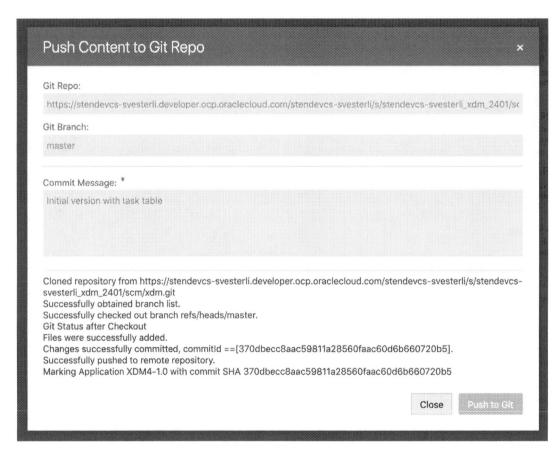

Figure 12-8. *Pushing changes to the DevCS Git repository*

Look for a Successfully pushed to remote repository message near the bottom of the Git repository interaction log for confirmation that your code was successfully pushed to Git.

Checking Status

When you have worked with your application in VBCS, you can always compare your VBCS environment with what is stored in the DevCS Git repository by selecting *Git Status* from the Git menu and then clicking *Retrieve Git Status* in the dialog box that appears. VBCS communicates with Git and shows you what has been added, changed, or deleted as shown in Figure 12-9.

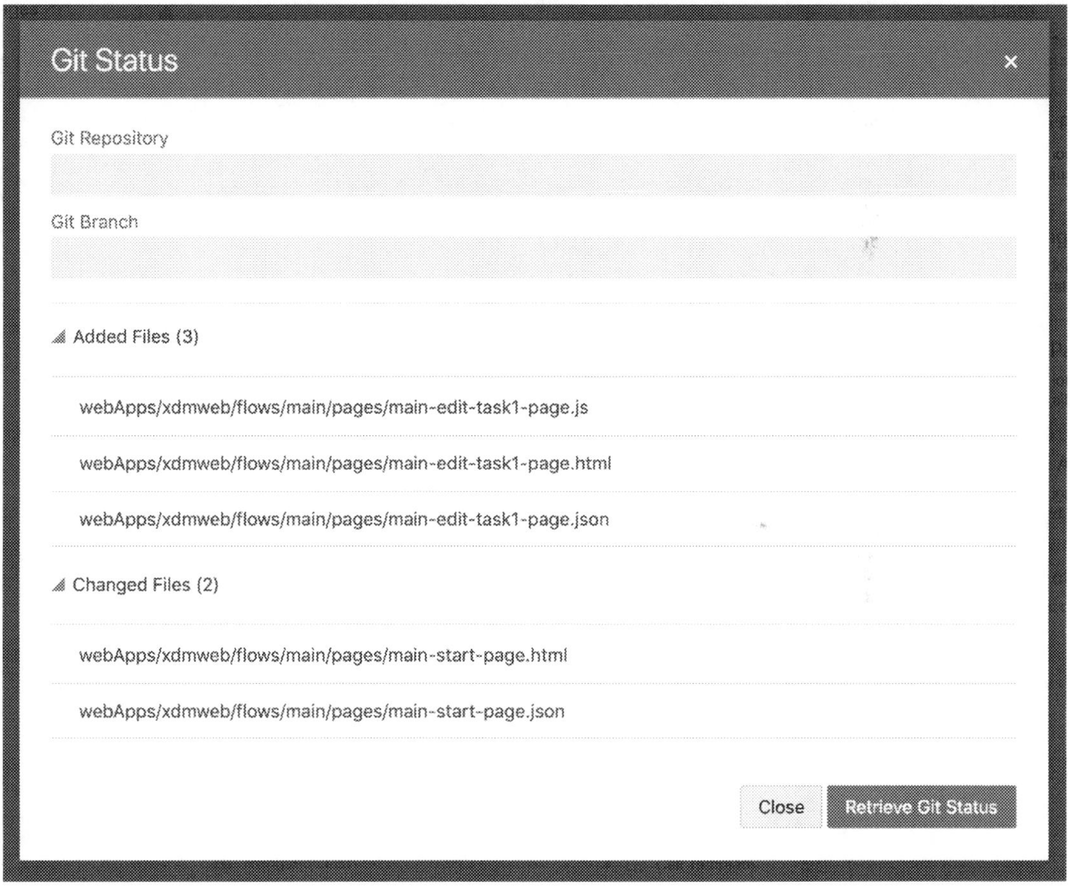

Figure 12-9. *Showing Git status*

Comparing Code

If you want to see the difference between your local code and the code in Git, you can choose *Git Diff* and click *Retrieve Diff* in the dialog box that appears. This will retrieve a detailed, line-by-line comparison between VBCS and Git as shown in Figure 12-10.

Figure 12-10. *Showing Git differences*

Getting Changes

You can also retrieve changes made in the Git repository that are not in your VBCS environment yet by choosing *Pull from Git* and then *Update From Git* in the dialog that appears. This can be used to retrieve an existing application in a new VBCS environment or to get updates made and pushed by another developer.

Dropping All Changes

If you should decide that you want to discard all changes since the last time you saved changes to Git, you can use the *Reset to HEAD* command from the Git menu. This resets your code to the state it has in Git, discarding any changes made in VBCS since last push.

Working with Git in DevCS

Developer Cloud Service of course also provides you a view into your code. As you can see in Figure 12-11, the Source view in VBCS shows you the exact files that make up your application, and that structure is reproduced on the Git tab for the project in DevCS.

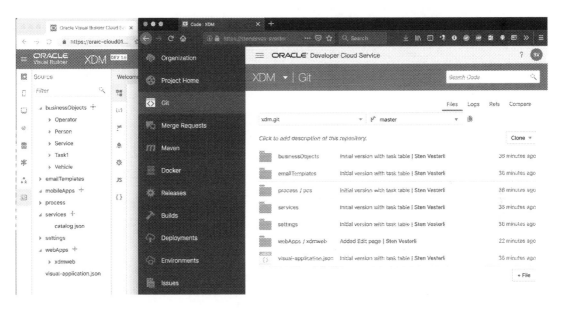

Figure 12-11. *Source view in VBCS and Git view in DevCS*

You can search your code in both VBCS and DevCS, but the DevCS search has the advantage that it includes the entire code of your application. For example, Figure 12-12 shows the result of searching for the string "My Application" that appears in a default application.

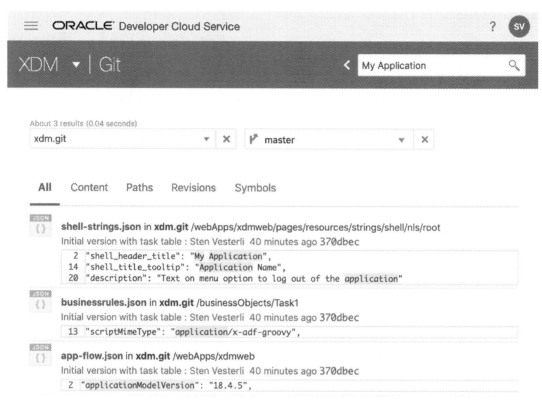

Figure 12-12. *Developer Cloud Service code search*

You can click the files DevCS has found and even make small changes to them directly from Developer Cloud Service. If you do edit the file, you will have to do *Pull from Git* in VBCS to see the change reflected in your VBCS application.

Note   In the version of VBCS current at the time of writing (19.1.3), the commands *Git Status* and *Git Diff* sometimes do not detect a change made through DevCS. However, a *Pull from Git* will always update your VBCS code.

Developer Cloud Service has many other useful functions and can show you a complete history of changes to files, compare versions, and much more. Refer to the Developer Cloud Service documentation for more information (https://docs.oracle.com/en/cloud/paas/developer-cloud/index.html).

Enterprise Development Workflow

Visual Builder Cloud Service makes a good effort to allow a small team to work together on the same application. If one developer makes a change, it is normally automatically propagated to the browsers of other developers, even without the other developer refreshing the browser. The version control capabilities also help ensure that VBCS is easy to work with.

However, for larger teams and in organizations with more formal requirements, this might not be sufficient. Fortunately, Visual Builder Cloud Service and Developer Cloud Service together can be used to implement an enterprise development workflow.

This section contains my recommendation for how to work with VBCS and DevCS together, but using the power of both tools, many other workflows are possible.

Setting Up an Enterprise Project

When you want to work with your project in both Visual Builder Cloud Service and Developer Cloud Service, you need to set up the project in both services.

Setting Up the DevCS Project

In DevCS, you create the project from the *Organization* tab as described earlier in this chapter.

If you want to manage your tasks and defects in DevCS, you can create them on the *Issue* tab. When you click + *Create Issue*, you are given a choice between the five issue types DevCS recognizes:

- Defect

- Epic

- Feature

- Story

- Task

You can choose to handle all work simply as Tasks, but DevCS also supports establishing a hierarchy of issues. Once an issue is created, you can open it and click + *Create Sub-issue* to create a new issue subordinate to the open one.

In a larger project, you will probably start with some *Epics* and break them down into *Features* and *Stories*. Some agile developers argue that features are part of stories, and some say stories are part of features – Developer Cloud Service allows you to have it either way. The hierarchy has a maximum depth of three levels, so you can choose *Epic* ➤ *Feature* ➤ *Story, Story* ➤ *Feature* ➤ *Task,* or many other combinations.

Setting Up the VBCS Project

In Visual Builder Cloud Service, you initially create a *master* project. Establish a naming convention, for example, `<project>_master`. Open this application and link it to the master branch of the DevCS project as described earlier in this chapter.

Caution   Visual Builder Cloud Service doesn't support simply switching development branches as other tools do. While it is possible to relink a VBCS project to another Git branch, this can lead to unpredictable behavior. Use a separate VBCS project for each branch.

Working on Features

A good enterprise workflow when you have access to a modern version control system like Git is to perform all development work on *feature branches*. You create a new branch for all work on the feature, allowing the developers working on that feature to finish it without unnecessary dependencies on other features. This also makes it possible to keep a master branch that only contains the code that is deliverable at any given time.

Developer Cloud Service presents you with an overview of all changes to the Git repository on the *Logs* tab. This tab can show both a list and a visual representation of the branches as merges as shown in Figure 12-13.

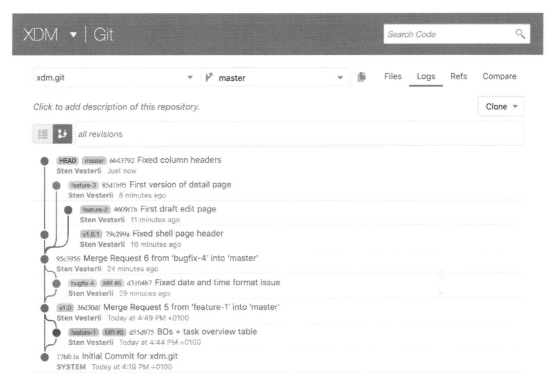

Figure 12-13. *Git branches and merges*

Creating a Feature Branch

When working with DevCS and VBCS, you create your feature branches in DevCS on the Git tab. The + *Create Branch* button is found on the *Refs* tab as shown in Figure 12-14.

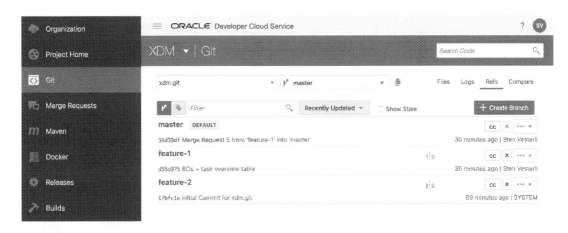

Figure 12-14. *Creating a new branch*

In the *New Branch* dialog, you select the base you want to create the branch from. VBCS projects tend to be simple enough that you can create all your feature branches from `master`, but in larger projects, you might have many "root" branches like `master`, `development`, or `test` to base new branches on.

Developing the Feature

When you have created the feature branch, you then create a new VBCS app for development of that feature. Again, you need to establish a naming convention, for example, `<project>_<branch>`. Open this application and link it to the relevant feature branch in DevCS.

Then perform a *Pull from Git* operation from the Git menu to pull the branch code from the DevCS Git repository into your new VBCS application.

This application will contain whatever features were already built, tested, and integrated because it branches off the `master` branch. You develop the new feature on this branch, and because you have your own branch, you are free to run the *Push to Git* command from the Git menu whenever you want.

Merging New Development from Master

Sometimes, work on a feature is affected by changes made in other features. In this case, you can use the merge request functionality described later to merge the master branch into the feature branch. You should only merge finished features from `master` into your feature branch – do not merge from one feature branch into another unless you want to truly combine the branches.

Reviewing and Integrating Features

When the developer or developers in charge of a feature say they are done and that the new code has been pushed to Developer Cloud Service, it is time to review and *merge* the new feature into the master application.

Requesting a Code Review

When new code is delivered to be included in an enterprise application on the `master` branch, it must first be reviewed. The functionality for handling this review is called a *Merge Request* in Developer Cloud Service.

To ask for a code review and merge, you open a merge request from the Merge Requests tab in DevCS by clicking + *Merge Request*. The New Merge Request wizard appears as shown in Figure 12-15.

Figure 12-15. *The New Merge Request wizard*

In the first step, you select a *Repository*, the *Target Branch* (normally master), and the *Review Branch* (the feature branch containing the new feature).

In the second step, you start typing the name of your issue in the *Linked Issues* field. DevCS will automatically search the issue in your project. Select the issue or issues that this feature branch addresses. You must also select one or more users that you want to review the code.

Note   You can only see and select the users that have explicitly been added to your team from the *Team* tab on the project home page as described earlier in this chapter.

In the third step, DevCS has automatically filled in a description based on the issues you selected in the second step. You can edit this text if you like, and then click *Create*.

Performing a Code Review

The person or persons you assigned the merge request to will see it on the *Merge Requests* tab in DevCS as shown in Figure 12-16.

Figure 12-16. *Merge request overview*

The reviewer can click each merge request to see the merge request details in Figure 12-17.

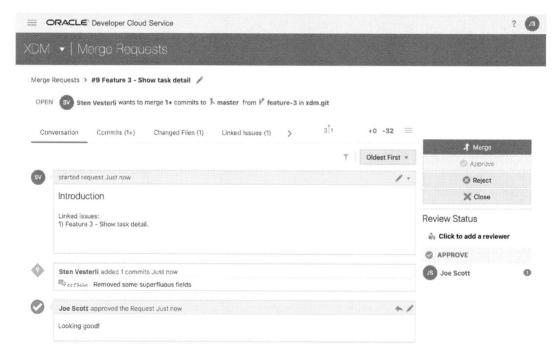

Figure 12-17. *Merge request details*

On the *Conversation* tab on this screen, the reviewer can provide comments to the developer, and the developer can respond. The *Commits* tab shows which commits this merge request applies to, the *Changed Files* tab shows all the file changes in detail, and the *Linked Issues* tab shows the issues that this merge request addresses.

When the reviewer is satisfied, she can click *Approve* (or *Reject*) to indicate that the review is complete. If the review was approved, the reviewer (or potentially a separate release manager) then clicks *Merge* to initiate the merge into the `master` branch. The *Merge* dialog appears as shown in Figure 12-18.

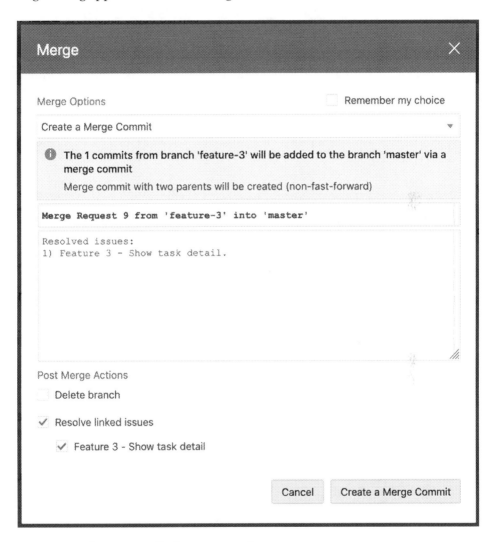

Figure 12-18. *The Merge dialog to complete a merge request*

You will normally leave *Merge Options* at *Create a Merge Commit*. This means that the reviewed feature branch is merged into the master branch and committed. DevCS suggests a default commit message ("Resolved issues: ...") that you can edit if you like. When you click *Create a Merge Commit*, the merge is completed, and the work on the feature branch is now part of the master application.

Publishing the Application

Your *release manager* is the person who decides when to release a new version of your application to test (and production). After each successful merge to the master branch, you could conceivably release the application, but that might be too often for the people in your organization tasked with testing it.

To keep your VBCS version and the code in Git aligned, you can use Git *tags*. The tag applies to a specific commit, so you add the tag right after the last merge commit that goes into the release.

When the release manager decides to release a version, he creates a new tag on the *Git* tab in Developer Cloud Service. This is done on the *Refs* sub-tab by selecting the *Tag* icon to the left as shown in Figure 12-19.

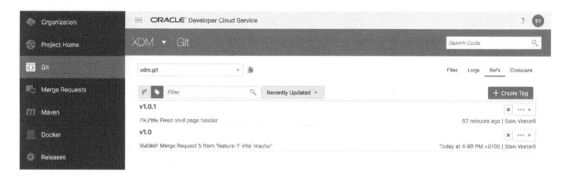

Figure 12-19. *Creating a tag*

Clicking + *Create Tag* opens the *New Tag* dialog. Here, you should provide a tag name in vX.Y format, for example, v1.1 and base the tag on the master branch.

Tip   Use version numbers in vX.Y format for new functionality and version numbers in vX.Y.Z format for bug fixes.

In the VBCS master application, you should now create a new version with the same version number as the version tag. Use *Link DevCS GIT Repository* from the Git menu to connect the new version to the master branch of your repository. Then do a *Pull from Git* operation from the Git menu to update it with the new functionality. Then use normal VBCS functionality to immediately *Stage* it and give the URL to the people charged with testing your application. When your test is completed satisfactorily, you can *Publish* the application version.

Handling Test Failures

In case the testing discovers something that must be fixed, you can either fix it in place or create a bugfix branch.

Simple errors like spelling errors or wrong labels for fields, menus, and buttons can be fixed in place.

Caution   Make sure you fix such errors only in the master branch. If you make changes to the same parts of the same file in both the master branch and a feature branch, you might get a *merge conflict* as described later in this section.

Simply make the change in the master VBCS application and push it to Git with a message indicating which issue it fixes. If you have logged the issue in DevCS, also mark it resolved there.

Tip   If your commit message contains the words `feature`, `defect`, or `task` followed by a number, DevCS considers that a link to a specific issue. If you have, for example, `defect 36` on your issue list, using a commit message like "`fixed defect 36`" will create a link from the commit on the *Logs* sub-tab on the *Git* tab in DevCS to the specific issue. You can then just click the link to go to the issue and change the status as needed.

If the necessary change is not trivial, create a new bugfix branch from `master` to implement the correction and follow the normal enterprise development workflow:

1. Create a VBCS application named after the bugfix branch, connect it to Git bugfix branch, and pull the code.

2. Fix the bug.

3. Go through the merge request workflow.

4. When the bugfix is merged into the master branch, create a new tag (in `vX.Y.Z` format) in DevCS.

5. Create a new version of your VBCS application matching the DevCS tag, link it to the Git repository, pull the code, and *Stage* the application for renewed test.

Merge Conflicts

If you have made changes to the same part of the same file in two branches, and Git can't figure out how to merge them, you will see that the Merge Request detail window doesn't allow you to perform the merge. Instead of a Merge button, you have a Show Merge Conflicts button as shown in Figure 12-20.

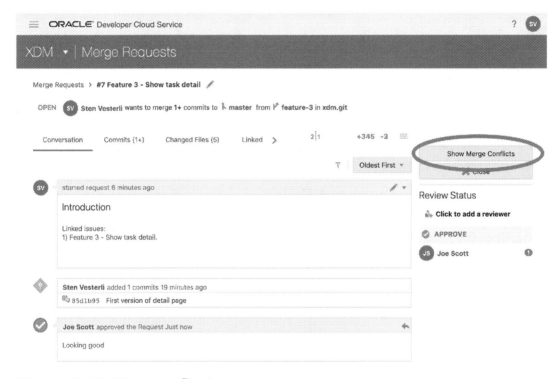

Figure 12-20. *Merge conflict in a merge request*

When you click this button, a dialog box appears with instructions on how to handle the merge conflict, as shown in Figure 12-21.

Figure 12-21. *The Merge Conflicts dialog*

If you are unfamiliar with using Git commands, it will be a good idea to find a colleague with Git experience to help you run these commands. They must be run from the command line on a development workstation that you have already cloned the DevCS repository to.

You can find the URL to clone from by clicking the *Clone* button next to the name of your repository on the project home page in DevCS. Copy the https:// address for your repository and then execute a git clone command from a command line on your development workstation. For my environment, it looks like this:

```
git clone https://<username>@stendevcs-svesterli.developer.ocp.oraclecloud.
com/stendevcs-svesterli/s/stendevcs-svesterli_people_2212/scm/xdm.git
```

You will be prompted for your password (the DevCS username is part of the URL), and then a local clone of the DevCS repository is created. From here, you can run the Git commands you need.

Handling Data

The Git operations in Visual Builder Cloud Service apply to your code, not your data. If your enterprise application makes use of its own data in business objects, you need a way to manage that data.

Development Data

Data created for exploratory testing by the developer in a feature branch should be considered transient. You can keep it around in the feature branch, but you will normally not be using this data as persistent test data. If you wish to move it to the staging environment, you will have to use the *Data Manager* to export it and then import it in the master application.

Test Data

Test data should be created in the staging environment for the master application. Each time you stage the application, you should choose *Keep existing data in Stage*, so your testers have a consistent data set to run their tests on.

Production Data

Production data is managed in the *Live* environment of your master application. When you publish the master application the first time, you should choose *Publish application with a clean database*. Subsequently, you should use *Keep existing data in Live*.

Moving Data Between Branches

As long as you do not make any changes to the fields in your business objects, the functionality *Export All Data* and *Import from File* (in *Data Manager*) can be used to easily move data between the VBCS applications corresponding to the different branches.

Handling Data Format Changes

Visual Builder Cloud Service handles additions to your business object structure well. When you pull a new version into the master VBCS application with additional business objects, new relationships, and new fields, they are transparently added.

If you add new mandatory fields to business objects that already contain data, the user will be prompted to provide the mandatory data the first time he tries to save a change to a record that is missing mandatory data. However, the application runs fine without error messages even though mandatory data is missing.

Note   VBCS will often refuse to remove fields from existing business objects. If you pull a change that removes one or more fields or business objects, run the *Git Diff* command to see if the fields and/or objects are actually removed. If *Git Diff* shows a difference right after *Git Pull*, you will need to make manual changes until *Git Diff* shows no differences.

Storing Data in Git

If you want to store your test data in Git, you can use the *Data Manager* and choose *Export All Data*. This gives you a ZIP file with a CSV with the data in each business object.

You cannot directly add a ZIP file to DevCS through the web interface, so you must add this file via a local clone of the repository. The preceding section on merge conflicts described how to create such a local repository. When you have it, you can add your data files in a new directory to this local repository and then do `git add,` `git commit`, and `git push`. This will push your local changes up to the DevCS Git repository.

Customizing the Build Process

The default way of building Visual Builder Cloud Service applications is through the VBCS user interface, where a developer chooses *Stage* or *Publish*. However, from version 19.1.3 of VBCS, it is also possible to automate this process using the Grunt build tool. This allows you to include VBCS applications in a CI/CD workflow.

Your application comes with a package.json file that the Node package manager (npm) can use to get and install the necessary Grunt tasks. The file looks something like this:

```
{
  "name": "vb-application",
  "version": "1.0.0",
  "description": "VB application",
  "devDependencies": {
    "@oracle/grunt-vb-build": "https://static.oracle.com/cdn/vb/tools/npm/
    grunt-vb-build/grunt-vb-build-19.1.3.3.tar.gz",
    "grunt": "^1.0.3",
    "grunt-cli": "^1.3.2",
    "load-grunt-tasks": "^4.0.0"
  }
}
```

To download and install the necessary Grunt tasks, you can run npm install from the root directory of the application (where the package.json file is located).

Once you have these tasks installed, you can run a Grunt command to build the application. For example, to build the application from the application root directory, you could run the following command:

```
./node_modules/.bin/grunt vb-build \
    --url=<url of visual builder instance> \
    --username=<username> \
    --password=<password> \
    --id=<your visual app ID> \
    --ver=<your visual app version> \
    --git-sources=<local directory for sources> \
    --optimize=<optimization>
```

The developer guide contains a section "Optimize Your Builds" that describes the available Grunt tasks.

Building in Developer Cloud Service

You can use Developer Cloud Service (DevCS) to automate building your VBCS application with Grunt. To do that, you first need to create a virtual machine template on the *Virtual Machine Templates* sub-tab found in the *Organization* area in DevCS as shown in Figure 12-22.

Figure 12-22.   *Creating a virtual machine template in DevCS*

When you have created the template, you go to the *Build Virtual Machines* tab to create at least one virtual machine.

When you have a virtual machine configured, you go to the *Build* area and create a new job. In the *Job Configuration* window shown in Figure 12-23, you first go to the *Git* tab and connect to your Git repository, and then go to the *Steps* tab and add a *Unix Shell* step that includes the npm install and grunt vb-build commands as shown in the figure.

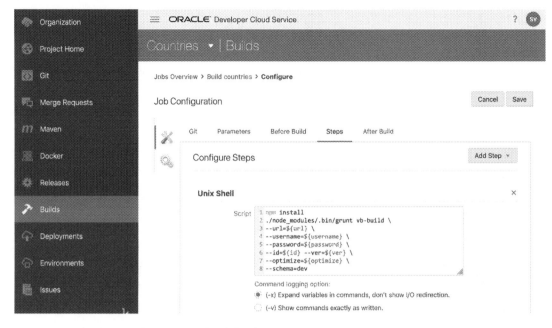

Figure 12-23. *Configuring a build job in DevCS*

The job configuration might look like this:

```
npm install
./node_modules/.bin/grunt vb-build \
--url=${url} \
--username=${username} \
--password=${password} \
--id=${id} --ver=${ver} \
--optimize=${optimize} \
--schema=dev
```

The preceding example uses parameter syntax to refer to parameters defined on the *Parameters* tab.

When you run a `vb-build` job like this, you will find that it stages the application in your VBCS instance. You can also run a `vb-publish` job to set the application live.

Saving the Build Output

If you want to run your application on another server outside VBCS, you can save the build output. Go to the *After Build* tab and add an *After Build Action* of type *Artifact Archiver*. Set *Files to archive* to `build/*.zip` to store all the compressed application files built by the build job.

Building Locally

In theory, you should be able to clone your Git repository to your local machine and run `npm install` and then `grunt vb-build` as described earlier.

In practice, I have not been able to make this work in the current version of VBCS (19.1.3). Oracle clearly states that this is a supported approach and the issues might be fixed by the time you read this book.

Deploying to Another Server

It is possible to deploy Visual Builder Cloud Service web applications to other servers, either in another Oracle Cloud Service, in another cloud, or on-premise. Business objects depend on Oracle Database Cloud and cannot be moved out of VBCS.

When you deploy a VBCS web application outside VBCS, there are two things to be aware of:

- Configure your VBCS application for anonymous access so you don't depend on Oracle Identity Cloud. If you need authentication, you must configure it on your web server or implement it programmatically.

- For any REST service connections you use, you must go to the *Authentication* tab and select *Enable Authentication Proxy* and choose *Direct (Bypass Proxy)*. This configuration means that your VBCS application will connect directly to the REST service without using the VBCS proxy. See Figure 12-24.

restV2 ✕

Service   Endpoints   Authentication   Headers   Transforms   Source

☑ Enable authentication / proxy
Authentication Mechanism

Direct (Bypass Proxy)   ▼

☐ Allow anonymous access

Figure 12-24. *Configuring a service for direct connection*

If you save the build result with an *After Build* step, you can download the application by clicking the *Artifacts* icon on the build results page as shown in Figure 12-25.

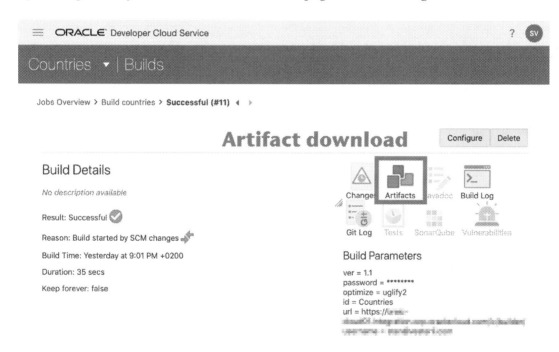

Figure 12-25. *Downloading build artifacts from DevCS*

For deployment, you should download the optimized.zip file. This file contains everything you need to run your application locally. Unpack it in a directory in your web server. If you place the application directory in the document root of your web server, the URL to run the application is /<name of folder>/webApps/<name of web app>/. You want to point to the directory that contains the index.html file.

Note   If you have problems running your web application locally using HTTPS, try changing the service connections to HTTP and run the application with HTTP. Once that is working, you are sure your build and web server is set up correctly and can troubleshoot any HTTPS issues.

Conclusion

In this chapter, you have learned how to leverage the connection between Visual Builder Cloud Service and the Git repository in Developer Cloud Service. You have also seen an example of an enterprise development workflow that uses modern Git best practice (features branches, etc.) and DevCS code quality features (merge requests, etc.). You saw how it is possible to customize and automate the build process and how to run a VBCS web application outside VBCS.

In the next and final chapter, we will discuss how to integrate Visual Builder Cloud Service with Oracle Process Cloud Service.

CHAPTER 13

Integrating with Process Cloud Service

Visual Builder Cloud Service is only one of many cloud services that Oracle offers. Another handy service is *Process Cloud Service* (PCS), which allows you to manage long-running processes that involve multiple steps and possibly multiple different people. If you have the *Oracle Integration Cloud* product, you have both VBCS and PCS as shown in Figure 13-1.

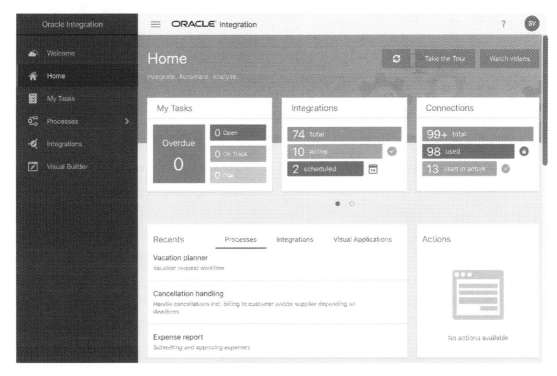

Figure 13-1. *Oracle Integration Cloud home page*

© Sten Vesterli 2019
S. Vesterli, *Oracle Visual Builder Cloud Service Revealed*, https://doi.org/10.1007/978-1-4842-4929-1_13

It is easy to integrate VBCS and PCS, allowing your VBCS application to interact with the processes managed by PCS.

About Process Cloud Service

You can consider Process Cloud Service a workflow engine. A developer develops *process applications* containing processes. Each process consists of a number of steps that can include both human and system tasks, including interactions with other systems as shown in Figure 13-2.

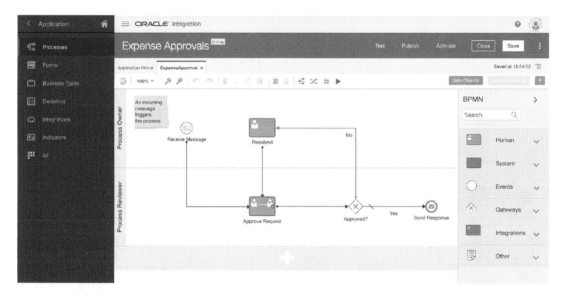

Figure 13-2. *A Process Cloud Service workflow*

Similar to VBCS applications, processes are developed, released to test, and finally deployed.

When a process is started, PCS creates a *process instance*. There can be many instances of a process, and each instance has its own data and its own state. For example, there might be eight expense approval processes waiting for approval, and three waiting for the submitter to provide more information and resubmit.

Connecting VBCS to PCS

If you have a default Oracle Integration Cloud instance, you have VBCS, PCS, and other services. They should already be integrated, shown by the fact that you have a process server connection on the *Processes* tab in your VBCS applications as shown in Figure 13-3.

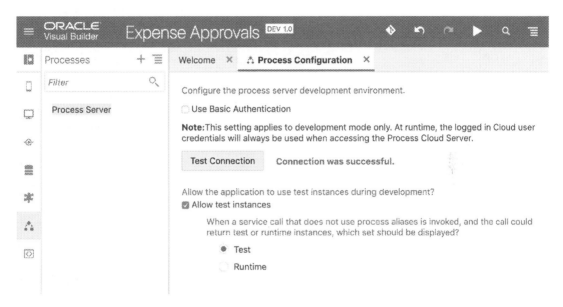

Figure 13-3. *Process Configuration*

You can click *Test Connection* and should receive the message *Connection was successful.*

Note   If you don't see a process server, you need to get your Oracle Cloud administrator to set up the connection between VBCS and PCS.

A VBCS application works with specific processes inside process applications. To establish a connection to a PCS process, you click the + sign next to the *Processes* header and select the process from the *Register Deployed Process* dialog shown in Figure 13-4.

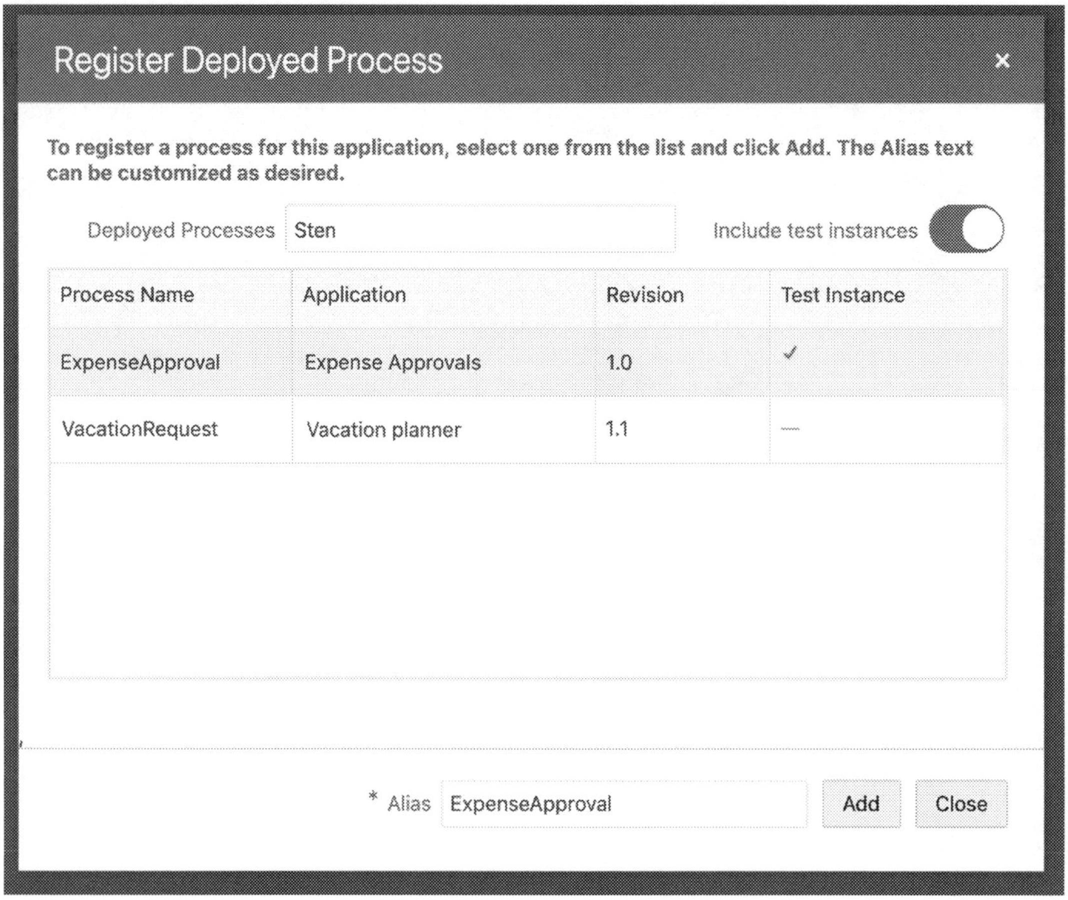

Figure 13-4. *Registering a process in VBCS*

You provide an *alias*, which is the connection to PCS. To connect a VBCS application to another process, you can remove the alias and register another process with that alias.

Once you have registered a connection, it opens in a new tab in the VBCS work area as shown in Figure 13-5.

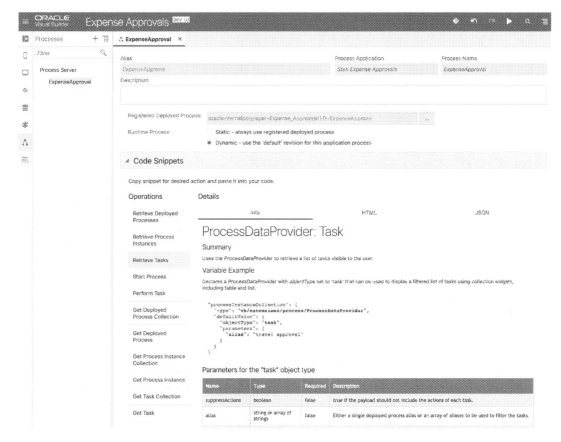

Figure 13-5. *A registered process tab*

Notice the *Code Snippets* part. Here, you can get information about various operations and copy the HTML and JSON you need to use that operation in a VBCS application. Code snippets are available to handle the following PCS operations:

- Retrieve Deployed Processes

- Retrieve Process Instances

- Retrieve Tasks

- Start Process

- Perform Task

- Get Deployed Process Collection

- Get Deployed Process

- Get Process Instance Collection

- Get Process Instance

- Get Task Collection

- Get Task

We will see how this works at the end of this chapter.

Starting a Process from VBCS

You can start a process from within Visual Builder Cloud Service using the code snippets described earlier, but it is easier to do from the visual logic builders in VBCS. You can start a process both from a user interface action chain and from a business component trigger.

Starting from User Interface

As you saw in Chapter 7, business logic in the user interface is defined in *action chains* connected to some user interface event (e.g., a click on a *Button*). In that action chain, you place a *Start Process* action in an action chain as shown in Figure 13-6. Note that the *Process* header to the left of the action chain work area contains some other process-related actions you can place in your action chain.

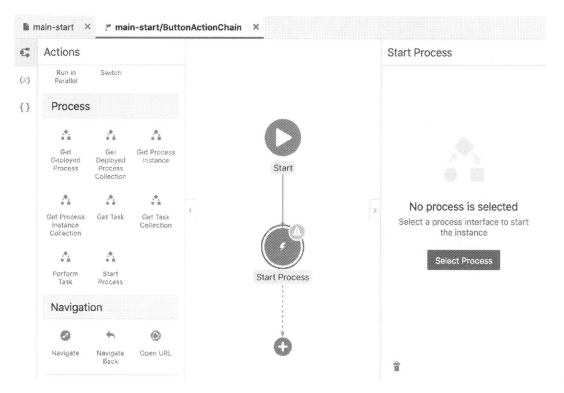

Figure 13-6. *A Start Process action in an action chain*

Then you click the *Select Process* button to map the action to a specific action. You select from all the available actions in the associated process server as shown in Figure 13-7.

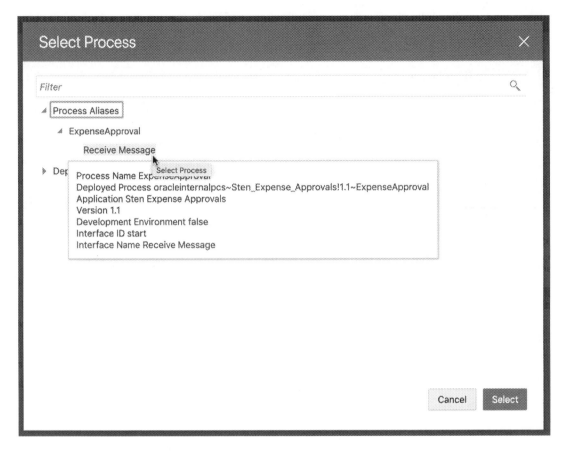

Figure 13-7. *Selecting a process for an action chain*

You select an entry point to the process – in the preceding figure, the process only has one entry point called Receive Message. When you have selected it, the input parameters will show up as NOT MAPPED as shown in Figure 13-8.

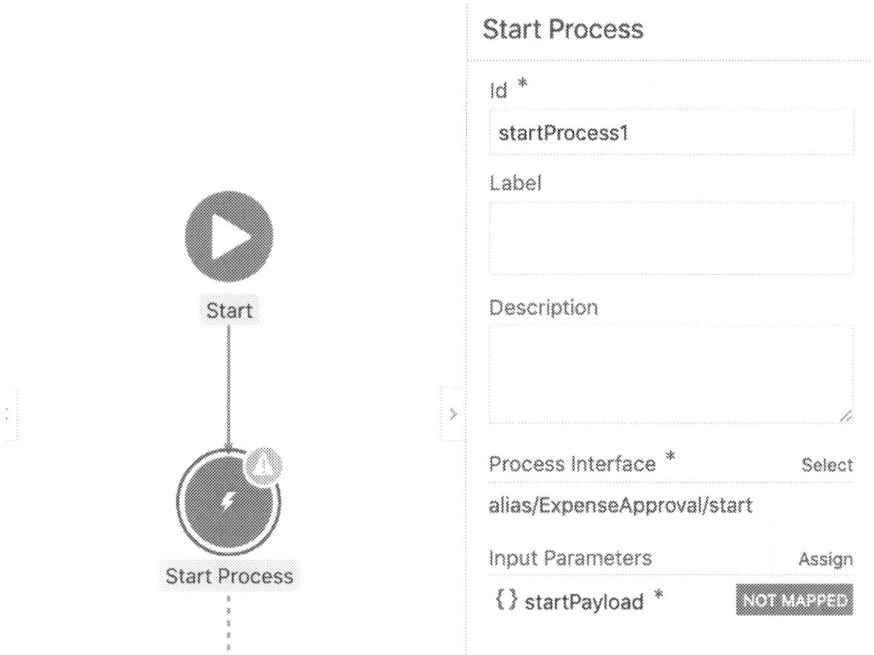

Figure 13-8. *A Start Process action with a process interface selected*

When you click the *Assign* link for *Input Parameters*, you can then use drag and drop to map existing variables to the input parameter to the process as shown in Figure 13-9.

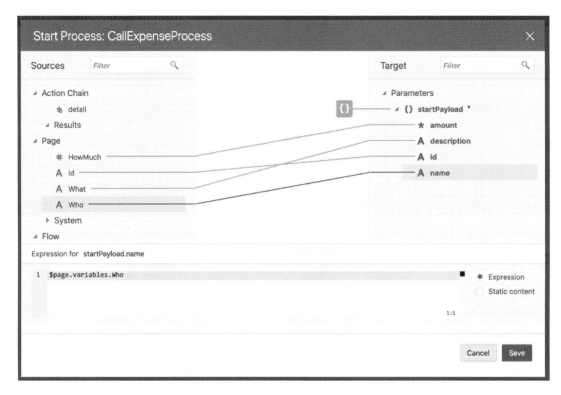

Figure 13-9. *Mapping input parameters to a process*

After the *Start Process* action, you might have success and failure branches. You can access the result from the start process under the Result node in the variables selector as shown in Figure 13-10.

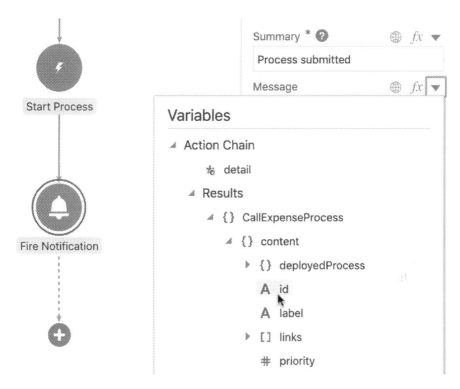

Figure 13-10. *Retrieving the ID of a process instance*

Starting from Business Component

As you saw in Chapter 6, you can also add logic to your business components on the *Business Rules* tab. For example, you can create an object trigger that is activated by a *Before Insert* event. That brings up the visual business object logic designer shown in Figure 13-11.

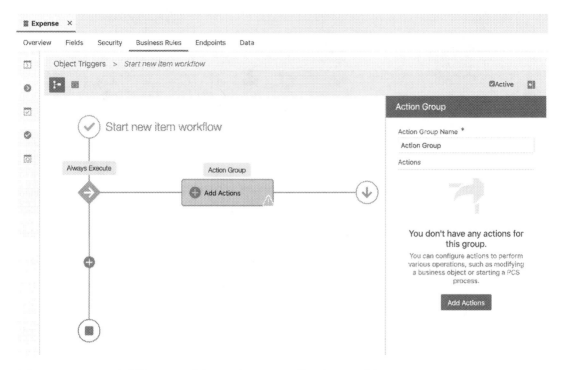

Figure 13-11. *Adding an object trigger to a business object*

When you add actions to triggers and validators, one of the options is to Start a Process as shown in Figure 13-12.

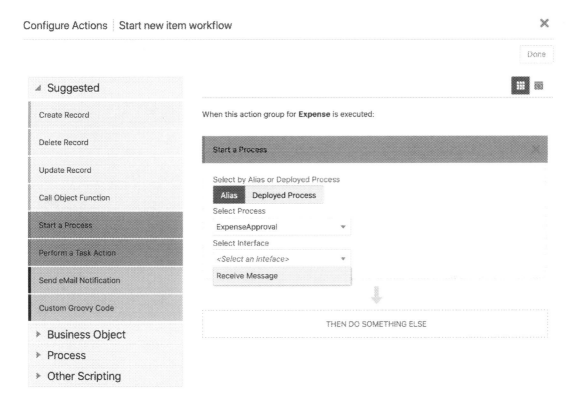

Figure 13-12. *Starting a process from an object trigger*

In this action, you can select an alias, a process, and an interface to trigger. After you have selected the process interface, you will have to map any parameters that interface uses, just like you would do in an action chain. In this case, you have access to the fields in the business object and not the components on the screen. The mapping could look as shown in Figure 13-13.

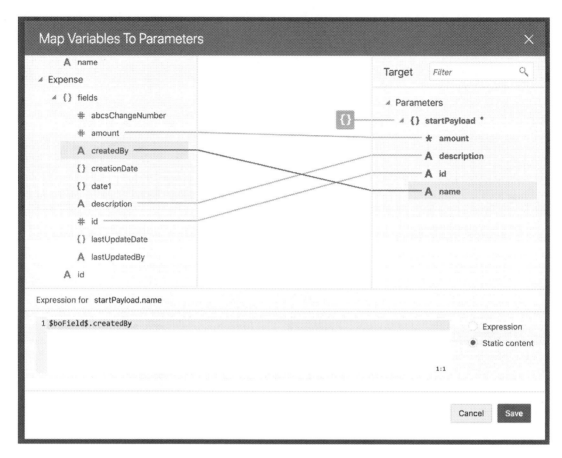

Figure 13-13. *Mapping process parameters in an object trigger*

Working with PCS Tasks

The typical reason to automate a process with Process Cloud Service is to make sure that system actions and human actions happen in the right order. When a process instance reaches a human task, processing stops and that task becomes available on the task list of the process for a user to take action on.

Building a Task List

To create a list of tasks assigned to the current user, you can use a collection component like a *Table* or a *List View* on a page. When you run the *Add Data* quick start, notice that you have the option to connect the collection component to several process objects. The task object selected in Figure 13-14 presents you with a collection of tasks.

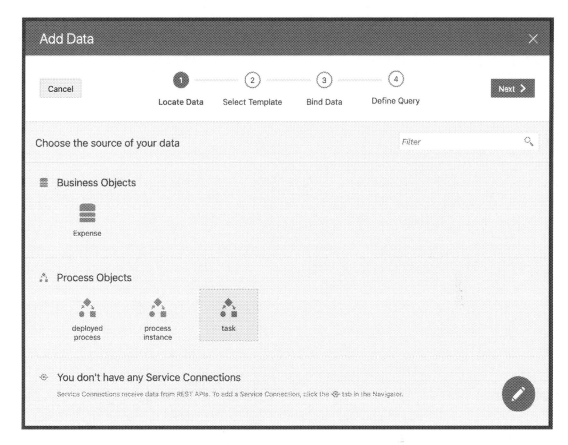

Figure 13-14. *Adding process data to a collection component*

In step 3 of the wizard, you bind data elements from the task to your VBCS components. The process developer determines the content of the task fields.

Note   In the *Define Query* step, you need to set the `alias` parameter to the `getTaskCollection` operation to the value of your process alias.

Working with Task Actions

Another aspect of the task defined by the process developer is the possible actions a user can take on a task (e.g., `Approve` and `Reject`).

When you have a collection of tasks selected in *Design* mode, you will notice that you find an *Add Task Actions* quick start at the bottom of the quick start list as shown in Figure 13-15.

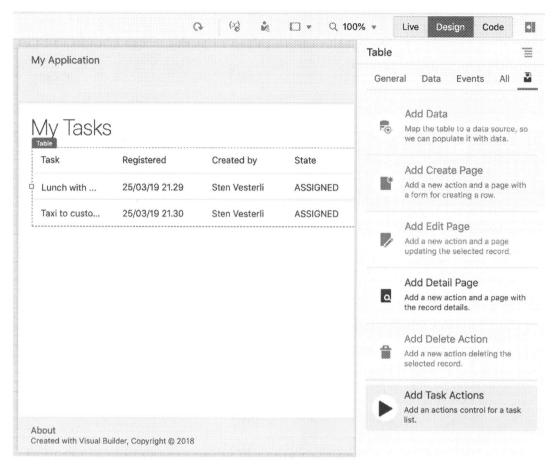

Figure 13-15. *Adding Task Actions with the quick start*

This quick start adds a single-select drop-down list *Choose an Action* above the list of tasks, showing the options the process developer has defined, and a *Submit* button. With this, you can select a task from the list, select one of the options, and submit your task. You will receive a notification that the action was successful, and the task disappears from the list (because the process has moved on).

If you want to tweak this flow a little, you can examine and modify the variable and the action chain the quick start has built for you.

Showing Process Instances

As an example of how to use the code samples you get when you connect a process with VBCS, let's have a look at a page showing deployed processes. These are all the processes the process developer has made available for VBCS developers to connect to.

In the *Code Snippets* section, you select the operation you want to use and then copy everything on the HTML tab. For *Retrieve Deployed Processes*, the HTML starts like this:

```
<div class="oj-flex">
  <div class="oj-flex-item">
    <h2>Retrieve Deployed Processes</h2>
    <p>Uses the <i>ProcessDataProvider</i> to retrieve deployed
        processes visible to the user.</p>
  </div>
</div>

<div class="oj-md-odd-cols-2 oj-flex-items-pad">
  <div class="oj-flex">
    <div class="oj-flex-item">
      <div class="oj-header-border"><h3>Parameters</h3></div>
        <div>
          <oj-checkboxset id="options" value="{{$variables.options}}">
            <oj-option value="extended">Extended properties</oj-option>
            <oj-option value="suppressUnregistered">
                Suppress unregistered</oj-option>
            <oj-option value="showProcessInstanceCount">
                Show instances count</oj-option>
          </oj-checkboxset>
...
```

On the page where you want this operation, you select the *Code* mode (top right, next to *Live* and *Design*). Replace everything on this tab with the HTML code you copied.

Similarly, select everything on the *JSON* tab under *Code Snippets*. For *Retrieve Deployed Processes*, the JSON code starts like this:

```
{
  "pageModelVersion": "18.2.3",
  "description": "A page that shows the deployed processes visible
      to the current user",
  "title": "Retrieve Deployed Processes",
  "variables": {
    "options": {
      "type": "string[]",
      "defaultValue": [
        "extended"
      ]
    },
    "selectedAliases": {
      "type": "string[]",
      "defaultValue": []
    },
...
```

On the page where you want the operation, select the *Metadata* tab in the tab ribbon along the left edge of the tab showing your page (the bottom-most one, below the JS icon for *Functions*). Replace everything on this tab with the JSON code from the service process.

When you run this code, you will see something like Figure 13-16.

Retrieve Deployed Processes

Uses the *ProcessDataProvider* to retrieve deployed processes visible to the user.

Parameters	Results

Parameters		
☑ Extended properties		
☐ Suppress unregistered		
☐ Show instances count		

Id	Aliases	Label
oracleinternalpcsplayer~Cancellation_handling!1.0~CancellationNotificationFlow		CancellationNotificationFlow
oracleinternalpcsplayer~CorrelationApplication!1.0~FormProcess		FormProcess
oracleinternalpcsplayer~Cancellation_handling!1.0~Invoicing		Invoicing
oracleinternalpcsplayer~EventBasedGatewayAndCorrelationsDemoApp!1.0~OrderProcess		OrderProcess
oracleinternalpcsplayer~Expense_Approvals_02!!1.0~ExpenseApproval		ExpenseApproval

Aliases

Deployed Process Ids

Details for 'CancellationNotificationFlow'

Name

Cancellation notification flow

Application

Cancellation handling

Version

1.0

Figure 13-16. *Code snippet page showing deployed processes*

Of course, you can modify the HTML code to get a different layout.

Conclusion

In this final chapter, you learned how to integrate Visual Builder Cloud Service with Process Cloud Service. These two cloud services supplement each other well – PCS is suitable for handling long-running work processes, and VBCS is useful for creating attractive pages for the necessary user interaction.

You now have all the information you need to put Visual Builder Cloud Service to work in your organization. With VBCS, you can rapidly build the applications the organization needs to innovate and thrive. Enjoy!

Index

A

B

W, X, Y, Z

Printed in the United States
By Bookmasters